RURAL COMMUNITIES

IN THE MEDIEVAL WEST

THE JOHNS HOPKINS SYMPOSIA
IN COMPARATIVE HISTORY

The Johns Hopkins Symposia in Comparative History are occasional volumes sponsored by the Department of History at the Johns Hopkins University and the Johns Hopkins University Press comprising original essays by leading scholars in the United States and other countries. Each volume considers, from a comparative perspective, an important topic of current historical interest. The present volume is the eighteenth. Its preparation has been assisted by the James S. Schouler Lecture Fund.

Aerial photo shows West Whelpington North, a village that was occupied from the 12th to the 14th century. Its stonebuilt houses, each within its croft, are grouped around a green. On the right are ridges and furrows.

Source: J. Steane, *The Archaeology of Medieval England and Wales* (Athens, Ga.), 146. Cambridge University Collection ATV 76.

RURAL COMMUNITIES

IN THE MEDIEVAL WEST

Léopold Genicot

*

THE JOHNS HOPKINS UNIVERSITY PRESS

BALTIMORE · LONDON

The Johns Hopkins University Press, 701 West 40th Street, Baltimore,
Maryland 21211

The Johns Hopkins Press Ltd., London

∞ The paper used in this book meets the minimum
requirements of American National Standard for
Information Sciences—Permanence of Paper for
Printed Library Materials, ANSI Z39.48-1984.

LIBRARY OF CONGRESS CATALOGING-IN-PUBLICATION DATA

Genicot, Léopold.
Rural communities in the medieval West / Léopold Genicot.
p. cm.—(The Johns Hopkins symposia in comparative history)
Rev. ed. of the author's James S. Schouler lectures for 1986–87.
Includes bibliographical references.
ISBN 0-8018-3870-3 (alk. paper)
1. Europe—Social conditions—To 1492. 2. Europe—Rural
conditions. 3. Villages—Europe—History. I. Title. II. Series.
HN373.G45 1990   307.72′094′0902—dc20   89-37340

CONTENTS

ACKNOWLEDGMENTS

Aɴʏ ʙᴏᴏᴋ has its prehistory. In the case of this one, the origins are simple. After finishing the third part of my *L'économie rurale namuroise au bas moyen âge,* which describes the legal, economic, and social status of *les hommes; le commun* (the common people), I proceeded to work on the fourth and last volume, which will be entitled *Communauté et vie rurales.* * This will not deal with individuals but with groups and their ways of life.

As is my custom, I first read a good number of studies on the rural community in the medieval West in order to become aware of all aspects of the subject—problems, methods of investigation, solutions or hypotheses advanced. At that very time, the Johns Hopkins University honored me with an invitation to give the James S. Schouler Lectures for 1986–87. I accepted and proposed that I should deal with the theme upon which I was engaged. The faculty agreed, and the Johns Hopkins University Press offered to publish the text of my lectures, enlarged and supported by references. We easily came to an agreement, and I proceeded to revise my lectures, to supplement, substantiate, and refine them.

So far as the contents were concerned, the task was not too difficult. It was made easier because, at the suggestion of my friend G. Constable, the Institute for Advanced Study at Princeton granted me a fellowship for the first term of 1987–88 and thus gave me the opportunity of advancing my researches under the best possible conditions.

As to form, matters were more difficult. It is always a daring enterprise to write in a foreign language. Fortunately, I had the help of two good friends. A former student of mine and now a most distinguished colleague at Johns Hopkins, Michael McCormick, read and corrected my English. Philip Harris, Deputy Keeper at the British Library, with whom I share so many pleasant memories, did the same for the notes.

I am indebted to so many other people, especially in the United States, that I cannot mention all of them. I prefer to express my

---

*The first volume was devoted to *La seigneurie foncière,* that is to say, the juridical and economic regime of landed property, the second to *Les hommes, La noblesse,* the nobility; they were published in Louvain in 1943 and 1960.

gratitude by praising their country—the country where two centuries ago the first democratic constitution in the world was composed.

RURAL COMMUNITIES
IN THE MEDIEVAL WEST

INTRODUCTION:

SUBJECT AND METHODS

W HEN, a century ago, medievalists pushed beyond the limits of political facts and ideas and turned to material, social, and economic life, they devoted their best research to the towns. Since 1050 or 1100, the towns had been—and in 1850 still were—the most vital element in western Europe and the most active factor in historical change. Yet most people in the Middle Ages—and until the eve of what we call inappropriately the contemporary era—lived in the country. In William the Conqueror's England, according to the Domesday book, 90 percent of the population lived in villages, hamlets, or on isolated farms. In the autumn of the period in an area as urbanized as the Low Countries, 64 percent still lived in such places.[1] In the fifteenth century as in the eleventh, rural communities formed the foundation of the economy, indispensable for every kind of activity.[2] So rural history is of great significance and deserves more attention than it has been given so far. Moreover, the rural community was less static than our predecessors thought and wrote. In the matter of settlement, for instance, the Middle Ages displayed as much dynamism as stability; even when writings, artifacts, and place-names concord to suggest permanence, these communities sometimes experienced a succession of decline and renewal.[3] These reasons make the rural past of the western Middle Ages an essential problem.

The first pages of this introduction explain and justify the choice of the term *community*. The second part speaks of methods, especially of documentation, underlines the difficulties of the subject—at any rate down to the eleventh century—and presents the means of facing and partly solving them. These considerations shape the book's plan.

*

T O DESIGNATE the basic rural collectivity in the Middle Ages, one would be tempted to use the word *village*. But the concept of village is extraordinarily ambiguous. Significantly enough, the *Dictionnaire de la géographie* gives no definition of *village*, and in the entry *hamlet*, distinguishes the two simply by the "lack of buildings of social or collective use, townhall, church, school" in a hamlet.[4] In the same way, other French geographers put forth as the distinctive mark of the village versus the hamlet "an administrative role" or "a community life."[5] For official censuses, specialists at the United Nations in 1970 used the word *locality* and proposed an extremely long and intricate description, whose length at least has the merit of underscoring the complexity of the matter.[6]

The right term must take that complexity into account. German scholars usually speak of *Gemeinde, Landgemeinde*—that is to say of a juridical organism, of public law. Sometimes, to escape from those narrow boundaries, they utilize the words *Genossenschaft* or *Gemeinschaft*.[7] Or they speak of *Dorf*, whose geographical connotation links it with economy and society: a *Dorf* is "eine irgendwie in sich geschossene Gemeinschaft von mit- und nebeneinander Bauern" (a community of peasants with and next to one another, in some way closed unto itself).[8] The French, the Italians, and the English are more prudent and less precise; they prefer the word *community*, which does not emphasize any single aspect, and which was the medieval term, at least from the eleventh century.

In the early Middle Ages, documents used the word *villa*, which meant, first, manor and, afterward, an inhabited plot of land: ("in villa et territorio" or, in France in the late Middle Ages, "à ville et à champs"). *Villa* developed at the same time a quantitative connotation, attested by the appearance of diminutives like *villula*.[9] In a further step, *villa* was replaced by *communitas* or *universitas*, a highly significant phenomenon, as eloquent as all semantic changes are. The further I go, the more convinced I am by the primordial importance of semantics in history. For me, there can be no real history without semantic investigation and no real semantic investigation without computers.

I shall return to the significance of the passage from *villa* to *universitas*. But my definition and the term I choose derive from the aforesaid. Not village, but community—that is to say, a group offering some specificity and being conscious of it. The specificity may spring from many sources: one collection of studies devoted to "les communautés rurales" presents some sixty conceptions of community![10]

Community may spring from geography and vicinity and, consequently, from identity of economic activity—normally, in the country, cultivating and pasturing. Community may spring from juridical status, falling under the same public and private law and the same political and administrative framework. In the Middle Ages, when all authority was founded on the ownership of soil and of men, juridical status derived from attachment to a manor or a lordship. I have in mind the famous French distinction between *seigneurie foncière* (precisely, in the medieval vocabulary, *trèfoncière*) and *seigneurie banale* (the medieval documents speak of *hautaine*). Community may spring from religion, from belief, and from their structures. This means, on the local level, that the parish is the community. It may spring from tradition, culture, and mentality, and from sharing myths, language, customs, and values. These common elements are not, of course, in opposition. On the contrary, several normally exist at once, which does not mean that their limits always coincide, that lordship and parish, for instance, have the same boundaries. The community is not only an objective reality; it is also a subjective one. Its common features ought to be conscious ones—and so generate solidarity.

According to some scholars, especially in Germany, a community's existence also requires a juridical element. Solidarity must lead to some power and some rules. The possession of authority—of some measure of self-government or self-administration, with a legal responsibility and *Zwangsgewalt* (coercive power)—is needed.[11] But is this not going too far? I prefer S. Reynold's position: a community is "a collectivity engaging in collective activities, activities which are characteristically determined and controlled less by formal regulations than by shared values and norms, while the relationships between members of the community are characteristically reciprocal, many-sided and direct rather than being mediated through official and rulers."[12] This question will need closer examination when we turn to the concept of *communitas* and *universitas*.

*

To CAPTURE and analyze these realities before 800 or 1000 is extremely difficult. Written documentation is poor, even for countries as rich in historical records as Italy and Spain. One example is the origin of parishes. In 1980, at Spoleto, A. Settia deplored "the lack of explicit evidence" on parishes for the early Middle Ages.[13] The hindrance is greater for northern Europe. At the same congress, C. Brooke described how he started from a list of religious circumscriptions set up in the thirteenth century and worked backward, with largely disappointing results.[14]

Written documents suffer from other defects, too. They are unilateral, since they only illustrate the structure and management of big estates, which were mainly, and for some countries even exclusively, ecclesiastical. The latest studies now make it more and more obvious that, in the early Middle Ages, those estates did not cover as much of the surface as our predecessors believed. In the ninth century, for instance, the manors of Saint-Bertin were still on their way to constitution or enlargement by absorbing little or midsized independent properties.[15] And these small properties were surely not organized and ruled like the huge ones belonging to abbeys and *potentes* (power-ful men). Written documents moreover speak with an awkward, poor, and therefore imprecise vocabulary, using the same word, for ex-ample, for kindred, however different, realities. And frequently they express Germanic conceptions and structures in Latin terms. Finally, they are too often examined with insufficient care, without there being drawn up—if possible with the help of computers—complete lists of technical terms and their interconnections.[16]

So written documents must be supplemented by nonwritten evi-dence. To be sure, that evidence is often fully understandable only with the help of written evidence. And despite the constant progress of the natural sciences, nonwritten evidence is still scarce, as the fol-lowing review of the different kinds of documentation shows.

The material remnants of the past are indispensable. They may be discovered and analyzed first of all by traditional archaeology, by the study of still-standing buildings, like keeps, and surviving objects, like jewelry. For too long, archaeology was interested almost solely in reli-gious and monumental achievements. Today, fortunately, it has ex-tended its scope.[17] It studies villages: their births, locations, structures, continuity; disappearances, desertions, destructions, and deaths—"Wüstungen des ausgehenden Mittelalters" (the desertions of the late Middle Ages), or more exactly, the recurring desertions in many peri-ods of the Middle Ages. It studies the buildings and their technical aspects. It studies houses: their implantation, whether clustered, like those at Brucato, or scattered, whether surrounded or not by a close, a garden, a plot of grass or land; it studies their plan, whether one construction or several; their dimensions, whether made to shelter a large family or a small one, whether it housed servants and cattle; whether it was used for all activities or only for a dwelling; it studies their materials, whether solid enough to endure a long time or nei-ther durable nor dear, inviting their inhabitants not to stay.

Archaeology studies the common places and buildings, whether they are in the center or on the border of the agglomeration, and whether they are factors of concentration or of dispersion into new nuclei, hamlets, or farms. Among these common buildings is the church. Of demographic significance is its origin, its space, its internal disposition (was there room, for instance, for the baptismal font?), and its trans-formations.[18] Also of significance is the cemetery or cemeteries, either coexistent or successive, their connection with the church's transfers, and their role in stimulating the gathering of the population, whether they were ringed by a wall and defended by towers and whether they included a spot for privileged tombs.

Archaeology also examines human productions, the artifacts found

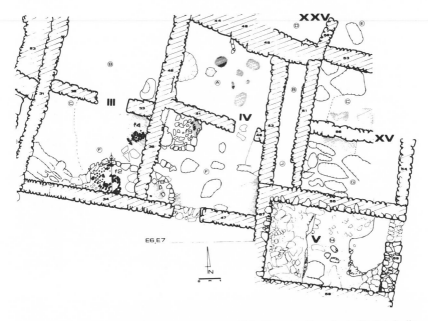

Figure 1. Archaeology and History. A house (IV) in Brucato, Castellacio (Sicily), built between the second half of the 13th century and the first half of the 14th century. The plan of this simple two-room house suggests differentiated functions. The southern room had a door leading outside and two hearths. The rear room, completely closed except for the door in the southern room, may have been used for storage and sleeping. The walls are bound by clay, and the floor is beaten earth.

Source: Brucato. Histoire et archéologie d'un habitat médiéval en Sicile, ed. J. M. Pesez.

in the ruins, like pottery—its material, facing, form, decoration, qualities or defects of fabrication, and so on. These artifacts are now analyzed with increasing precision by the chemical and physical sciences.[19] They bear witness to material culture, which is so revealing of the past—of daily life, relationships, beliefs, and mentality.[20] And they are helpful, even necessary, for establishing with other evidence (especially coins) the excavations' stratigraphy and so for dating the finds, particularly the buildings, with an exactness that makes them usable. Too often an archaeologist's report will say that a keep, for instance, was erected "sometimes in the eleventh century," and historians find they cannot really use such a vague indication. And finally (to summarize, for my list is far from exhaustive), agrarian archaeology examines the ground and the marks cultivation has left in it, primarily the crêtes de labour (ridges, furrows), Ackerberge (their depth and broadness), and whether they were dug systematically and therefore intentionally.

To disclose these traces and, in a broader way, to prepare, confirm

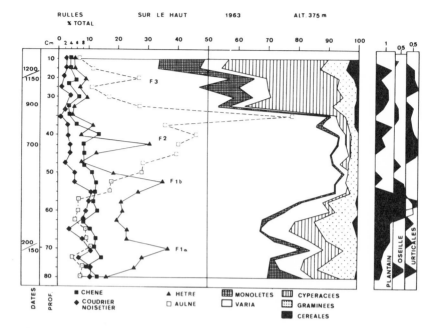

RULLES   SUR LE HAUT   1963   ALT. 375 m
% TOTAL

Figure 2. Palinology and History. Pollenogram for Rulles, in southeastern Belgium. It reveals the patterns of pollen deposits—and therefore relative significance of different species over time—and accordingly the fluctuations in occupation and exploitation of the soil. The vertical axis shows the timeline from Augustus to the Black Death, next to the depth at which the pollen was deposited. The horizontal axis indicates the percentage of total deposits represented by each pollen. Hardwoods are located to the left of the graph and reveal the extent and make-up of the forest. Pollen from cultivated land is displayed on the right side. The three additional columns on the far right document are drawn on a larger scale because these plants are less abundant; the percentage of greater plantain, sorrel, and nettles proves a particularly intense presence of men and cattle.

Fluctuations are provoked by changes in natural conditions, like exhaustion of the ground and especially variations in the climate, and by human activity. For instance, advance of the beech suggests a wet climate. And of course demographic progress compels to assert forest and convert the waste into pastures and fields. Of particular significance for the history of a rural community, its origin, its development, and its way of life is, first, the respective importance of uncultivated and cultivated land and, second, of graminae (monoletae is a kind of fern) and cereals, that is to say of pastures and fields.

Here the correlation of species reveals three main phases in the history of Rulles' cultivated areas: advance under the *Pax Romana*, retreat from ca.350–400 to 800, and renewed advance from 800 on, phases that written evidence does not mention and archaeological remnants hardly suggest.

Source: Drawn by M. Couteaux, Department of Earth Sciences, Catholic University at Louvain la Neuve.

and supplement its excavations, archaeology is backed up by the airplane. Photographs from the air help select places in which to dig. They also show marks that do not appear on the soil and so reveal the plan of an agglomeration and the organization of its fields. This work has advanced thanks to British and Italian specialists.

Recourse to earth sciences is more recent and in full development.[21] Pedology analyzes the soil's fitness to produce food and sustain people. Palinology, which, thanks to its latest progress, is no longer confined to sump holes or bogs, establishes the evolution of vegetation, especially of the plants used to make bread, with a chronology now precise enough for historians. Thus the graph of pollen deposits at Rulle, in southern Belgium, paints a remarkable picture of agrarian decline and growth. Ecology formulates laws governing relations between botanical species, mainly trees, which explain the transformation of the forests and woods that were indispensable for a medieval community's survival. Archaeobotany examines, for instance, the composition of the hedges that once enclosed most houses and many villages; the number of botanical species found in each hedge reveals its age.[22] Combining all kinds of elements with modern observations, historical meteorology discloses changes in climate that may account for the desertion of regions or places.[23]

Medievalists are also beginning to link with the medical sciences. Archaeozoology is already a cornerstone for solving the fundamental problem of the respective importance of hunting, cattle rearing, and cultivating, and of the different species of domestic animals. And it may prove the persistence of traditions and belief, for instance, of the kosher diet in Sicilian villages reconquered by the Christians.[24] As for humans, osteologists' analyses of bones from churchyards in Saxony and Spain have produced remarkable results on life expectancy in the early and late Middle Ages and on the causes of mortality. Hungarian and Swedish researchers endeavour to measure the dimension of settlements by combining anthropology and the archaeology of tombs.[25] These only hint at the possibilities opened by somatic and psychological medicine.

Since Marc Bloch's "Caractères originaux de l'histoire rurale française," rural history also scrutinizes early maps and, above all, because they exist for every locality, cadaster surveys. The use of these surveys, however, requires attention to the traps of retrospection—all the more since the geographical framework and its disposition changed more frequently and radically than was thought one or two generations ago.[26]

Finally, place-names provide precious witness: on the one hand, macrotoponomy (names of villages and hamlets) is used, despite the difficulties in interpretation and datation and the problems arising from instability;[27] on the other hand, microtoponomy (the names of parts of the field, of *Gewann*, of *saisons*, and of *campagnes*) illuminate, for instance, assarts or new clearings.

The list is long and rich. Nevertheless, gathering such witnesses does not capture the origins of most medieval rural communities, all the more since the witnesses do not always concord: archaeological evidence and place-names sometimes are contradictory, to give but one instance.[28] And too frequently they lack the chronological precision necessary for ranking the data and establishing their connections, interdependence, and causal ties.

Deficiencies of documentation are only the first barrier in the search for the roots and the development of the rural communities of the Middle Ages. There are two more: the complexity of the reality and the diversity of the cases.

Complexity: I touched on the point with regard to specificity as basis and criterion of a community. Now—to use medical or chemical metaphors—the factors underlying the coagulation, precipitation, and evolution of a peasant group are still more numerous. Natural conditions may dictate movement within a more or less large area either by precluding return to an earlier spot or by failing to foster sedentariness. Hills or open fields; dry or wet soil; wealth or poverty of the stream network; abundance or scarcity of forest, underwood, and glades, all these cause people to gather or to scatter. The past also weighs, insofar as it is heavy enough to decide people not to break decisively with the inherited forms of the settlement: *Kontinuitätsfrage*, the permanent problem of continuity! The economic and social structures are no less influential: systems of property, possession, and power; forms and strength of personal entities, tribe, and family. The mentality and habits of an aboriginal or immigrant population interfere, too: the intensity of the sense of association and the scale of values cannot be ignored. Here, as always in history, all aspects of collective life are involved as they act and react to produce certain phenomena.

They act and react in different ways, with varying importance and producing different results. The diversity from case to case is amazing. For Italy in the early Middle Ages, two young scholars, trying to draw from archaeology the map of the conversion of the country, write: "the examples adduced suffice to discourage any generalization whatsoever."[29] Another states that Toubert's picture of the *incastellamento* in the Latium does not, despite its author's assertion, fit the whole peninsula and, in particular, the Po plain.[30] For England, C. Brooke observes that huge parishes, expanding over several—up to twenty and more—villages or hamlets, existed side by side with very small

ones.[31] And Th. Mayer, one of the leaders of the preceding generation of researchers in Germany, concluded at the end of a long career
mainly devoted to the origins and nature of the *Landgemeinde* that
"even common general characteristics appear to be excluded."[32]

*

THIS OVERVIEW explains and justifies the plan of the book. The rural
medieval community's multiple components may be gathered into
three main groups: first, geographical and economic; second, juridical,
political, and administrative; and third, religious. They form the sub-
stance of three chapters entitled, in the period's own key words: *universitas, bannum, parochia*. The three aspects are barely clear before the
second millennium: "So little is recorded about local communities before about 1100 that it seems pointless to pile speculation upon speculation by saying more."[33] The rare data and certainties and the more
abundant hypotheses are presented in a preliminary chapter called
villa. And as the country did not and could not live in isolation, a last
chapter will put it in its broadest context, which the medieval documents named *terra*.

The size of this volume obliges us to concision. Shades and nuances
have been scratched out and only the main lines drawn, illustrated
with concrete cases. The emphasis falls on problems and methods.
Questions, suggesting means and ways of investigation, aim at, rather
than propose or impose, solutions.

Many of the examples come from northwestern Europe and especially Belgium and its neighbors, countries that I know best after fifty
years of research and where I more easily find instructive and en-
lightening cases.

For the same reason of brevity, the references have been drastically
limited. Mentioning all the valuable studies on every point would be
impossible. I have only noted, on the one hand, recent syntheses provided with good bibliographies and, on the other, precise, sure, il-
luminating monographs.

1

VILLA:

ORIGINS DOWN TO THE

TENTH CENTURY

*

Under the conditions described in the Introduction, it is difficult, even impossible, to apply one valid, ideal method for discovering the situations and events contributing to the formation of rural communities, to date their appearance, and to measure their relative importance in a quantity of cases sufficient to grasp the rules or patterns—if they exist—for the genesis and early development of these communities. We must be satisfied with collecting elements toward a furthering of the discussion.

Roughly speaking, there are two possible origins of rural communities: (1) spontaneous formation, without compulsion or interference by an external or superior power, and through the sole pressure of necessity—that is, the struggle against nature and competitors; or (2) artificial formation, at the initiative or under the guidance of some authority, lay or religious. Both are examined below and some general views are proposed. These views will be checked, supplemented, and confirmed or invalidated, in the following chapters.

*

Spontaneous formation would have relied upon natural and human factors that invite people to settle—whether the settlements were clustered or scattered, permanent or temporary.

Nature's role has already been evoked. Water is the first element; it is indispensable for humans and their livestock. In many places, it was also used to irrigate fields, improve pasture, and fill fish ponds, which were numerous in the period. In other areas, amid marshes or along the sea, water was dangerous. In order to exploit its advantages and to defend against its perils, cooperation was needed—and people were obliged to unite. In Spain, following the Arab example, it was used cooperatively for improving cultivation. In the Netherlands, an assembly was formed for maintaining fields and winning new ones. Until the late Middle Ages, this assembly was significantly called *buurschap* (group of neighbours). It watched over dams, streams, roads, and fences and, broadly speaking, made its decisions by the way of *willekeuren* (by-laws).[1]

The composition of the earth affected water's presence or absence, abundance or scarcity; chalk and limestone, for example, reduced the possibility of finding springs or digging wells and obliged people to assemble in villages. Vice-versa, water made soil more fertile or less fertile and could force a community to move after a few decades.[2] The impulse to move on might have been strengthened by awkward methods of cultivating, which exhausted arable land, and by the short life span of the houses, which were built with materials that decayed or rotted within one generation. In fact, in some regions the custom was to construct a new house when the son succeeded his father in his holding.[3] From a purely material viewpoint, leaving fields and home was not a loss, hence the instability of settlement evidenced by recent excavations.[4] The chemical interaction of soil and substratum was also decisive for the kinds and importance of the forests. People tended to assemble and live in the glades and to join together to enlarge their community by the hard work of assarting.

The orographic system also influenced settlement and its forms. In the mountains, people tended to live in small independent communities, which frequently compensated for their weakness—and defended their autonomy—by banding together. These communities favored stability and conservatism. The plains, on the other hand, knew no frontiers or fixedness. The Lombardy of the Po and the narrow Pyrenean valleys illustrate these phenomena.[5]

But according to Vidal de Lablache's famous aphorism, "nature proposes and mankind disposes," in settlement no less than other areas. The first human agent was the family, which varied in its structure and evolution.[6] Was it large or small? Patriarchal or conjugal? Unicellular or pluricellular (limited to parents and unmarried children or uniting relatives lacking their own hearth, agnates and cognates, and even servants under the authority of the ancestor or the master)? The question has been and remains eagerly discussed. From a careful examination of the Polyptych of Irminon, so often invoked in this debate, a Russian scholar, who applied the methods of anthroponymy, affirms the predominance of exploitations in common and notes that the document ignores the conjugal house or family. But one of his fellow countrymen observes that cultivating in indivision does not imply cohabitation.[7] A French medievalist introduces the same distinction and, confronting written and archaeological evidence, asserts that in the Carolingian period the patriarchal family was the exception.[8]

Recent excavations have yielded more data on house dimension and disposition. Some were up to one hundred feet long and were probably built to shelter many people. But their size might only signify that they were the houses of rich men, which is also attested by the privileged tombs. Or it might express the constitution or consolidation of a landed aristocracy, a phenomenon we shall encounter again. To judge, one would have to know with precision the percentage of this kind of residence in each country in each period between antiquity and the ninth or tenth century. Or this pattern might have been a vestige of—and a witness to—a first stage in settlement, when large families lived and tilled in common, according to a rule or a custom of maintaining the patrimony intact. In a second phase, law and practice—which did not always coincide—could have changed.[9] The inheritance, over generations of division, could have divided the large family into conjugal cells, which would have multiplied the smaller houses that apparently predominated in the Carolingian period (if those rude huts were really dwellings, and not workshops). If this view is exact, the family formed the nucleus of primitive human establishments in the early Middle Ages, and probably much before, and generated small agglomerations when it divided into distinctive branches. This view is lent support by the toponomy of the kingdom of Valence, by the form of the hamlets of Auvergne, and by the configuration of northwest German villages into *Langstreifenflur* (long strips) derived from the fragmentation of the *Grozsblocke* cultivated by large families into *Streifenparzellen*.[10] Such a development would not have broken the ties between relatives, who remained legally, economically, and sentimentally linked. No plot of land, for instance, might be sold without their consent (*laudatio*), and it might be bought back by any of them. The familial idea and ideal still inspired the *affrèrements* and *consorzie* in France and Italy in the second millenium, even as *frater* replaced *monachus* in the religious vocabulary.

It is hardly conceivable that even large families lived alone for centuries on isolated farms. Many must have wished, or been forced, to join forces to aid each other, to share or lease implements or livestock, to coordinate agricultural labor, to provide for their common defense, and to intermarry. So vicinity could become another force operating on settlement. Actually, in the early Middle Ages, proximity may have been no less important than kinship,[11] especially since, after a possible decline, the population had probably been growing since

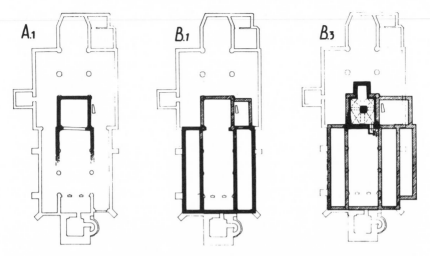

Figure 3. Demographic Growth Attested by an Expanding Parish Church. Progressive expansions of the floor plan reveal the congregation's continuing growth, which in turn suggests growth in the rural population. In the church of Gerpinnes (Belgium, Hainault), the expanding floorplans of the Merovingian (A.1), Carolingian (B.1), and pre-Romanesque (B.3) buildings can be detected in the Romanesque structure.
    Source: J. Mertens, "L'Église Saint-Michel à Gerpinnes," *Bulletin de la Commission royale des Monuments et des Sites,* XII, 1961, 206.

the eighth century.[12] Here again archaeology is most helpful, since, for instance, it can uncover transformations of the parish church that reflect demographic patterns, as at Gerpinnes (see figure 3).

Whether the economy was also progressing and promoting the demographic wave is a controversial question. Some scholars maintain that the Merovingian or at least the Carolingian times were a period of economic depression.[13] Others, on the contrary, assert that, especially from the seventh century, the West, in its northern as well as southern parts, expanded;[14] that colonization occurred, favored by a change in the climate, which became moister and warmer[15] and was stimulated at the end of the Merovingian epoch—according to a highly debated view—by a technological revolution, which would have transferred supremacy from the south to the north.[16] Some hesitate choosing between the two theses.[17] In the present state of knowledge, the theory backed by demographic and economic arguments seems to be better substantiated. At any rate, barbarian laws and other written documents of the period not infrequently mention *vicini* (neighbors), and the archaeological evidence increasingly and impressively argues for the growing predominance of hamlets in Spain, England, Germany, Italy, and elsewhere.[18] We shall return to this point in the next chapter, when discussing what Italian historians call *incastellamento* and a French historian has baptized *encellulement* (closing up into a cell). In any case, vicinity kept its importance in the following centuries. Until the end of the Middle Ages, the rural community was called *buurschap* in the Netherlands, *Nachbarschaft* in Schleswig-Holstein, and *veziau* in the French Pyrenees.[19] In other regions, *vicini* played at least some part in many matters concerning the collectivity: administration,[20] justice,[21] and above all management of the *communia* (the commons). Many local customs recognized two kinds of *retractus* (buying back a plot of land within a year from the sale), since they allowed neighbors as well as relatives to redeem a piece of field alienated by a peasant or they simply prohibited sale to a stranger.[22] In some affairs, they allowed some groups of *vicini* the right of bringing cases before a court.[23]

In every time and in every country, common possession or use of land constituted a cornerstone of the collectivity. Many theories have been built about the system of landed ownership before and during the Middle Ages. In the mid-nineteenth century, the founders of economic history spoke of a primitive communism and held that the whole surface (*Mark*) pertained to the *Markgenossenschaft*.[24] The *Mark* consisted of the infield, which was regularly cultivated, and the outfield (*Allmende*), or fallow lands and forests, which were sometimes tilled and were continually used for pasturing, timbering, collecting wild fruits, cutting turf or peat, and collecting firewood. Such a thesis is obsolete. Tacitus's famous sentence in his *Germania*, "Arva per annos mutant" (they exchange fields annually), is no proof that the fields were collective property. And no historian would write today that the *Mark* was the foundation of the *Genossenschaft* and generated the rural community.[25] Did even the commons date from antiquity? Bognetti asserts it did in Italy.[26] Some scholars apparently agree, some do not.[27] To be sure, the right to commons is attested in the Carolingian period.[28] And in the ninth century, in Languedoc, the Pyrenees, Catalonia, and northwestern Spain, the collectivity owned or farmed a part or the whole of the soil.[29] One would be tempted to generalize from those centuries and regions to previous times and other countries, but the retrospective method is always dangerous.

Mentality and traditions probably played a secondary but not negligible part in settlement forms and in the precocious birth of nucleated agglomerations. Meitzen's thesis on the ethnic character of different kinds of settlements or the theory opposing Latin concentration and German dispersion are no doubt false or exaggerated.[30] Nevertheless, Tacitus might be quoted here too, and excellent archaeologists are of the opinion that the barbarians introduced in the North a new type of settlement that mixed village and farmsteads.[31] Here we are dealing with habits deriving not from race but from fundamental conceptions regarding people and society, reflected in law and custom, that favored individuals or groups and that influenced the settlement and its evolution, especially in the rules that governed landed succession (i.e., partible or indivisible inheritance).

To sum up, kin, interest, necessity of mutual aid, the holding of commons, and traditions incited or compelled peasants to join together spontaneously and to act collectively. To what extent and in what way? Were peasants completely free in all matters, independent of everyone except public authority, the king and his officials, enjoying a real self-government, debating and determining every question of general interest, endowed with full judicial capacity? Let us admit that on the central Rhine in the seventh century some collectivities intervened in some areas: prosecution of trespassing and quarrels about boundaries or transfers of landed property.[32] That does not imply total liberty. Let us concede that Bavaria and Flanders on the threshold of the Middle Ages knew some communities of free peasants; but they were few, and they were integrated into the seignorial system under the Carolingians.[33] At first sight, the Italian case seemed clear, but nowadays, when the origins of the "associations of free tillers of the soil who spontaneously enjoyed self-administration" are studied, it appears that the data on them only date from the twelfth century.[34] In Carolingian Roussillon and Catalonia there existed collectivities of peasants whose *boni viri* attained a judicial authority, but it was a limited and not really official one.[35] Finally, in northwestern Spain there were free rural entities, but by the ninth or tenth century they were slowly and insidiously being permeated by the lords.[36]

*

A SEIGNORIAL system—lords, private and local authority, as it were—leads us to the second possibility for the birth or development of the rural community, that is, by a leader.

In an agricultural or pastoral economy, this was naturally the owner or one of the owners of the land, either a descendant of a leader who, before the Middle Ages, settled there with his retinue, or a newcomer who emerged from the collectivity during the early Middle Ages by accumulating fields and mastering the commons. This raises two sets of much discussed problems: (1) the legacy of antiquity, especially in the Roman Empire, and the continuity from antiquity into the Middle Ages; and (2) the process of the concentration of landed property from the fifth to the ninth centuries and the constitution of what the Germans call *Grundherrschaft*.

In studying the system of landed property and forms of settlement in antiquity in areas incorporated into the Roman Empire, scholars often focused their attention on the *villae,* the manors held by a lord and managed with the help of slaves or tenants. Yet such *villae* did not cover the whole land. They did not eliminate the *vici,* communities of free peasants, some of which had even been established in the *villae.*[37] Moreover, all the so-called *villae* were not big estates; many, perhaps the majority, were of modest size.[38] Around Trier, one can distinguish small isolated buildings on the hills and on the less fertile soil, *villae* of middling importance on the plateaus and better ground, and impressive manors in the valleys, the remnants of which are frequently covered by the centers of modern villages.[39] Besides, in the late Empire and its disorders, many *fundi* (estates) were abandoned or occupied by squatters.[40]

In the fourth century, little dwellings and huts multiplied, apparently independent of a manorial regime.[41] No less than seventy-eight instances of this kind have been counted in the Pays de France, north of Paris. They were called *casae* if they were alone and *loci* when two or three were grouped together on new sites.[42] Finally, all *villae* were not concentrated in one point; excavations have turned up many that had several cemeteries.[43] In England, many *villae* were multiple estates, with a central settlement and a number of dependent ones.[44] Under such circumstances, they might have formed the base or roots of some, but not all, medieval rural communities.

What about deduction from later evidence? This raises the problem of continuity from antiquity to the Middle Ages, which is still debated.[45] Some accept, some deny a continuity; some give a cautious answer, distinguishing periods, areas, and cases. As a matter of fact, one ought, since all aspects of the past are involved, to differentiate among fields, institutions, social structures, the economy, thought and letters, beliefs, festivals, and so on; between regions and sites, particularly towns or country; and between periods. As far as the economy is concerned, the trends often did not develop the same way in industry, trade, and agriculture. It is necessary to avoid confusing settlement, dwelling, field layout, and systems of cultivation and management. The inhabited center of a *villa* could disappear or be converted to a cemetery, while the fields continued to be lived on and tilled.[46]

The coincidence of boundary between a Roman *villa* and a medieval manor, or the proximity of classical and Frankish remains, is no proof that occupation and cultivation continued without break.[47] The landscape, "that most subtle and fragile of all historical documents,"[48] was all too often reshaped not only in the Middle Ages by the medieval lord in order to unify his territories and enhance their productiv-

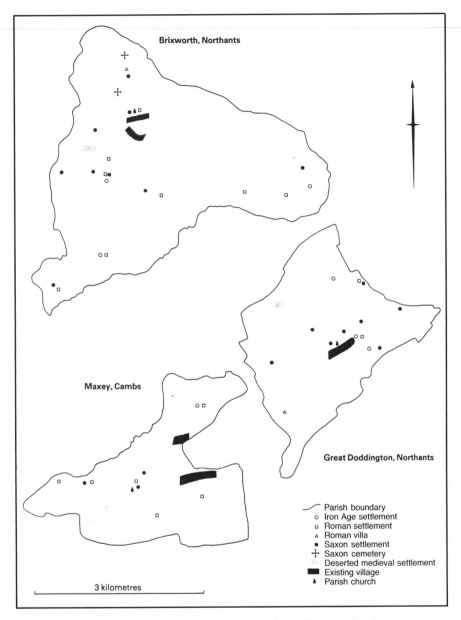

Figure 4. Continuity or Instability in Settlement. In the three villages, shifts of settlement sites are confined within small distances of a few thousand meters. Continuity from Iron Age to Middle Ages through Roman and Saxon periods combines with instability.

Source: C. Taylor, *Village and Farmstead. A History of Rural Settlement in England,* London, George Philip and Sons, 1983, p. 113.

ity but in later centuries. Mention of many localities of classical origin first appears in medieval texts, and not a few Roman sites survived in the Middle Ages under a new place-name. To add to the difficulty, there was great variety in the matter: variety in form and size of settlements (modest farms subsisted near deserted big estates,[49] so concluding from one kind of farm to another would be an error); variety from region to region; variety from place to place. In Lombardy, the *vicus* was revitalized by the invaders, and great landed properties, until the Carolingians, no longer covered huge and compact areas made up of several adjacent *fundi*. In Romania and other countries under Byzantine authority, the *fundi*, with their *latifundia* or *masse*, survived and hindered the formation of independent rural communities.[50] Around the lake of Garda there was continuity in some places and breaks in other places.[51] England shows the same contrasts, but here continuity frequently coexisted with movements from the chalk downs to the bottoms of the valleys.[52] Even in Italy, the taciturnity of written witnesses prevents too peremptory an assertion.[53] Spain allows more solid views: in the coastal regions and in mountainous regions like the Douro Valley, the Roman system kept the upper hand.[54] In the Auvergne, too, the contrast persisted from antiquity until the tenth century between rich soils intensively occupied and poor soils sparsely inhabited.[55] And of course continuity was greater in the Romanized parts of the West.[56] At any rate, not all medieval villages derived from antique *villae*. Some, perhaps many, sprang up after the fall of the Roman Empire.

They were located in the intervals between ancient *villae* or on virgin grounds in younger regions.[57] And in Italy, some antique *villae* that had been deserted and whose fields had been abandoned were reconstructed.[58]

The initiative for these new *villae* came from the *potentes*, whose existence is unquestionable in the fifth century, and certainly in the sixth. The written evidence of that time constantly mentions *nobiles*, and excavations have uncovered privileged burials surrounded or flanked by graves of warriors and by tombs devoid of any jewel, furniture, or vessel, sheltering the remains of poor people—servants, slaves, serfs of the *familia*—the retinue. In Arlon in the southeast of Belgium, nineteen rich burials, some of them extraordinarily so, took place between the second quarter of the sixth century and the end of the seventh, next to the local aristocracy's church.[59] The origins and status of that nobility are today the most debated problem of the early Middle Ages. Was it an *Uradel*, an ancient nobility from German antiquity, which derived its privileges and its independence from birth and blood and which possessed an *allodium*, or free property? Or was

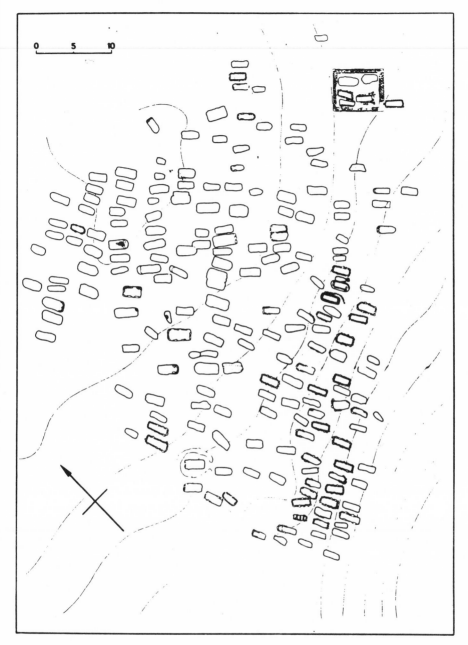

Figure 5. Aristocracy in the Frankish Period. In death as in life, Frankish grandees remained close to but separate from underlings. Note how the aristocratic graves are distinctively grouped within the small funerary monument on the cemetery's eastern corner.

Source: A. Dierkens, *Les deux cimetières mérovingiens de Franchimont (Prov. de Namur). Fouilles de 1877–1878*, Namur, 1981.

it a *Dienstadel,* an officials' nobility, composed of *convivae regis,* companions and officials of the barbarian kings, and deriving its position from royal gifts and concessions? Or was it a class inheriting its legal rank from the *senatores* of the late Empire? Space is lacking here to enter into these extremely intricate questions.[60] Suffice it to say without hesitation that a caste was present and was increasingly powerful in the first phase of the period we are interested in. During the same epoch, too, some peasants combined chance, skill, and energy to emerge from among their equals and develop their possessions and power. So, for instance, the *boni homines* became progressively distinct from the *cetera plebs* (the rest of people) in the Pyrenees.[61]

There were two main ways the *potentes* created new *villae.* The first was to absorb more modest establishments. It was followed no doubt by ecclesiastical institutions. And perhaps too by laymen, but we do not know much, if anything, about them. Under the Merovingians, freeholdings could be found in the territory of a *villa.*[62] The polyptychs of the Carolingian religious chapters and monasteries reveal that the big estates consisted partly in mini domains, or large tenancies, which seem to have been peasants' properties that were not yet well integrated.[63] And Charlemagne's capitularies strove to defend the *pauperes liberi homines* (the common people) against the great landowners.[64] The second method of creating new *villae* was to appropriate uncultivated land and to allot it to one's men, one's *Haus*—hence the term *Hausherrschaft*[65]—and to free people, who in that manner became the lord's tenants, and to promote or command its reclamation, the *auszerer Landesausbau.*[66]

In both systems, the subjection to the same owner created or strengthened the link among the *potente*'s dependents and, when manor and village coincided, among them and members of the whole rural community. The link deepened by a reshaping of the estate's organization, by the diffusion (or more likely, the creation and diffusion) of the so-called classical, domanial, or bipartite system, with the division into demesne and tenancies. The tenancies were granted to tenants who, in return, had to cultivate one lot of the domain or work on it a fixed number of days per week. The origins of that way of managing a manor are another subject of controversy. A legacy of antiquity? Perhaps in Italy.[67] But elsewhere? Relying on descriptions of landed properties in charters is more valid than one might think at first blush, because the descriptions were not stereotyped.[68] It seems more and more certain that there was no identity between the *fundus,* with its slaves destitute of personal property, and the Frankish *villa,* with its characteristic partition and the connection between its two elements. The latter appeared in some regions in the sixth century, spread in the seventh, and gained the upper hand in the Carolingian era.[69] It supposed a uniformity in size and value of the holdings. These were remolded into *mansi,* "hides," *Hufen,* "manses,"[70] which worsened the pressure on the population. These transformations helped concentrate hamlets and farmsteads into *Verdorfung,* (the constitutions of villages), beginning in some cases in the sixth century[71] and developed in the seventh,[72] but reaching their full impetus only after the ninth century.[73]

Old or new, *villae* were, in the ninth century, the normal type of settlement and management. Of nine localities composing in the thirteenth century the castlery of Couvin, close to the modern Belgian-French frontier in a rather infertile region, eight were mentioned between 780 and 870, and seven were called *villae.* In 862 in the Ardennes, an area not any more privileged by nature, the abbey of Stavelot possessed five *villae* with thirty-two to sixty-two *mansi* and ten *loci* with five to ten *mansi.*[74] Of course, the meaning of *villa* was manifold. In the *Lex Salica,* it applied to diverse realities.[75] But more and more it came to mean a manor[76] and even an agglomeration of some importance—a village or, more frequently, the nucleus of a future village.[77]

In fact, *villae* did not cover the whole ground. There were a few *vici* of free peasants and more *loci.* But, as the estates of Stavelot suggest, these were less numerous and smaller, and they lacked churches. Nor did the *villae* always coincide with the whole agglomeration.[78] Many agglomerations were divided into several manors. Not a few manors were made up of *mansi* pertaining to several agglomerations. Of course, partition or dispersion could appear or increase with successions and gifts. But some manors kept their initial structure.

Nevertheless, the *villa* at the close of the early Middle Ages was the usual framework for rural society. It was used to localize goods: "in villa et territorio," as the acts specify. The *villa* lent its limits to other structures. It soon was identified with the village. On the whole, it was the nucleus that gradually incorporated free peasants and free properties into one collectivity.

*

ANOTHER entity—the parish—intervened in the birth, or at least in the maturation, of the rural community (at any rate from the Carolingian period). The parish grouped together the whole people, however they lived—concentrated or dispersed, in villages, hamlets, or farmsteads. It put on everybody's shoulders the same burdens and duties, both moral and material. It drew or invited precise boundaries. All of these generated or nourished a collective conscience.

The rural religious network developed slowly, without any systematic and detailed plan, and under the impulse of many factors, the most influential of them being administrative and judicial structures, economic activity that animated roads and markets, population growth, the dynamics of the clergy, the power and ambitions of the upper class, and the piety, whether orthodox or deviant, of the common people.[79] Churches had been erected in late antiquity in the countryside, probably many in populous Roman Britain and a few elsewhere, mainly but not exclusively in *vici* and *castra* (boroughs and castles).[80] More were built in the fifth and sixth centuries by bishops, by the faithful, and, increasingly by landowners.

The bishops continued creating *ecclesiae* in the boroughs, the *matrices ecclesiae* (mother churches) of the future, or the Italian *pievi* (parishes). Peasant groups combined their finances to support a priest to take care of their spiritual needs and help them meet their religious obligations. In the Pyrenean valleys, for instance, in the ninth century or before, some communities were *fundatores* or *edificatores* (founders or constructors) of churches. These churches were the *allodium* (the free property) and *dos* (dowry) of the *plebs*, the *populus habitancium*. These inhabitants chose the officiants of their churches.[81]

Above all, the *potentes* founded their own *tituli*, *capellae*, and *basilicae*—their domestic—or private—sanctuaries. These *Eigenkirchen* were built in the center of large estates or at the junctions of several minor ones.[82] The reasons for building private sanctuaries varied: some *potentes* wanted to satisfy their personal religious needs or wishes and were inspired by a real devotion; others aimed to attract people by facilitating the observance of their religious duties; others wanted to maintain a cult or perhaps memorialize their ancestors.[83]

At the end of the sixth century, in the diocese of Auxerre, of 20 new churches, 8 were established in boroughs and 12 on estates. A hundred years later, the diocese counted 37 churches, 13 in the boroughs and 24 on manors.[84] In the seventh and eighth centuries, the proportion of churches on estates continued to grow. And in the ninth century, a capitulary ordained that each *novae villae* be endowed with a church.[85] From the seventh to the ninth centuries, 300 churches were built in the diocese of Limoges and 200 more were promoted from private to public sanctuaries; together, that makes 500 new parishes founded in the Frankish period out of 1,000 for the whole diocese.[86] Little wonder the capitulary of Pitres, in 869, demanded "ut presbiteri parrochiani suis senioribus debitam reverentiam et competentem honorem impendant" (that parish priests pay due reverence and appropriate honor to their lords).[87] In that period, the density of the church network differed from region to region. On an average, it was less loose than might be expected. In Ortenau between the Rhine and the Black Forest, in a square space of thirty kilometers, twenty-nine parishes were built in the seventh and eighth centuries, nineteen in the ninth and tenth centuries (mostly on royal fiscs), and thirty-three in the eleventh, twelfth, and thirteenth centuries, thanks especially to the initiative of princes.[88] Even in a rather rough region like the Ardennes, of the 127 parishes in Bastogne and Stavelot in 1807, 40 existed in the Carolingian period.[89]

From the Carolingian period, the parish played a major part (one is tempted to say the major part) in country life, mainly as a consequence of measures promulgated by lay and clerical authorities during the Carolingian period.[90] In that disorderly field, as in other ones, the dynasty intended to introduce order. It was helped by the hierarchy, which wished to foster and check the religious life. The dynasty was backed by circumstances—for instance, by its military needs, which justified the obligation of the tithe.

The first measure to establish order was to fix the canonical rank of each church and to define the status of private sanctuaries and their relation to public ones and to the *matrix ecclesia*. The churches were placed in one of two categories, and some moved from the first to the second. At Anthée, on the central Meuse, for instance, an oratory erected on the foundations of a *fanum* (a Roman sanctuary) and belonging to a *potens* who managed what had once been a huge Roman estate, probably gave way to an edifice apparently linked to the bishop, which in time became the parish sanctuary.[91]

The ecclesiastical organization was also modified, as in Italy, where continuity in that respect from antiquity to the Middle Ages seems to have been less certain than has been believed.[92] The bishops kept the upper hand in this area. They tried not to obliterate the rights and interests of the *matrices ecclesiae* but made some concessions to the private oratories. From the fifth century, the priests of the *vici* and *castella* were allowed to baptize; their power to do so was confirmed in the mid-eighth century, and their use of this power is attested by the presence of font stones in rural churches.[93] In 529, the Council of Vaison permitted parish priests to preach.[94] But the Carolingians compelled the congregation to hear mass on Sunday in the *matrix ecclesia* and to confess and receive communion in it on the main feast days.[95] These prescriptions were probably not strictly obeyed: a capitulary in the mid-ninth century deplored that "quidam laici ac maxime potentes ac nobiles . . . juxta domos suas basilicas habent in quibus audiunt officium" (certain laymen and especially the powerful and the nobles have their own churches next to their homes in which they hear the divine office).[96] The *matrix ecclesia* also required that funeral rites be performed there but did not succeed: the faithful maintained the right of electing their burial place and, from the eighth century at least, many tombs were disposed around domainal churches.[97] So Hincmar of Reims prescribed that every *capella* "tantum atrii habeat ubi pauperculi qui suos mortuos longius effere non possunt eosdem ibi sepelire valeant" (should have enough yard where the poor who cannot transport their dead to a greater distance might be able to bury them).[98]

There were other means to enclose, control, and restrain the faithful. The doctrine on marriage and its sacramental value was proclaimed by the church.[99] And the parochial synod was introduced, which all believers were bound to attend in order to denounce the "crimina notaria et manifesta" (the notorious and evident public trespasses of the moral rules).[100]

All these duties were met and all these ceremonies were performed collectively: baptisms, funerals and even, for major and public sins, the antique penance assembled the whole community.[101] So too the processions: for the offerings (which probably did not take root in Gaul and Spain except at funerals) and for holy communion. But the liturgy was not in the vernacular, and the mass especially became a matter for the clergy. In the canon of the mass, *sacramentaria* of Frankish origin added to "qui tibi offerunt" (the faithful who offer to you) the words "vel pro quibus tibi offerimus" (or for whom we offer to you). It was the priest who offered, no longer the laity.[102]

Above all, the tithe was imposed. It had been executed since the seventh century by the Frankish church. It was made compulsory in 765 and definitively so by the capitulary of Heristal in 779. At the same time, the parish ceased being personal and became territorial. It became necessary to lay out its limits: "Ut terminum habeat unaquaque ecclesia de quibus villis decimas recipiat" (Let each church have boundaries from which *villas* it receives tithe) declared the *capitula ecclesiastica* of 810–13.[103]

The limits could be those of the *matrix ecclesia*, established in administrative and judicial centers,[104] or of a *basilica* or *capella* that had been promoted to the rank of parish (a parish of the second generation, according to G. Fournier's expression).[105] In Carolingian times, parish limits were those of the *villa* which normally included several small settlements. Sometimes there were manifest or latent conflicts, especially since the church attracted people from localities lacking a sanctuary and thus helped reshape the landscape.[106] At any rate, the boundaries inserted the peasants into a firm framework. In the majority of cases, the *villa* preceded the parish and gave the latter its boundaries. But the parish in its turn supported the *villa*. And with its

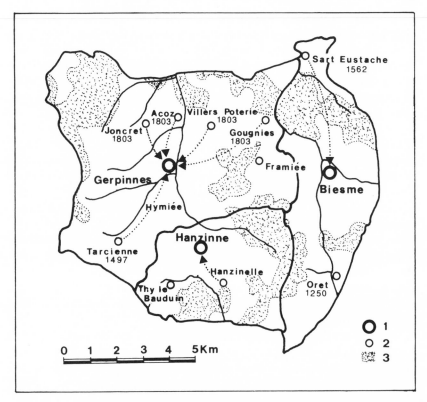

Figure 6. Estates and Parishes. This map reveals how centers and boundaries of estates and parishes could coincide. In this example, the centers of three early medieval, fiscal estates in the Entre-Sambre-et-Meuse region coincided with the location of the *matrices ecclesiae* (1), and the approximate boundaries of both institutions were essentially the same. Parish churches and chapels subordinate to the *matrices ecclesiae* are shown and, where known, the date when new parishes were created is given (2). Known forest areas are indicated (3).

Source: A. Dierkens, "Note sur un acte perdu du maire du palais Carloman pour l'abbaye Saint-Médard de Soissons, ca.745," in *Francia* XII, 1984, 640.

common obligations, with its ceremonies marking life from birth to death, with its well-drawn limits, it was possibly—indeed probably—in most countries the first formation that unified the whole community and made it to some extent conscious of itself.[107]

*

Does the present state of knowledge preclude generalizations? And will generalizations always be impossible because of the weakness of our documentation? I don't know. I dare only propose some cautious and partial conclusions.

The birth and childhood of the rural community were very complex phenomena, which witnessed the action and reaction of many forces of different kinds, varying strengths, and uncertain chronology, especially in regard to the consciousness of constituting a distinct entity. Consciousness is a collective and psychological fact, which, like all such facts, is difficult to date and locate—to insert exactly into time and space.

The first consequence of such complexity is the diversity of specific situations and the pressing necessity for monographs.[108] The second consequence is the uncertainty of the process of community formation and development and of the stages reached by the end of the tenth century. In younger regions, most communities probably originated either spontaneously, from families that became large and separated into distinct houses and that for different reasons joined each other; or authoritatively, by a traditional or emerging aristocracy who appropriated the common territory and distributed it to *familia* and to free peasants or who appropriated the free smallholdings. Older communities, especially in the romanized countries, derived from *villae* that survived the late Empire or that were created in the early Middle Ages.

Those communities that were united more or less strongly, gained more or less liberty and became more or less conscious of their specificity in natural conditions—a need for defense against the sea or amid the marshes, as in Friesland, or the need for irrigation, as in Catalonia, or the possibility of escaping all external powers, as in the mountains of northwestern Spain. Their specificity also entailed human circumstances (fear of raids for instance). Some communities enjoyed only the use of the common, without the right to dispose of it. Some were integrated into the domainal system, which abridged their liberty but unified to some extent the use of the soil and the status of the people. Some maintained or obtained a limited political, administrative, and juridical capacity, as in Bas-Languedoc.[109] Likewise, in Catalonia, some took oath to nobody but the public power, and they could take action in the official court against anyone.[110] Finally, some were effectively autonomous, as in Friesland, the country without lords, and in the Pyrenees. But these were few, very few. Most communities were part of a manor. This was probably, in most cases, the first step on the path to a real community, from a material viewpoint. The parish was the second step, from a perspective of consciousness and self-awareness. However, it was not the last step. Given the scattered settlement, the diversity in the status of people and in the conditions of cultivation, the weakness of the people vis-à-vis the owner of the land and, soon, of the air, their lack of juridical status, and the absence of their own organized bodies, the way to the *universitas* was still long.

Insufficient, questionable, disappointing conclusions? No doubt. But are historians bound to the possibly impossible task of distinguishing and dating every phase, at the risk of disconnecting factors that operated in symbiosis? Is it required and reasonable, for instance, to separate manor and parish?

And finally, historians have to avoid a common error: to devote the best of their attention to the origins of any phenomenon. Origins of the Middle Ages, origins of the towns, origins of nobility and chivalry: our books are full of origins. Even though it be new, every phenomenon is a permanent creation, and its development is not less important than its appearance or emergence.

It is with that reassuring reflection that we leave the origins of the rural community and the Dark Ages to enter into the sometimes less than bright light of our second millennium.

2

UNIVERSITAS:

ECONOMIC ASPECTS

*

FROM THE twelfth century on, two words have been associated with *villa* and other designations of the rural community: *universitas* and *communitas*.[1] *Universitas* was used in the *Liber diurnus*, the early medieval formulary of the papal chancery: "convenientibus nobis, id est clero, axiomaticis etiam et generali militie ac civium universitate."[2] The term appeared afterward in diplomas delivered in the second half of the eleventh century to Italian cities.[3]

Universitas was not connected with *villa* before 1150 or 1200. In Belgium, whose documents prior to 1200 have been put into computers and for which a thorough enquiry is thus feasible, the correlation was not made until 1224, when the *universitas ville* of a village near Namur claimed some rights to a wood owned by a monastery.[4] In Italy, the first instance of the expression is found in a document from 1194, where the bishop of Trento intervened "vice totius communie universitatis," (in the name of the university of the whole commune), probably because this group did not enjoy a juridical existence.[5] In Germany, in a charter dated 1163, the archbishop of Trier, as lord of Merzig, disposed by virtue of his "judiciaria potestas super homines" (judicial power over men) that, in that little place, the manager of the *hunria* was not qualified to interfere in matters that "universitas populi a nobis convocata dixerit ad suum officium non pertinere" (the university of the people that we have convoked has declared do not pertain to his office).[6] Here, too, the *universitas* did not act spontaneously. And in Alsatia, the *communitas ville* was not mentioned until the thirteenth century.[7] A collection of all such mentions would confirm— and lend precision to—this date.

It would also help to establish the meaning of *universitas* and *communitas*. Of course, a shift in the words does not imply, at least immediately, a change in structure, especially when the words are adjectives and not substantives: *nobilis* is less significant than *nobilitas*. We are here in the field of German conceptual history, the *Begriffsgeschichte*, which leads from words and concepts to realities.[8] At any rate, one is always bound to hunt out the technical words that cover a specific meaning, to discover that specificity and its possible evolution according to time, space, and literary genre. In the present case, we ought to know the exact meaning of the two words when they are connected with *villa*—whether they applied to a factual or legal reality, whether they were synonymous, or whether *communitas* designated a kind of second-level community, less perfect in its constitution and consciousness, while *universitas* had a more juridical connotation.[9]

Whatever the definitions, the terms denominated a true community, with territory, mutual assistance, rights and duties, and self-consciousness. The community was especially qualified to act in juridical affairs, like making binding agreements, buying, and appearing in a court. When, how, and in what measure did the community acquire that ability and exercise it? Thanks to or under the pressure of economic, political, and religious developments? This chapter is restricted to economic reasons. The first and most consequential consisted of the increase in population, which affected settlement by encouraging the concentration of people in villages, the production of food, and the reclamation of wasteland and innovations in cultivation—which in turn imperilled the common and the structure of the society. The growing mobility of people and goods also acted to create or deepen the gap between the rich and the poor.

*

THE PHENOMENON of the population increase remains clouded.[10] Its beginning, according to Marc Bloch's famous—and questionable—*second âge féodal* (second feudal age) was in 1050. But for a long time the nonwritten evidence (for instance, the successive enlargements of Merovingian rural churches) has suggested an earlier date. And recent research confirms that everywhere in the West the phenomenon started in the tenth century, or the ninth, or even earlier. In England, the Domesday Book attests to huge reclamations long before 1066;[11] and in Portugal, assarts are mentioned in the oldest charters, around 1000.[12]

What were the causes and conditions of the increase? Some factors were natural. Climate improved, reaching its optimum between 1150 and 1300.[13] This made previously infertile soils tillable and drastically reduced the frequence of crop failures to one year in twenty, even in upland areas.[14] Some factors were technological. Improvements in cultivation, which are examined below, enhanced the yield ratio and allowed the land to feed more people and to feed them better. Life expectancy may have lengthened, a population trend perhaps offset by a lowering of the marriage rate. The mortality rate was also down, though still formidable by modern standards.[15] Whether the improvements provoked or allowed demographic advance or demographic pressure forced people to innovate is an open question. Psychology also intervened. Many children were born: in noble families whose genealogies can be drawn up, we find five adults in each generation down to 1250,[16] perhaps because children were considered to be wealth, not burdens. Finally, the decrease in violence[17] and the renewal of the economy also played their part.

The rhythm, if not all the phases, for the movement, is better known. Through and despite fluctuations caused mainly by public disorders,[18] human density did not gallop as in nineteenth-century Europe but grew steadily over three centuries or more, apparently reaching its maximum speed in most countries from 1150 to 1250.[19] In England, where the figures are the least questionable, the population grew from a little over a million in 1086 to nearly four million in 1347.[20] In several especially infertile regions, population was around 1,300—as high as in the nineteenth or twentieth centuries—or even higher in the mountains. The rise of rents and entry fines and the reduction in the dimension of holdings eloquently witness the phenomenon's strength. This strength gradually became an almost unbearable pressure. Then the demographic flood slowed from the mid-thirteenth century, except in less favored and less occupied regions, like the Dauphiné. Reclamations slackened or even ceased, rents and wages were lowered, and marginal fields were abandoned.[21]

With the fourteenth century, the movement inverted. The climate became colder and wetter, as attested by the adaptations in the plan of houses to defend them and their crofts against water and humidity— for instance, by digging or deepening drainage ditches.[22] It invited or forced the abandonment of fields located above 900 to 1,200 feet.[23] Crop failures multiplied, reaching one out of three in the uplands. Internal and external wars disturbed the economy. Prices fluctuated more and more, making transactions speculative. The birth rate declined for various reasons:[24] overpopulation, late marriages, age differences between spouses, or the desire to maintain wealth and prestige by avoiding partitions of the inheritance. Perhaps children were no longer considered an advantage but a burden. Perhaps, too, there was a general atmosphere of low energy brought on by a flourishing of regulations of every kind.[25] Above all, public plagues raged: famines, epidemics, especially the Black Death and its sequels in 1360, in 1369, and in every generation until the fifteenth century.[26] A new invocation was added to the litany: "A fame, peste, et bello libera nos, Domine" (From famine, plague, and war deliver us, O Lord).

*

BUT BEFORE reaching that last stage, the continuous population advance had launched a lot of consequences of primary importance for the peasantry. It had affected the way of life and settlement patterns. Aside from a few exceptions due to special circumstances—Sicily, for instance, where the Normans did not succeed in linking *villeins* and holdings[27]—population growth contributed to the decisive victory of sedentariness, which marked an essential step in the coalescence of the peasant community. As for settlement patterns, the phenomenon was more complex and requires some development.

According to a growing number of scholars, guided by archaeologists and geographers, from the ninth or tenth centuries onward—if not before in parts of England and the districts around Trier and Marburg in Germany—the West passed from dispersion to concentration of the population.[28] Was the movement spontaneous or compulsory? Was it generated by the peasants? Or was it generated by the lords, eager to gather and muster their dependents in order to dominate them and improve the production of their lands? The answer is likely that the lords were the principal actors, not only in this change, but in others that we shall consider.

The causes or occasions of clustering are not always obvious. Some historians explain the evolution simply by the growth of population.[29] But populated regions are not always regions of nucleated vills. Other scholars invoke technological improvements requiring mutual aid: the passage from pasturing to tilling, changes in the manner of cultivation, a shift toward a cooperative and productive agriculture, the adoption of heavy ploughs, the introduction of the open-field system.[30] But that system also operated outside villages. One could also think of social habits or trends, like the desire for living together in community, under the shadow and the shelter of the church and near ancestors buried in the cemetery. However, the main factor apparently was the need for security, even if troubles did not always and everywhere hinder dispersion.[31]

The political "failure" of the Carolingians paved the way to internal disorder, inflamed by the weakening of public authority, and to external attacks by Vikings, Hungarians, or Saracens, even if raids and the construction of fortifications did not always exactly coincide. Dispersed in agglomerations, the biggest of which rarely counted more than forty or fifty dwellings and, for the most part, in mean hamlets or isolated farms, people were unable to defend themselves. Not infrequently, destruction offered the opportunity for reshaping the settlement. Some villages were vigorous enough to ring their inhabited portion of the land with walls or palisades[32]—the German *Etter*. But *Etter*, we shall see, has a more juridical than military significance; it marks the limits of the enfranchised part of the territory. And above all, the lords erected castles, the famous *incastellamento*.

These last have in recent decades generated a new branch of archaeology and history, castellology. From the tenth century to the thirteenth and later, thousands and thousands of fortified buildings arose in the countryside of the West. To determine the reasons for—and the significance of—the phenomenon, it is indispensable to distinguish kinds of fortifications, periods, owners and locations.[33] Keeps, castles, moats, *maisons fortes*, and *sites fossoyés* (those surrounded merely by a ditch) differed in size, structure, and aims.[34] The keeps opened the way; in a second stage, they were enclosed with a belt of towers and ramparts; the moated or ditched sites, sometimes preceded by a wooden dungeon, multiplied from 1200 or 1250.[35] The initiators were the heads of noble lineages and were successively in a more and more modest manner imitated by juniors, knights, officers, vassals, and eventually in the late Middle Ages by well-to-do farmers.

The location of the castle varied; it normally moved from the *curtis*, the very center of the agglomeration,[36] to the edge of it, often on poor, marshy, wooded spots. This movement may have been related to late land reclamations, the intensification of agriculture, or the development of pasturing.[37] The motivations of the builders were primarily political: mastering a region (as shown by the military elements in the structure of early castles and the kings' and princes' care in controlling them). Defense against peers or, at a lower level, against rustlers or thieves could also inspire building, not to mention the attraction of people anxious for protection and security. More and more, display of rank or riches figured in the construction. Of course, these purposes could coincide, as in the foundations of the *villes neuves* we shall encounter below.

With what results? Many scholars, mainly in France but also in Germany and Italy, are convinced that the first fortified edifices, keeps and castles, became the base of authority and of the *seigneurie banale*, and that they also provoked changes in the parochial network. Those aspects will be met in chapters 3 and 4. Here we are only concerned by the influence of the *incastellamento* on the concentration and the layout of villages. Many keeps and castles effectively drew to their walls people in search of quiet and protection to the extent that they were willing to pay tallage to the local lord or *salvamentum* to a foreign magnate in order to live "safely."[38] These castles became the centers of

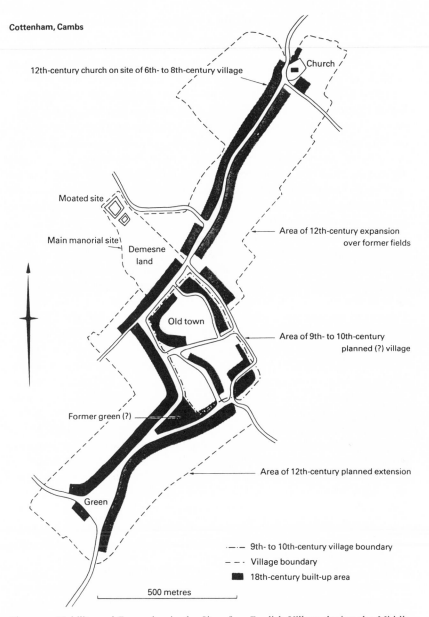

Cottenham, Cambs

12th-century church on site of 6th- to 8th-century village

Church

Moated site

Main manorial site

Demesne land

Area of 12th-century expansion over former fields

Old town

Area of 9th- to 10th-century planned (?) village

Former green (?)

Area of 12th-century planned extension

Green

·—·— 9th- to 10th-century village boundary
– – – Village boundary
■ 18th-century built-up area

500 metres

Figure 7. Mobility and Expansion in the Site of an English Village during the Middle Ages. Transfer of settlement center from its original site of the 6th to the 8th century—still marked by the location of the village church—toward the moated defensive works and demesne during the turbulent period of the 9th to the 10th century. From here, the village expanded northeast and southwest in the 12th century, until it finally absorbed the original site.

Source: C. Taylor, *Village and Farmstead: A History of Rural Settlement in England*, London, George Philip and Sons, 1983, p.157.

new settlements.[39] In some cases, they also led to a remodeling of the territory.[40] In other countries and other cases, they influenced neither settlement nor layout.

Nucleation proceeded in different ways. Old sites, favored by natural or human conditions, grew by *Landesausbau*, (enlargement of extant settlements).[41] Dispersed places agglomerated from polyfocal to unified settlements. New vills or new wards (*villes neuves*) were founded in the intervals or on the edge of old localities.[42] The reasons were not only, not even primarily, economic and financial, but also—and probably more frequently—political, military, and administrative.[43]

Nucleation gave the opportunity, if it did not impose the necessity, for shaping or reshaping the village's layout. Whether a rural community could not exist without a planned organization is questionable.[44] At any rate, a more or less precise and detailed plan is noticeable since the eleventh century. A fundamental distinction existed henceforward between the inhabited part and the rest of the territory, between what French language documents call "le champ et la ville." The vill was often surrounded by a road, a ditch, a palisade, a wall, the German *Etter,* and was frequently delineated by crosses or some other marks.

The village normally—but not always—was centered on the church and the churchyard, the castle and the lord's farm, or a green. Occasionally it contained common buildings, like a town hall. The dwellings—with their toft (*pourpris*), including house, outbuildings, garden, and yard; and with their croft, which was also enclosed but of bigger size—succeeded each other along a street or on parallel or radial roads. In some regions and in the vicinity of the cities, the arable land was partially specialized, in *pagos* for one kind of plantation[45] or in larger concentric circles planted in vegetables, vineyards, and cereals.[46] The field was divided into blocks, as we shall see later. Around the infield lay the outfield, common pastures, wasteland, and woods.

Of course, all people did not live in villages of this kind. In some regions, settlement remained dispersed thanks to natural conditions, as in the French *bocage,* with its watered land; or thanks to individualism, as in the old Narbonnaise, where disorder and caprice apparently presided.[47] Hamlets still prevailed. In Cornwall, for instance, they made up 75 percent of the settlements at the time of the Black Death.[48] Besides, many villages were of modest size: a dozen hearths, or even fewer.[49] And in its last stage, the demographic advance generated the constitution of hamlets and farmsteads around nucleated agglomerations. Thus old settlements sprouted new shoots. From 1150 to 1300, eight courts were created in the outfields and forests of a vill called *Novilia francorum hominum* (of the noble men), to distinguish it

Figure 8. German "Etter." A wooden fence encloses the vill of Birkenfeld (Franconia). Such a barrier demarcated the inhabited territory of the village from the uninhabited fields. Its significance was both legal and practical.
Source: Würzburg, Staatsarchiv, Würzburger Risse and Pläne, 1/221. Map of 1552.

from another Noville pertaining to knights. Six of the courts were created by younger sons of the local noble family, and two were created by religious institutions near Namur, at a distance of some ten miles.[50] In the same county, twenty-two out of twenty-five keeps were erected on the margins of villae.[51] This word and the word hamyal (hamlet) appeared in a charter dated 1393: "villes, manoirs et hamyals del franchise."[52] In Italy, monks created grangiae (barns) according to the Cistercian model, and furthermore, both members of the low aristocracy and rich citizens created isolated farms by reclamation or by sewing wild pieces of land, in order to increase their productivity.[53] In the same country, many peasants, deprived of their possessions, left the fortified heights, abandoned the villages and castelli—where henceforth only small landowners and craftsmen stayed—and descended into the plains to dwell in houses dispersed around the estates (the poderi).[54]

On the other hand, demographic pressure, civil disorders, and poor soil, which was more or less rapidly exhausted, provoked in most countries, but not everywhere,[55] the desertion of hundreds and hun-

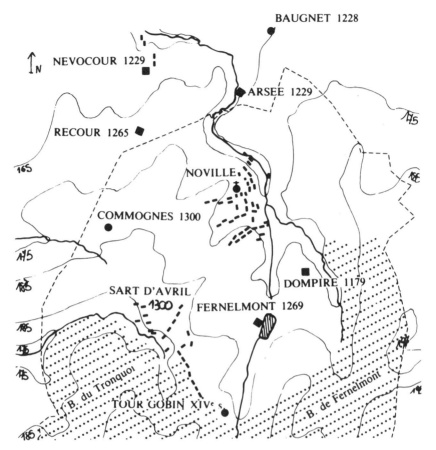

Figure 9. Evolution of a Village in the 12th and 13th Centuries: Noville in the County of Namur. *Nova villa,* the "new vill," with, in its very center, the church devoted to St. Stephan and the castle of a noble seigniorial family, was, before the 11th century, the nucleus of a village. When population grew and children became numerous, the lord gave a part of the territory in the forest outside of the inhabited area to his younger sons, who with a small retinue created hamlets or farmsteads, as did two religious institutions of Namur (17 kilometers from the village), that were endowed or purchased land and built a *grangia.*

Source: L. Genicot. *Le destin d'une famille noble du Namurois,* in *Annales de la Société archéologique de Namur,* XLVI, 1952, p. 150.

dreds of spots, most of them of small size, and the concentration in more fertile or better defended agglomerations.

On the whole, the growth of population and its geographical consequence, especially from the tenth to the thirteenth centuries, narrowed and strengthened relationships among peasants.

*

POPULATION growth also forced the production of more food, achieved by cultivating new land and by improving the yield ratio through technological progress.

New land was brought under cultivation by clearing woods and moors, by draining marshes and turf pits, and by damming coasts and shores. The process intensified in the tenth century: in 960–65, Bishop Éracle of Liège gave back to the monks of Lobbes all the fields his predecessor had appropriated "tam in sartis quam in sylvis et villulis ipsius ecclesie" (in the assarts, the woods, and the small villas of the monastery).[56] And the process continued until the mid- or late thirteenth century, supported by technological progress and improved climate, which made clay soils and highlands tillable.[57]

According to scholars who deliver impressions more than evidence, this process was continued spontaneously by individual peasants. However, these scholars underestimate how difficult assarting, which necessitated pulling out trees by the roots, was, especially with medieval tools,[58] and how difficult it was to claim land from the outfields or at the village's border. Indeed, around 1143, the Landgraf of Thüringen prohibited "sibi subjecti extirpatores" (assarters subject to him) to reclaim land without his permission.[59] In Surrey, fines were inflicted on those bringing land under cultivation without the lord's allowance.[60] If we had elsewhere not only the usual seignorial charters but also court rolls, which have survived in England, we might possibly discover such infringements on the commons, but they would surely be minor.

In my personal research, I encountered the following evidence: In the early thirteenth century, a peasant suffered from paralysis and could no longer "novale quod excuderat excolere" (cultivate the new land he had cleared); about 1000 and also in 1208, small groups of *quidam* or *commanentes incolae* "quosdam sartos sartabant" (were assarting certain assarts); and between 1289 and 1294, a vill community reclaimed some ten acres of woodland. Above all, owners of the soil planned, initiated, stimulated, and directed all these activities.[61] In the village of Haltinne, a property of the Count of Namur, the fields were divided into *quartiers*, that is to say, quarters of a hide, and in *terres de sartes,* and each inhabitant held the same proportion of both. This arrangement excluded reclamations by individual tenants or by the collectivity.[62] Despite Montalembert and his *Moines d'Occident,* the lords involved were not mainly monks, except for new orders during a period following their foundation, or for the first Cistercian granges.[63] They were lay lords. In the instance of Noville given above, six of the hamlets were created by the local noble family.[64]

By combining old land surveys, old maps and sketches, old place names of the microtoponomy, and old rent rolls, one could calculate the approximate importance of the clearings. In Haltinne, the *quartiers* covered 785 acres and the *terres de sartes,* 522.5. But on the estates of the Bishop of Worcester, out of 30,000 to 40,000 acres of cultivated area in 1299, perhaps only 2,000 acres had been cleared in the previous century, and half of the new lands were inferior to those settled earlier.[65]

In the long run, the process imperilled the commons, which were vital for the peasants to graze their cattle. Cattle were needed both for cultivation and, for many peasants whose holdings were desperately small, merely for living. In Flanders in the late Middle Ages, cereals constituted only 63 percent of the diet.[66] Moreover, flour does not provide enough of the necessary calcium. In the county of Namur about 1400, 80 to 85 percent of the villagers also had a cow, one or two pigs, and one or several sheep.[67] Under such circumstances, the rural population could not accept the reduction of grazing land, and since the eleventh century, conflicts had burst out about the rights to common land. The *Miracula sancti Foillani,* written a little before 1100, narrates a controversy between an *ingenuus* (a noble), the owner of three-quarters of the vill of Fleurus, and the canons of Fosses, proprietors of the rest, who rejected the assertion of the first that the whole territory was "publica pascua totius fisci nullique fas esse ibi vel aedificare vel arare" (public pastureland of the entire fisc, and no one was permitted either to build or to plough there). In 1127, the founders of the abbey of Solières, near Huy, gave to the sisters some rights in the woods of the "allodium, ibi tantum ubi est incisio rusticorum totius allodii" (allod, only there where there is a clearing of the peasants of the whole allod).[68] From the eleventh century, the Italian *vicini* also fought for the defense of their common rights against the lords.[69]

With the passage of time, the struggle was no longer between opposing lords but between the peasants and anyone who threatened their grazing rights. The peasants struggled against lords who converted land into fields and later tried to profit from the rise in prices for meat and wool by developing cattle rearing.[70] In England, the Statute of Merton allowed lords to modify the commons only if they proved that their free tenants had enough pasture and wasteland for their cattle.[71] The peasants also struggled with outsiders, especially the newly founded religious institutions, which coveted the commons for their flocks.[72] They struggled with adjacent villages, which claimed some right to the woods, the limits and status of which had been vague during the time of sparser population.[73] They struggled with migrating flocks, which were taxed when passing through.[74] They struggled in all directions: Italian *statuta* of the fourteenth century are full of prohibitions against clearing the woods.[75] Collecting and chronologically ranking all traces of such differences would be an excellent method for testing the growth and strength of community feeling.

In the late Middle Ages, a new set of phenomena exposed the commons to another danger. The progress of breeding, the rise in wool and meat prices,[76] and the constitution in the community of a group of well-to-do farmers pushed the owners to enclose their properties and thus to save them from the grazing of the common flock. Such flocks had perhaps never been permitted to pasture on the demesne: in the region of Namur, for instance, a tax called *restor* was paid for restoring the damages made by tenants' cattle to the lord's fields.[77] At any rate, from the thirteenth, fourteenth, or fifteenth century, the *herde banale* (the common flock) was in certain places no longer admitted on estates, which were henceforward surrounded by hedges or ditches.[78] In the same county of Namur, a sentence pronounced in 1376 denounced the attempts of rich people to enclose their fields to escape the common rights.[79] And in 1414, a *homme de loy* (a descendant of a knight) tried to possess his own flock without paying any tax if his cows and pigs pastured "sur son hirtagez ens ses enclos" (on his properties within his closes).[80]

Gaining new fields and defending the commons fostered the growth of the *universitas villae*. Assarting was not infrequently a collective endeavour. Controlling water demanded a huge and permanent struggle.[81] Maintaining the common uses required the collaboration of members of the whole group. The *universitas* sometimes acted in court, even against the lord, to get *Weistum* (a judicial document, attesting its rights); in 1443, for instance, all the "masuirs et habitants" or "tous ceaz qui sont manans et tokans feu et logeans" (all people who dwelled and had hearth and lodged) of the vill of Ohey required from the mayor and the aldermen an official declaration on the uses of the woods.[82] The *universitas* often compromised with the lord, abandoning to him a part of the outfield and wood and obtaining the disposal of the rest "en franc alleu" (in frank almoin), as a charter of 1283 explained.[83] It took *ad censum* (perpetual) and afterward *ad firmam* (temporary) lease of the commons, occasionally the demesne,

Figure 10. Improvement of Agricultural Tools. The medieval "pick" was made of iron and fitted to a wooden shaft. With it in his right hand, the peasant cut ears of grain at the bottom and, with a hook fitted to a short stick, brought them together. So he got more straw to make manure. This represents more sophisticated and thorough use of the entire plant, which in turn enhanced yields.

Source: Mayer van den Bergh Breviary, Antwerp, Museum Mayer van den Bergh, cat. no. 946, f.5r. Cliché ACL M.4156. From about 1530.

or even the whole manor.[84] Sometimes it bought the disputed land. At some sacrifice, it normally succeeded—except in Italy and in Flanders—in preserving, at least partially, its commons.[85] So the first efforts deployed to cope with the demographic flood were a crucial element in the birth or the consolidation of the rural community.

*

THE SECOND set of measures supported or imposed by the growing difficulty of finding wasteland and woodland to clear were the improvements of cultivation that produced the same effect.

The improvements were manifold,[86] but their chronology and geography remain less than precisely known. Marling combats acidity of the soil by infusing nitrates in it. Renier de Saint-Jacques of Liège mentions in his *Annales* the discovery in 1213 of that fertilizer in his country.[87] A large heavy plough drawn by eight oxen could be put into operation.[88] Horses were substituted for oxen and cows; quicker and stronger, they labored longer but were more expensive in every respect.[89] Iron replaced wood in tools, especially the plough and its share, which made furrows deeper and turned the ground better.[90] The number of ploughings of fallows increased up to four and even to six a year.[91] Farmers sowed thicker in the hope of harvesting more.[92] Wheat was scattered in the place of spelt or rye or barley, as the *grand bailli* (the first official) of the county of Namur experimented in the second half of the fifteenth century, without great success.[93] Peasants mowed no longer at the top but at the bottom of the ears, to get straw for litter and manure, as seen in late medieval iconography. Irrigation increased, and trees were planted in the fields to provide leaves for fodder.[94] Selecting and cross-breeding aimed to make cattle more productive.

But the most promising progress was the introduction of crop rotation. Convertible or alternative husbandry, which from time to time changed fields into meadows, was practiced in the early fourteenth century by Battle Abbey.[95] The robbed cultures, so-called because parts of the spring fields and fallows were robbed to sow green plants

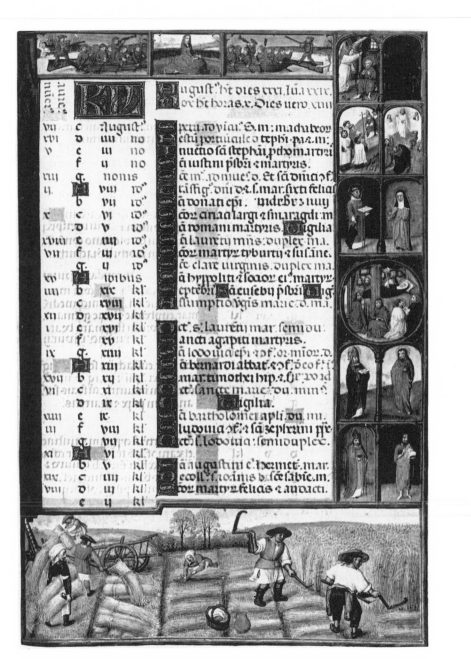

(peas, clover, and vetch), replenished nitrogen in the soil and supplied fodder. The system appeared in the early thirteenth century on the estates of the Bishop of Winchester[96] and in the region of Lille, where peasants were allowed to seed a part of the fallows.[97] The practice then was to spread to more fertile soils. On some manors of Glastonbury island, in Somerset, in 1312–13, legumes occupied twenty-nine to thirty-three percent of acreage sown. In 1401–02, the domains of the Baron of Neubourg produced 440 bushels of wheat, 14 of rye, 14 of oats, 42 of barley, 25 of white peas, 128 of grey peas, and 102 of vetch.[98] In some parts of central Italy, Flanders, and England, the fallows was entirely seeded by the end of the Middle Ages.[99]

Spring fields and fallows imply three field rotation, the adoption of which was very influential on the rural community. The problems of its origins, diffusion, and effects are eagerly discussed. According to an excellent specialist, the origins "will never be solved; documents are few and their meaning is uncertain."[100] Did it date from the Roman period or from the early Middle Ages, when increase in population, partitions of inheritance, and allotment of the *Allmende* (commons and clearings) divided the *Groszblock* (the block of land cultivated by the large family) into *Streifenparzellen* (strips)? Or was it when the *Ackerstreife* (narrow strips) generated the *Gewannflur* (field of furlongs)?[101] At any rate, three field rotation was practiced in the Carolingian period, at least on the *culturae* (the demesnes of the manors). The polyptychs of that time explicitly mention it or hint at it, as in the *Descriptio villarum* of Lobbes in 868–69.[102] The practice gradually spread over most territories. Some passages in the writings of the eleventh century could be interpreted as referring to it;[103] and archaeological and physical data seem to bear sure testimony of it in that time, especially for England.[104] In Picardy, the first mentions date from 1148–61.[105] Some regions passed from the two field to the three field system only in the thirteenth century, or even in the fourteenth, like Micheldever.[106] Some partially maintained the earlier system.[107] Large pieces of land persisted and even continued to dominate in the French *bocage*, for instance. Some new blocks were cut by clearers; others were formed in the late Middle Ages by well-to-do peasants or by urban citizens who patiently and cleverly acquired and stitched together several adjacent pieces and tried to enclose them. And some regions never adopted the three field rotation system (in England and Spain, for instance); or limited it to a kind of soil (in Frisia, to sandy soil); or abandoned it before the end of the Middle Ages and gave to the peasants full liberty of cultivating at their will (for example, in Flanders).[108]

Theoretically, the new system was attractive. It pushed the percentage of cultivated land from fifty to sixty-six, without exhausting the soil. But it required fertile heavy clay soil and did not fit light, thin, more easily leached soil, especially on steep slopes.[109] And the yield ratio was lower on the three field than on the two field system; if it was reduced from 4 to 3.25, the profit was minor, even null.[110]

Moreover, the three field system normally entailed a reshaping of the layout (*Vergewannung* or *Verzelgung*)[111] and a redistribution of cultivated land. It could operate in any structure, but it better fitted a landscape of open fields. When and where the remodeling occurred is another debated problem. "Any discussion on either the dating of the layout or the circumstances of its origin must be a matter of speculation."[112] The layout came perhaps from Roman times, and the reshaping took place, at least in England, in the eleventh century or even as early as the ninth. But normally it became widespread only in the thirteenth century.

The tilled plots were grouped into three fields (*soles*, *Zelge*), in the technical meaning of the word; or in a multiple of three, respectively, for winter cereals—wheat, spelt, barley, and rye—for spring cereals—mainly oats—and for fallow. The fields were divided into furlongs, the form and size of which differed according to physical conditions. The furlongs in turn comprised sellions, long and narrow strips of a variable surface, sometimes separated by a balk, a noncultivated streak.[113] This layout was neither rigid nor static. The surface sizes of the fields were not equal and could change by clearing or by furlongs that passed from one cereal cultivation to another.

That arrangement made desirable, if not necessary, a uniformity in cultivation, which was also required by the common uses. The fields were to be sowed with the same seed "comme dessus et dessous" (alike above and under) as adjacent plots. And they were to be harvested at the same time, to allow the common flock (*herde*)—made up of all the cattle of the village—to graze on them. In the same way and for the same reason, all meadows were to be mowed and hayed together. Collective matters required collective decisions—by whom, we shall see later. Such a system of cultivation and the regulation of the activity of all the members of the village—even of the workmen and the merchants, since everybody tilled at least a small spot of land—strengthened the common spirit and attitudes. But this system was not practiced everywhere. Some parts of Kent or Norfolk knew neither common rotation nor common pasture on the fallow strips but an unlimited individualism, which favored innovations and raised the productivity of agriculture.

To some extent, technological improvements also fostered unity. To profit from them, peasants had to help each other, especially to form a team for ploughing. The 1289 rent account of the Count of Namur

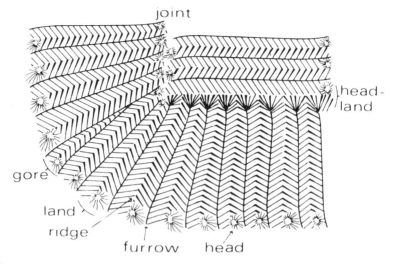

A

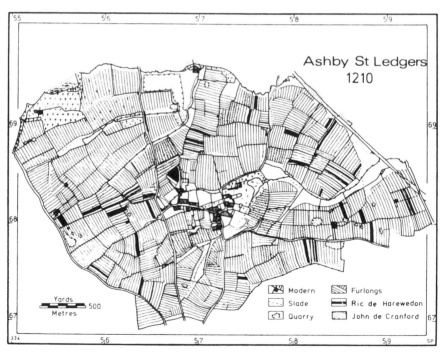

B

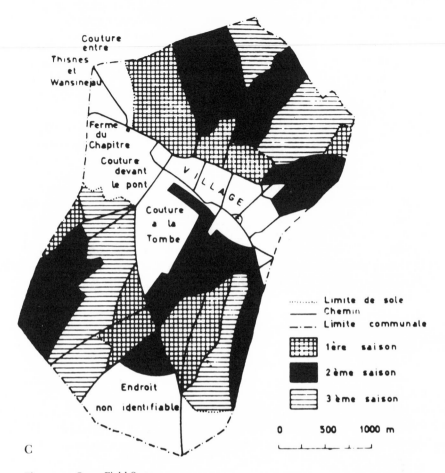

Couture
entre
Thisnes
et
Wansineau

Ferme
du
Chapitre

Couture
devant
le pont

V I L L A G E

Couture
a la
Tombe

Endroit
non identifiable

.... Limite de sole

———— Chemin

—.—.— Limite communale

▦ 1ère saison

■ 2ème saison

▤ 3ème saison

0   500   1000 m

C

Figure 11. Open Field System.

A. Diagram of principal features. The cultivated land is divided into long, narrow strips, the ridges starting from a head accessible with a plough and covering a gore limited on both sides by slight ditches that collect the rain and at its end normally by a little hillock formed by the accumulation of earth at the turning-point of the plough. A set of strips makes a furlong that joins another set (see 11B). A set of furlongs makes a *cultura*, *couture*, field uniformly cultivated (see 11C).

B. Layout of a village and demesne. Reconstruction of the village and demesne of Richard de Harewedon in Ashley. John de Cranford gave to the vicar one-third of the demesne in the early 12th century. The graph shows, first, the partition of the land into furlongs and the furlongs into ridges and, second, the presence in the village of several demesnes—not lordships—that are not a block but consist of many little pieces scattered in many furlongs and that were formed by inheritances, gifts, or purchases.

C. Layout of a village: Thisnes in the county of Namur in the 14th century. The three contiguous *coutures* are the big fields of the owner's demesne. The other fields are grouped in *soles*, which are subdivided into three *saisons* for winter grain, spring grain, and fallow.

Sources: D. Hall, "Fieldwork and Documentary Evidence for the Lay-out and Organization of Early Medieval Estates in the English Midlands," in *Archaeological Approaches to Medieval Europe*, (Studies in Medieval Culture, Kalamazoo, 1984, pp. 54, 60); M. J. Bodson, *L'évolution d'un paysage rural au moyen âge* (Centre belge d'histoire rurale, no. 3, Louvain-la-Neuve, 1965).

is full of items relating to the payment of the tallage: "Se doi bor-
gois jundgent ensemble lours chevaus et fachent une kerue communs
por iaus deus, chascun d'iau doit 18 deniers" (If two burgesses join
their horses and make a common plough for both, each must pay 18
pence).[114] In Normandy, cultivators "associabant equos ad carrucam"
(pooled horses for ploughing) and grouped together for other tasks.[115]
So too in Italy there was the *societates plovi*.[116] And in central France in
the late fifteenth century, four or five horses—rarely fewer—were
put to a plough, and *laboureurs*, who were more than half of the population, associated to form teams.[117]

But if those changes increased the output of crops,[118] they were also
expensive. The landowner possessed the money required for improvement. He could lend to his farmers equipment, cattle, seed, and
even cash.[119] He could introduce agricultural improvements, in draining or irrigating for instance, which were not as common as one might
expect,[120] or invest in tilling rather than in animal rearing, which was
even more unlikely, especially for upstarts and urban citizens. Cistercian monks, English earls, and patricians of Metz and other cities built
vaccariae and *bercariae* for cows and sheep but cared less for improving their farms.[121]

But the masses? How would they get a net surplus with their mean
holdings? Rents were lowered from the eleventh century onward, no
doubt, but profits from their reduction supposed two conditions that
were not always satisfied, especially in the late Middle Ages: perpetual
lease concessions and rents in money. Borrowing? Many peasants did
so. In the mid-thirteenth century, seeing during a pastoral tour that
the grain was growing in a promising way, Eudes Rigaud, Archbishop
of Rouen, noted in his calendar: "de blado poterunt vendere usque
ad solutionem debitorum vel circa" (they will be able to sell from their
wheat enough to pay off their debts, or nearly).[122]

One hundred years later, the bulk of the loans advanced by the
capitalists of the mighty city of Tournai were contracted by countrymen of the vicinity for short terms until the next harvest.[123] Obviously,
such loans were not contracted to make improvements but simply to
make ends meet. At the same time, cultivators in the region of Toulouse pawned their prospective crop to guarantee their debts and,
around Albi, 40 percent of the short-term loans bestowed by "bank-
ers" were not reimbursed after three years, and 52 percent of them
were owed by countrymen.[124] Financially, because they were short of
money, and psychologically, because they were diffident about changing their traditions, most peasants were hostile to innovation. In such
a way, the technological progress might help dig a ditch in the rural
collectivity between the rich and the common people.

The open-field system and compulsory rotation could act in the same way, if they were not identical for the whole village or if they did not really apply to all inhabitants. One might imagine a priori that regulation differed from sector to sector of the village—differed, for instance, between the nucleus and the surrounding hamlets. But the evidence does not support such a view: not one document mentions boundaries between the sectors or assemblies of inhabitants of each sector. But some persons and some lands could escape the common rotation and regulation—some lords, perhaps, or their farmers, at least on their demesnes; or in the late Middle Ages, some owners of big estates or capitalists of nearby towns who chiefly wished to develop cattle rearing at the expense of farming in order to take advantage of the divergent evolution in prices. So economics lead society—to the conditions of the life of country people and to the possibilities of clashes in the community.

*

STARTING from an economic viewpoint, one immediately thinks of rich and poor. However, wealth and need were not the only foundations for differences among peasants. Status, real or artificial, kinship, and vicinity might also oppose or unite people. Let us review these factors of the social structure in the countryside, in order to draw some conclusions from them.

Demographic advance was an element of the general advance across all sectors of the economy. Another aspect of that phenomenon, which did not affect only and mainly the rural community, consisted of the growing penetration of money into all material activities. This brought, as a sequel, the increasing mobility of people and goods.

The progress of the monetary economy in the countryside is not as obvious as it has often been asserted. Rents, for instance, were indeed, in the first stage, more and more stipulated in coins instead of grain. But when the progressive and deep debasement of money made evident the danger of such a practice, people went back to grain, especially—and significantly—in the vicinity of cities.[125] And did markets really multiply, mainly in the thirteenth century?[126] Or were many strictly local markets, the existence of which seems to be witnessed by the use of local measures for grain in the eleventh and twelfth centuries, replaced by less numerous and better furnished and better located boroughs, with their place market and day market?[127] Besides, did the bulk of the peasantry enter into regular and active connection with the markets? They had so little to sell! But commerce, no doubt, developed from 1000.

A land market also developed. In England, where the evidence is particularly rich, Peterborough Abbey, between 966 and 975, bought a great deal of land in order to consolidate and enlarge its estates.[128] On the continent, registers for enrolling the operations of landed property appeared in the early thirteenth century.[129] In 1289, the Count of Namur owned in his *mairie* of Anhée thirty holdings of twenty-five acres and more, twenty-six holdings of which did not apparently exist in 1265.[130] Several factors explain this phenomenon: reclamations; sales by old families who paid for partitions because of excessive expenses and unskillful management; the desire of upstarts in both countryside and towns for investing in real estate; abandonment or direct exploitation by some lords (some, on the contrary, enlarged their demesnes in the thirteenth century);[131] economic recession, which accelerated the speed of transactions; increasing taxation, which overburdened the properties; and passage from perpetual concessions to tenure at will.[132]

But measuring its volume, its velocity, and its phases and deducing from these elements the size of agricultural exploitation and its possible evolution from the eleventh to the fifteenth centuries are another endeavour, filled with traps.[133] Owner and tenant *ad censum* (as named) in a rental do not always coincide; a canon of an urban chapter, for instance, did not cultivate land; subtenants were sometimes numerous and unknown.[134] Patronymics were not immediately fixed, and they often used the same place-name for people without family relation. The registers were not all precise, complete, and exact; they mention partakers without giving their number; they forgot some operations; they often maintained the name of a tenant a century after his death. A peasant could hold tenures in several villages. The amount of the census greatly varied. The rents, which multiplied in that period, diminished the profit from a field.[135] Perpetual concession did not hinder changes of tenancy. And, inversely, concession at will did not mean necessarily a rapid succession of holders.[136] The deeds themselves prove how deceptive rentals could be.

One thing is unquestionable: as soon as the documents give indications and sometimes figures on the distribution of fields, they show a disequilibrium. This is true for the polyptych of Prüm, for Villance, in the Ardennes in 893.[137] This occurs also in the Domesday Book of 1086.[138] And, after opposing *divites* and *pauperes*,[139] documents beginning in the eleventh century, from Burgundy and Auvergne to Italy, distinguish *laboratores*, *manuoperarii*, *bubulci*, *manuales*, and *bracentes* (owners of oxen, and afterward of horses, and people laboring with their hands).[140]

Did the repartition of the soil change the condition of the common people when the landed property market developed? This market was not really accessible to peasants hungry for land. They lacked the money to buy land as its price rose ceaselessly: in Normandy it multiplied by six, even ten, in the thirteenth century.[141] Could they take a holding *ad censum* (for census or rent)? That required draft animals and implements, to get more than a tiny piece. Could they farm a part of a demesne? Demesnes were nearly exclusively leased as a block. What about clearing? When made collectively, reclamations only aggravated the disequilibrium among tenements.[142]

Under such conditions, a few skillful men profited from the development of the landed property market to no longer build *seigneuries* (manors in the strict sense of the term) but what I call *domains*, combining every kind of field: allodia, fiefs, and holdings.[143] Among them were both high or local officials, like the mayor of Thisnes, who in 1274 bought from his master, the Count of Namur, fifty acres, which he paid off within eight months.[144] There were also peasants like Hugo Cok of Codicote, who in 1277 was the least taxed for the tallage in the village, but who, from that date to his death in 1306, took at rent or lease three "places," one "messuage," twenty acres of fields, and one fisher's shop.[145] And above all, from the mid-thirteenth century, citizens of big cities like Metz and Ghent[146] and of middle-sized towns like Dinant and Bouvignes profited. In 1289, ten of the thirty holdings of the Count of Namur in Anhée (twenty-five of which were recent formations)[147] were in the hands of inhabitants of Dinant and Bouvignes, which are about six miles apart.

For the common people, on the other hand, things were less favorable. The average size of the tenements perhaps increased in the beginning: the middle class was more numerous in England in 1086 than two centuries before.[148] But in the long run, the movement apparently inverted in England and everywhere else in the West.[149] Reclamations could not match the demographic surge. When the latter ended in the late thirteenth century, the surfaces of most of the exploitations were extremely small, as illustrated by some villages in England and Belgium. One may estimate that 5 to 10 percent—or exceptionally 15 percent—of the population was made up of well-to-do peasants who held local offices, had a war-horse, and imitated or even approached the aristocracy, like the *caballeros villanos*.[150] Fifteen to 30 percent of cultivators disposed of 17.5 to 35 acres, enough to make a comfortable living. Thirty-five to 40 percent of *manuoperarii* were lucky when they made ends meet, while 20 to 30 percent of *pauperiores, Kossäter, malnutriti*, and cottars stood upon or below the poverty line (the *barre de subsistance*).[151] Condemned to starvation? Not to that extremity, in spite of the assertions of most scholars, who judge from nothing but the size of the tenements and yield ratios calculated for

TABLE 1. NUMBER OF HOLDINGS (EXPLOITATIONS)
IN THREE ENGLISH VILLAGES

	Number of Holders, as Percentage of Inhabitants			
Size of Holding in Acres	Pinchbeck 1259	Spalding		Sutton 1304
		1259	1287	
less than 1	9.1	34.5	32.4	23.6
1−3	29.8	27.2	31.5	31.5
4−5	18.2	10.1	11.9	17.6
6−10	15.7	10.3	9.9	15.2
11−20	14.7	5.2	7	8.5
21−30	7.8	5.4	4.1	2.4
31−60	4.7	7.2	3.2	1.2

Source: H. E. Hallams, "Some Thirteenth-Century Censuses," Economic History Review 10 (1957−58): 343, 349.

manors and who do not take into account that cultivating with the spade yields much more than using a plough and that grain was not, by far, the only food at the disposal of nearly everybody.[152]

Historiography marks the late Middle Ages as a period of crisis, especially in agriculture.[153] Famines and plagues, above all the Black Death and its sequels, killed probably one-third of the population. Settlements were deserted and fields abandoned. More generally—and too little emphasized by some scholars—the value of land fell and rents drastically diminished.[154] The activity of the land market logically improved for the peasants. The upper class went on constructing domains (poderi). In the Po valley, the first family of Valera combined and tilled properties, fiefs, and land taken on lease.[155] In the northern, most fertile, part of the county of Namur, high officials, knights or hommes de loy of knightly origin, some peasants, and above all citizens of the capital practically monopolized estates of any importance.[156] As most of them did not dwell on the premises and were engaged in other activities, they gave the domains on lease to bouviers (farmers) or land stewards, who—one, two, or three per village—were the cream of the crop. At a lower level, the middle class gained in number and strength. In Normandy in the fourteenth century, the percentage of

HERCHIES   HALTINNE

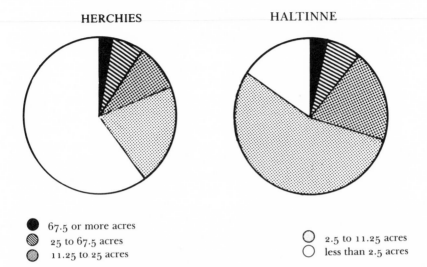

● 67.5 or more acres
◍ 25 to 67.5 acres
◍ 11.25 to 25 acres

○ 2.5 to 11.25 acres
○ less than 2.5 acres

Figure 12. Size of Land Holdings at the End of the Period of Expansion. These graphs show the extreme fragmentation and small size of the bulk of landholdings in two 13th-century villages in southern Belgium resulting from the great demographic surge. Note as well the narrow slice occupied by the category of the largest exploitations. The graph for Herchies (Hainault) represents the situation in 1267, that for Haltinne (Namur) in 1289.

Source: L. Genicot, *Racines d'espérance*, Brussels, 1986, p. 54.

people holding from 15 to 37.5 acres increased from thirty-four to forty-three, and the figure for men who held less reduced from forty-eight to forty-one.[157] In the East Midlands, well-to-do cultivators henceforward formed half of the population and extended their tenements.[158] In the county of Namur, the proportion of *cherruiers* possessing a plough increased notably from 1289 to 1410.[159]

In contrast (not necessarily in contradiction) the situation of smallholders worsened. They lacked money and the labor force for enlarging their tenement.[160] In Flanders and Brabant, the proportion of holdings of less than 4 acres or between 4 and 9.5 acres grew, respectively, from 21.4 to 35 percent and from 21.5 to 26.3 percent from the second half of the fourteenth century to the first half of the following one.[161] Asserting that legal serfdom was replaced by economic serfdom is a striking but somewhat exaggerated expression, except perhaps for the people tilling the *poderi*.[162] Claiming, as many scholars do, that in the late Middle Ages or even before riches weighed more than status in society is more questionable still, as we shall see when discussing the legal aspects of the rural community.

What seems to be beyond doubt is that the distinction between rich and poor became more acute in the last phase of the Middle Ages and that a few "high men, colored and sanguine" of the Canterbury Tales (*labradores acomodatos*) dominated the collectivity. But before examining their position, one has to point to another possible division introduced or accentuated by economic progress: the intervention and the arrival of newcomers.

Intervention concerns the persons just mentioned, who accumulated lands and built domains or who, not infrequently, acquired the seignorial rights from impoverished nobles or knights.[163] Most did not establish themselves on the spot: at the end of the fourteenth century, there were no members of the gentry residing in 122 of the 135 villages of Gloucestershire.[164] Personal ties collapsed between the masters who were more investors than lords—who, for instance, did not elect their tombs and found their anniversary in the parish church[165]—and the peasants, whom they did not know. And the social climate deteriorated.

Common people also came from outside, strangers whom the community distrusted.[166] The reason for the distrust was perhaps the scarcity of land prior to 1348,[167] or because the village was compelled to sustain them if they became needy,[168] or, more deeply, because they could imperil the collectivity's unity and traditions.[169] The collectivity often controlled the sale of real estate and gave a right of preemption to relatives and neighbors.[170] Or it dictated that buyers make their residence in the village.[171] Or it imposed, especially in the franchises, the oath that they did not act "in fraud of anyone or anything."[172] Or it submitted the installation of newcomers to a deliberation of the local assembly.[173] Or it reserved the participation in that assembly to descendants of local families.[174] Many lords adopted the same policy when they suspected that the newcomers would try to evade dues, such as *formariage* or *heriot;* or, if they were serfs, try to escape their status. Or they feared that the strangers would not perform the services required from the tenements. Nevertheless, newcomers were numerous. In Weston, in the Fens, in the second third of the thirteenth century, of the sixty-five boys who became adults, thirty-one emigrated.[175] In 1425 in Florence, 20 to 25 percent of the families were *tornati* (immigrants), who for the most part came from the *contado* (the territory surrounding the city and subject to it).[176] About 1450, in Holywell, of the families cultivating more than eighteen acres, 53 percent had lived in the village for more than a century, 23 percent had arrived more recently, and 17 percent did not reside in the village.[177] The village was by no means an *isolat* (a closed entity). But there is no evidence of it being disturbed by the immigrants.

Really dangerous, on the other hand, for both local lords and rural communities, was the *bourgeoisie foraine* or the *bourgeoisie du roi.* It sub-

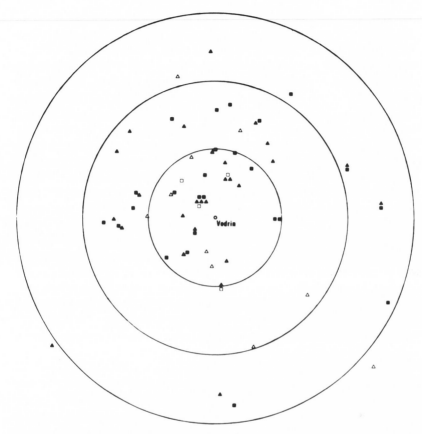

■ Founders of "obits" before 1350

▲ Idem after 1350

□ Debtors of "obits" (who cultivated a tenement charged with an annual rent for "obit"), before 1350.

△ Idem after 1350

Figure 13. Natives and Strangers in the Rural Community in the Late Middle Ages. The rural community was not "isolated." The Obituary of the parish of Frizet (close to Namur) proves that the immigrants were numerous but that most of them came from adjacent villages. The document listed the "foundations," from 1325 to 1525, of annual Masses commemorating deceased members of the community and the payments due for them. A quarter of the Masses were founded by families with at least one member not born in Frizet. The three circles, the radius of which is 10 kilometers (situated outside of the graph are Liège, Louvain, Hautepenne, and Trivière, all more than 30 kilometers away), show that, of the founders or debtors prior to 1350, 35% came from less than 10 kilometers, 39 from 10 to 20 kilometers, 16 from 20 to 30 kilometers, 10 from more than 30 kilometers; after 1350, the figures are 39, 15; 32, 5; and 16, 12.

Source: L. Genicot, *Une source mal connue* (50), p. 108.

tracted from the local dues, taxes, services, and courts. Princes and cities used it to enlarge their authority.[178] The lords attempted to prohibit it but without success. Under their pressure, the Count of Hainault forbade it in 1195. But from 1358 to 1364, Ath, a modest town of Hainault, received 636 new burgesses, of whom 600 were *forains*.[179] Things went even further in the Duchy of Luxemburg: from 1429 to 1450, the small town of Laroche admitted 451 *forains;* in 1561, 60 percent of the rural population held that status; and there were two categories among the peasants: the *forains,* who were free from the *aide,* and the rest.[180]

More or less privileged were the *feodati* (vassals), the *hommes de fief* or *hommes d'alleu* living on a fief or an allodium, clerics, especially priests, officials, crossbowmen, and specialized workmen, mainly pit men.[181]

At the top, the *cerocensuales* or *sainteurs,* pertaining to a saint, also had a status of their own; at the bottom in the franchises were the *manants* and, everywhere, the serfs. We shall meet them in chapter 3, in dealing with juridical conditions, and in chapter 4, in answering the question which cannot be solved before studying lordship and parish: what exactly was the community, and who was a member of it?

A final distinction existed in some villages that apparently became clearer and more important at the end of the Middle Ages: that is, the distinction between people who enjoyed the common uses and those who did not. The first were *mansionarii, masuirs, Hüber,* and *Markgenoten,* and the second were *manentes. Mansionarius* obviously derived from *mansus,* and in the strict sense of the term applied to the people who disposed of a *mansus* or a part of a *mansus* and therefore the oldest fields of the village. But the word took on a broader meaning, designating all the tenants of the lord. The *manentes* resided there and breathed the air of the lord but did not cultivate his lands.[182] In the Netherlands, the *mansionarii* were called *Markgenoten,* and from the thirteenth century, they formed a *communitas quae dicitur mark,* or, in Dutch, a *markgenotenschap.* Their association was officially recognized, and it decided the use of forests, woods, moors, marshes—of anything constituting the *mark.* In the fifteenth century, it sometimes became powerful enough to eliminate the *buurschap* and take the direction of the community.[183] In the same perspective, Germany at the same time, after the "crisis" of the fourteenth century, opposed *richtige Bauern* to the rest of the population.[184] In Westfalen, the *Markgenoten* were distinct from the *Kossaten,* who in the terms of a *Markenrecht* (law of the commons) of 1339 "hebben nen recht in eken ofte in boken" (have no right to acorns [for pigs] or to wood [for timber].[185] In Bavaria, the *Dorfeinwohner* possessed an *Ehostatt* (a house with its toft) and the *Dorffremden* did not.[186] In Provence, the juridical language distinguished the *privati* (who dwelled within the ramparts) from the *extranei* or *forestieri* (who resided in the hamlets and were not integrated into the community).[187]

*

ALONG with these elements of distinction, if not perhaps of opposition and conflict, there existed elements of coherence: family, neighborhood, common needs, rights, and duties.

The family, which was based upon living together "au même feu et au même pot" (around the same hearth and table), upon patrimony, upon remembrances (the knowledge of ancestors down to the fifth or sixth generation is astonishing), was more than ever the basic cell of society. Its dimensions depended upon many factors: quality of the soil, size of the exploitation, amount paid to the owner, and inheritance customs.[188] Texts[189] and archaeological sources (surface and plan of the dwelling houses)[190] attest that a couple with unmarried children and often elderly parents was the norm. Following the example of the Mediterranean countries,[191] the Church of the Gregorian reform had made marriage a sacrament, founded on the *dilectio* of the sole husband and wife, acting through their *consensus* and joining them for ever and ever. Civil law restricted the *laudatio parentum* (consent of the relatives) to make transfers of goods and—according to the wishes of the clergy—gifts easier and in that way made the economy more fluid.[192] And it limited to the nobility the *vendetta,* which too often degenerated into endless disorders.

Even so, lineage subsisted. If any member of it needed judicial or financial help, all the relatives gave their aid. Even in the south, lineage partly recovered its role in the late Middle Ages.[193] To face the difficulties of that period, especially the demographic recession, and also to escape heriot and taxes, people closed their ranks. The number of multiple houses increased.[194] And in some countries, fictitious kin, significantly called *frérèches* (brotherhoods), flourished.

Vicinity, too, remained important throughout the Middle Ages.[195] In Italy, the rural community was called *vicinia* until the twelfth and even into the thirteenth centuries.[196] Neighbors attended every life event: birth, wedding, death. They frequently gave advice, mainly about marriage. They helped in misfortune, like fire and murrain. And in some countries, they kept until the end of the period the right of substituting themselves for the buyer in transfer of a house or landed property.[197] In some parts of Germany, the *Nachbarschaft* (grouping the *Hufner*) played the part of the *Gemeinde* (the community).[198]

For above families and neighbors stood the community, which

TABLE 2. FAMILY SIZE AND WEALTH
AROUND LUCCA, 1411–1413

Family Size	Wealth [1] (in lire)									
	0	1–10	11–20	21–40	41–60	61–80	81–100	101–150	151–200	201+
1–3	43.9	47.5	45.1	42.2	34.1	20.4	26.4	18.5	25	0
4–5	31.7	30	25	22	23.1	32.6	23.5	18.5	8.3	10
6–8	19.5	20.7	22.1	22.7	21.9	36.7	35.2	22.2	41.6	40
9–11	4.8	0.5	6.7	9.7	12.1	8.1	5.8	22.2	8.3	30
12 +	0	1	0.9	3.2	8.5	2	8.8	18.5	16.6	20
Total percentages [2]	11.1	24.8	14.1	20.8	11.3	6.6	4.6	3.6	1.6	1.3

Source: F. Leverotti, "La famiglia contadina lucchese all'inizio dell '400," in R. Comba, *Strutture Familiari* 129:255.

[1] "Wealth" understood as land, cattle, and/or personal property but not resources. Land could be tilled by peasants for rent, leased, or held by joint tenancy (in *livello*, *affito*, or *socieda*).

[2] There are obviously two groups in the population of families: one group with total wealth of less than 60 lire and the other more than 60 lire. The first group comprises 71% of the 737 families.

created manifold links among the inhabitants. First of all, as some documents that call it *pax* (peace) [199] clearly imply, the community had to keep peace by preventing internal conflict and external disorder caused by strangers. The charters of franchises that created a local court or fixed its competence are full of clauses for avoiding or punishing insults, quarrels, feuds, and clashes of every kind, which the court rolls prove occurred frequently in the atmosphere "of excessive violence characteristic of the epoch." [200] If anyone assaulted a member of the community, "tota villa eum insequetur facto post eum clamore hahai," or as the French say, "au son de la cloche" (the whole village will go after him when somebody cries hahai or when the bell of the church rings). If the citizens caught him, they would deliver him to justice.[201] If an inhabitant did not take part in the chase, he was under penalty of exclusion from the village. The charters imposed, too, the obligation to testify before the court. In some regions, especially in Flanders and Hainault, they allowed as well the "droit d'arsin et d'abattis de maison" (the right of firing and destroying the house of the foreign enemies).[202]

The community used these and other means to defend its personal and property rights against the lord or the prince and their officials,[203] in court or, if the justice was inefficient, by force, "pour garder ses franchises" (to preserve its privileges).[204] The community also defended its common uses and properties against landowners and adjacent villages, for it could be astonishingly rich. The sources of a community's wealth were possibly rents from leasing the commons or selling the trees of the commons; fines for fraud in the use of measures, for public insult, and for violating the custom regulating the use of the commons, if these fines were not appropriated by the lord; escheats at least in partition with the lord; and proceeds from local taxes on the consumption of bread and beverages (the so-called *firmitates*, French *fertés*). Such taxes were assessed to erect, enlarge, and reinforce fortifications. We do not know if they were assessed in the country before the thirteenth century or if they were assessed without interference of the lord or with his approval.

At any rate, the village was able, with the money locked in the *arca communis* (the common safe), to buy landed properties and to construct or to fit some common building or place, fountain, mill,[205] oven, bridge, laundry, market, and occasionally a town hall. A town hall was not normally needed, since the local assembly usually met in the nave or the front of the church or in the hall of some important person. The village was capable of lending money to those who required financial help, even the lord for important amounts or of pledging on the latter's behalf. On the other hand, it could contract debts.

All these operations suppose the designation of proxies to appear in court or before a notary or before the lord for discussion of the status of the dependents. In the same way, the community had normally to choose at least the lower local officials, who were charged with watching over the fields and leading the common flock.

One of the community's main tasks lay in the economic sector. It regulated the common uses, deciding, for instance, whether the pigs would be put in the forest, when, and how many; or at what time the common grazing on fields, pastures, and wasteland would begin. Such determinations comprised the bulk of the rules inscribed in English by-laws.[206] It also supervised the observance of the common field rotation and organized the collective defense against nature.[207]

The village also assumed a so-to-say public responsibility in financial and military obligations to the prince. It assessed and collected taxes, especially the tallage, when it was *abonné*—converted into a fixed amount for all inhabitants and annually divided among them. Or it was collectively liable for the payment of the seignorial rents and the performance of statute labors. It was the unit in executing military service, whether, as in England following Henry III's order of 1242, the election of a few soldiers,[208] or whether sending all male adults into the army "sous la bannière" (behind the local standard).[209] In Thuringia, it had to provide for a car.[210] In other parts of Germany, especially where authority and territory had been parcelled out, the *Landgemeinde* assumed the maintenance of public peace, and, by the end of the Middle Ages, the rural population was militarized.

As for justice, the local court, its competence, and its procedure, whether it was allowed or not to meet spontaneously without the lord's presence or agreement, whether it was endowed or not to exert some kind of legislative power through *statuta* or *ordinationes* (by-laws) is discussed in the following chapter.

Finally, the community interfered in the daily existence of everyone and in the great events of the collective life. In marriage, for instance, some villages exacted a gift to validate a union with an outsider.[211] More generally, the male youth controlled and censured marriages, especially remarriages of widows, in order to reserve girls, women, and fields for the village. And the whole population celebrated religious and profane feasts, which flourished from the late Middle Ages.

It may be that the layout of the village reflected that progress of the common spirit. Houses were no longer built haphazardly: they were now grouped and ordered around a green or along a street.[212] In the same way, place-names often referred to the village and its plan, not to the seignory.[213]

All this clearly shows the reality of a *universitas* conscious of being a distinct group, considered as such by others who had confidence in its obligations, promises, oaths, and pledges. It enjoyed a juridical ability, attested occasionally and tardily by the possession of a seal: most rural communities used to borrow the seal of some *authentica persona*—a person or institution invested with public faith—whose documents constituted public authority: nobles, and afterward knights, priests, notaries, mayors, and aldermen acting collectively. A few of these actually had a "commun sael de le ville" (the seal of the village).[214]

All this presumed also an organization to express—in the form of one or several assemblies—and if possible to enforce the wishes and the will of the community. Some of these existed before the eleventh century[215] and continued without losing or limiting their freedom. Others survived but were appropriated and more or less distorted or diverted, first by the lords and then by the peasants themselves. New organizations were born by the action of the latter to curb seignorial power.

The emergence, or strengthening, of the rural community was not the fruit of economic forces alone. It was also, at least in the same measure if not in a greater one, the product of a confrontation of lords and peasants and of political events and movements that were translated into law or custom. The following chapter will analyze this aspect of rural development during the core of the Middle Ages.

3

BANNUM:

LEGAL ASPECTS

*

IN THE POLITICAL—or perhaps more exactly, the juridical—field it is difficult in the Middle Ages to distinguish policy and law or public and private law. Many medieval rules—in the matter of succession, for instance—pertained, according to our modern conceptions, to both sectors. The phenomenon that no doubt exerted the deepest influence on the rural community was the creation of what, for some thirty years, French historians (inspired by C. E. Perrin's *Recherches sur la seigneurie rurale en Lorraine*) have called the *seigneurie banale*, because it was founded on the *bannum*, (German *Bann*), the right of ordering and prohibiting under penalty of sanction.[1] That explains the title of this chapter and its structure as well. First was the emergence of the *seigneurie banale*. Second was its impact on the rural community: the promotion of unity by introducing a large uniformity in the personal status of the peasants and by obliging them to react, a reaction requiring unanimity to succeed. Third, the result is summed up in the relations between the lord and the community, relations expressed by the position of the lord versus that of the rural assembly or assemblies.

The *seigneurie banale* (for the *seigneurie foncière* as such could not generate a *seigneurie banale*) was, no doubt, inconceivable without a territorial base, ownership of some land.[2] It did not float between earth and heaven, but required the possession or the dependence of people, or, as German medieval lawyers used to say, the ownership of the air the people breathed: "Luft macht eigen, Luft macht frei" (the air makes one a serf, the air makes one free). And the *seigneurie banale* nearly always leaped across the boundaries of its material base and spread over several *seigneuries foncières*. A village we already have met, Noville les Francs Hommes, counted in the thirteenth century eight *cours foncières* or *cours censales* (courts of tenants), but only a single *cour hautaine*. To use a metaphor, there were two stories of *seigneuries:* on the ground floor, an abundance of *seigneuries foncières* and on the next floor the *seigneuries banales*, normally one in each village. The *seigneurie banale* and seignorial rights were a product not of ownership of the land but of possession of the *bannum*—some documents say of the *dominatio* or of the *districtus*.[3]

In which ways had the *bannum* in the tenth century and after come into the hands of many persons? This problem is connected with that of the nobility.[4] Lordships could be created by concessions of public authority, as the Carolingians did as their power declined. English kings behaved similarly toward their warriors.[5] So, too, did kings, especially in Spain,[6] princes,[7] and lords of lower rank in subconcessions, down to the end of the Middle Ages and beyond, to gain support or to reward a servant: obtaining the *alta justitia* introduced into the nobility. Usurpations by officials or by *potentes* were another route to lordship, opened by the weakness of central authority. This is the classical French theory. In contrary fashion, most German scholars maintain that the *Bann* was an attribute of all nobles, who were endowed with it by birth, by blood (*von sich aus*). But they did not exploit it, to borrow the term of Perrin, before the tenth or eleventh century—before the crisis of the supreme power in the north as in the south, on the Continent as in England.

Then the times favored such exploitation, politically and economically. The public climate had deteriorated and normal authority was unable to maintain peace, order, and justice. Documents are full of complaints and accusations against the "potentes qui solent circa se manentes qui sui juris non sunt magis opprimere et eorum incommoda semper sua commoda putare" (powerful men accustomed to oppressing those who live near them and do not enjoy their status and who always reckon as their own advantage the disadvantage of the others);[8] or against the "milites qui sicut mos plerisque militaris ordinis est, pro quaestu suo causas odii in rusticos quaerere, minis ac crebris insultationibus a plerisque quae sibi necessaria sunt extorquunt (the knights who, as is the custom of most of the knightly order, seek opportunities for disturbing the peasants for their own profit, and extorting their needs from many by threats and frequent injury).[9] Of course, these documents were written by clerics, who were prone to exaggerate and who more or less distorted reality. But the adjectives given by the common people to the *consuetudines*—the seignorial rights—are significant: *violentae, injuriosae, iniquae*.[10] Such a situation facilitated the *exactiones*, the first commonly used word for designating the tallage.

At the same time, the situation obliged the masses to solicit or accept the protection of a lord: the tallage was justified as the price paid "ut homines a quibuscumque deffenderet ipsos inquietantibus" (so that the lord might defend them from whoever were bothering them).[11]

For people "living under the crosier," the protector was theoretically the *advocatus*—the lay noble, initially of secondary rank,[12] whom chapters and monasteries, rich and forbidden to bear arms, asked to watch over their persons and goods in exchange for some properties or rents. Now, instead of defending, he nearly always oppressed; he exacted illegitimate dues, and he set an example, if necessary, to his fellow noblemen.[13] To restrain his abuses, the religious institution elaborated and often forged a document listing the office's duties and rights. Those *règlements d'avouerie* might serve as the prototype of the charters of franchises.[14]

The rest of the population frequently sought refuge in the shadow of the castles, which multiplied after the eleventh century.[15] The part they played in the country life and above all in the formation of the lordships is much discussed. Two aspects are clear.[16] On the one hand, the castle was a shelter; it provided security and defense. Too often, historians see the castle only an instrument of oppression, of *Bauern-bedrückung*, and forget, neglect or conceal that it gave needed protection to the peasants.[17] A passage of a charter delivered in 1138 by the Bishop of Liège deserves to be quoted on this point: "Quia villa . . . a castello remota omnium injuriis patebat, visum nobis est eandem villam sub castello collocare"[18] (as the village . . . remote from a castle was open to injustices by all people, it seemed wise to locate it at the foot of a castle). On the other hand, the castle was a means of imposing undue taxes; it was "omni adjacenti provincie infestum"[19] (hostile to the whole adjacent region); everywhere, the "munitio vicinos affligebat" (the fortification was afflicting its neighbors). And it was also a den, a haunt, within the tower or walls of which a lord dared to defy, and frequently succeeded in defeating, public authority. So there might well be a tie between it and the "exactiones et usurpationes." Hence most French scholars nowadays present it as the root of the *seigneurie banale* and name it *seigneurie châtelaine*. The term is not a very happy one. The connections were effectively frequent between both realities. Two quotations are appropriate here regarding the castle, even the simple moat, as the origin of the *seigneurie banale:* "cela se peut en divers lieux dès le XIe siècle, c'est certain par la suite, pas partout" (it is possible in some places by the eleventh century, it is sure for following period, but not everywhere); and "il castello diviene il piu efficace supporto per la formazione di distritti signorili" (the castle became the most efficient support for the formation of the seignorial districts). Two concrete cases for a part of Germany and an Italian city: Brandenburg and Parma.[20] But the links were not everywhere and at every time causal. Many holders of the *bannum* did not possess a castle or a keep.

Potentes could (and most of them were forced to) profit from the political possibilities, thanks to or because of the economic climate. Economic expansion penetrated into the countryside, increased opportunities of selling in the markets, and made money more abundant—or rather, less scarce. When the peasants disposed of more pennies, the master of the *bannum* could exact more from them. Simultaneously, statute labors were drastically reduced in most regions of the Continent.[21] The Carolingian obligation of working three days a week on the domain disappeared. The new obligation imposed not only on the tenants but on all men by virtue of the ban (the *corvées banales,* often confused with the old *corvées cens*) was very light: a few days every year.[22] So the peasant could invest more energy in his fields and produce more. Or he could give more of his time in other forms to the lord.

Was the latter also driven by the decline of his land rents, fixed forever in money sums and gradually losing their purchase power through the slow but continuous devaluation of the *denarius,* the penny? And did he try to compensate for the fall of his real income by creating, increasing, or generalizing personal taxes? That is probable; but to be sure we should trace the chronological debasement of the *census.* At any rate, in the late eleventh or in the twelfth century, the census amounted to a very small part, hardly 3 percent, of the renting value.[23] And it yielded much less than the seignorial rights in the strict sense of the word—tallage or toll, for instance.[24]

Many lords were also driven by the constriction of their property. It continued to be divided by inheritance, by gifts to religious institutions that would pray for the donor, and by the constitution of fiefs for their retinue. So in most cases, as we saw before, the *seigneurie foncière* no longer coincided with a *villa* or a parish. Yet the diminution of its resources went hand in hand with a continuous augmentation of expenses for military purposes or for display: improved armor or the development of the keep into a fortress;[25] participation in tournaments; foundation of a family monastery or, more humbly, of a small regular or secular chapter; decoration of the great hall; and so on.[26] Did the two movements combine to provoke or promote a change of the lordly mind-set? Did the aristocracy pass from a warlike mentality to the appetites of a businessman? And in that way, did the nobles "exert pressure on the productive forces" and "give a decisive impulse to the economy"?[27] One would be willing to agree with that view, to some extent. But did the nobles of the early Middle Ages really despise money? At any rate, many knights of the later period were at the same time professional warriors and gentlemen farmers—and the chronological priority of the new expenses is not proved. One instance of the prudence required by these questions: a specialist of medieval fortifications suggests that equipment, especially of a defensive nature, soon became more highly perfected and expensive; but a specialist in armament does not see in it any notable progress from the tenth to the twelfth century.[28]

Chronology! To construct that puzzle of motivations, it would be necessary to follow the chronological history of the *consuetudines, condictiones, coutumes, condicie*. They did not all appear at the same time. In the Empire, the banalities, the compulsory use of the lord's mill, bakehouse, and brewery—which derived from an old custom and did not directly take money out of the pocket of the peasants—may have been the first to show up, in the mid-tenth century.[29] For France, an attentive analysis of some quotations in recent monographs suggests that the *consuetudines* initially consisted in the performance of a task, especially erecting, enlarging, reinforcing, or maintaining the keep or castle; or in the delivery of a part of the peasants' production: grain, cattle, or eggs. Thus it was in Poitou, Anjou, Auvergne, and Champagne. The first Anjevin text giving some information on their nature, in 1007–26, calls them "bannum, carrucam, corvatas, biduanum et omnem vicariam" (ban, plough, statute labor, jurisdiction). In Champagne before 1030, the *consuetudines* obliged people to shelter the *advocatus* and to work for the maintenance of the castle and the transportation of goods to it. From 1050, they included serving with arms. Only after 1075 did they imply paying an arbitrary tallage.[30] So tallage came with a second wave, after one or two generations or more, when money had become more present in the countryside; characteristically, it was always fixed and paid in money. It seems that the possessors of the *bannum* shaped their requirements to fit the capacities of the peasantry, who were able at first to give labor and goods of their own production and, later, when the economy had been expanding a long while, money—more money than the few pennies paid in the Carolingian period.[31]

Generally speaking, the *consuetudines* appear in surviving texts from the Rhineland about 950 for the banalities and after 1000 for the other rights; in Normandy, Brittany, Poitou, Auvergne and Catalonia from 990 to 1000; and in the Meuse valley, which is less rich in documents, in the mid-eleventh century.[32] The vocabulary confirms the dates given by the charters: in the eleventh century, tallage, for instance, was called *accidentalis questus* (occasional demand).[33] Seignorial rights were *male consuetudines*. In Spain they were *mals usos* or, still more eloquently, *malae inventiones* in a Poitou charter from 993–1039.[34] Bad: that means new; for to the medieval mind every innovation was undue and unlawful.[35]

Consuetudines were not entirely new, however, and they varied greatly. Some derived from the public law, if we dare to use the term. Let us leave aside the question of justice, to avoid or skirt the problem of the existence and status of private courts in the early Middle Ages. But there is no doubt for the *gistae*—the right of exacting accommodation and nourishment, and for the *ost*—the requisition of men, horses, and wagons for the army. A second group originated in private custom: the burdens which weighed on the *servi* and the *cerocensuales* (the serfs of a lord and the men of a saint), especially the heriot and the *forismaritagium* paid for permission to marry outside of the *familia* (the extended dependency group),[36] and some statute labors that until now had been performed only by the tenants of lands and were henceforth imposed on all the inhabitants by virtue of the *bannum*. A third category was made up of apparently new rights: *tallia* and *banalitates*. The Carolingian period had known *exactiones*, which may possibly have paved the way for the tallage,[37] but no document proves a real connection between both taxes. And if use of the lord's mill, bakehouse, and brewery was probably common for practical reasons long before the eleventh century, it was not compulsory. To sum up, there was in Italy the required oath to be faithful to the lord and to defend his goods and rights[38] and in Belgium there was *commans et corvées*—the lord's right of commanding anything and exacting any kind of work.

But different as they were, all those rights formed an ensemble—all were *consuetudines*. Or, to pick more revealing expressions out of charters from 1343 and 1243, they were "chouses qui touchent à haulteur de seigneur" (things pertaining to the lord's jurisdiction); or "rustice servitutes quae ultra debitum censum terrarum a rusticis exiguntur" (rural servitudes, which are required from the peasants beyond the rent of the lands),[39] because they burdened not only the tenants but all the *rustici*. Noblemen were exempt. So to escape them became the most obvious mark of nobility; to be a *liber homo* meant henceforward to be free of these obligations. Knights, too, were exempt when they reached the threshold of the nobility; they would no longer be subjected to "consuetudines indecentes quae contra militarem ordinem mihi usurpaveram injuste" (the indecent customs which I [the count of Namur is speaking in the charter from 1212, which liberated the *milites de familia* from the heriot] unjustly for myself usurped against the knightly order).[40] Also exempt were priests and, to some extent, all clergy, and the owners of freeholds or fiefs not subject to banalities.

But *homines* and *servi* shared the same position in that matter. We shall see it immediately when we consider the consequences provoked by the introduction of seignorial rights.

But to understand all those consequences, one ought to gauge the weight of seignorial rights. It is commonly written that they were "crushing." The assertion must be carefully checked, for the data and conclusions, or rather opinions, do not concord. In the county of Namur, tallage in the mid-thirteenth century and until the end of the Middle Ages was not at all overwhelming compared with the prices of goods and services.[41] In contemporary England, it was of "no small weight" on some estates.[42] In the same time and country, entry fines were moderate, but on the manors of the Abbey of Bec they aroused severe opposition.[43] Still, in that time and place, the sum of all the seignorial rights amounted to half of the peasants' resources, at least for the *villeins*.[44] In the kingdom of Valence, it was "not unreasonable."[45] To judge, therefore, it is indispensable not to generalize from a few big estates to the bulk of all cases, not to neglect the part played by individuals and their hesitation and wavering—Saint-Amand and Battle Abbey are good examples[46]—not to forget that there were many forms of exploitation, not to ignore that the masters did not always exact all they were allowed to demand. As the rental of the Count of Namur from 1289 says, "cette droiture est à prendre à le volenteit do signour solonc le poir des gens dont om le prent" (this right is to be taken at the lord's will, according to the possibility of the men from whom it is taken).[47] And, finally, one ought to take into account the possible evolution, mitigation, or aggravation of seignorial rights, which explains the diversity in communities' attitudes versus their lords.

*

IN TWO main ways, the emergence of the *seigneurie banale* contributed to the birth, maturation, or reinforcement of the rural community.

At first, it largely unified the status of all the *rustici*. From the Carolingian period, opposition between *homines* and *servi* had weakened. It had disappeared in the classical distinction among *mansi ingenuiles*, *serviles*, and *lidiles*.[48] Most Italian documents no longer alluded to it.[49] Now a decisive step occurred. *Homines* and *servi* were bound to perform the same work and pay the same taxes under the same conditions and for the same reason: because they breathed the same air of the same lord. And those tasks and taxes constituted the bulk of the obligations to the lord. So status was largely identical for all members of the community, who were all called *rustici* in Italy or *Bauer* in Germany—and probably elsewhere.[50] Status was not constituted by "charges caractéristiques du servage" (dues characteristic of serf-dom).[51] Tallage and heriot were "servitudes appartenans à payer à gens de basse loy" (taxes to be paid by men of lower law), who were not members of an enfranchised community.[52] It was only in the four-teenth and fifteenth centuries, when serfs were very scarce and all the more despised, that the expression *macula servitutis* (stain of serfdom)—another term to hunt in the documents—appeared and that some lawyers established a connection between tallage, heriot, and serfdom.[53] The confusion became complete with the early mod-ern *feudistes*, who, like all jurists in every period, were concerned pri-marily with elaborating a coherent legal system.

So there were no taxes characteristic of serfdom and no *servage gé-néralisé*, as Marc Bloch asserts. *Liberi, coloni, mancipia,* and *servi* did not, in the post-Carolingian anarchy, mix in a social and juridical melting pot. All peasants did not fall into and join in one unique class in the tenth century. Serfdom apparently died out in some regions, like Poitou and Provence.[54] But it survived in many others and was still important in the thirteenth century in England, which by the end of that century counted between 25 and 72 percent *villeins*[55] and in vil-lages like Villeneuve-Saint-Georges, next to Paris, where there were eleven *servi* in the Carolingian period and thirty-three in 1250.[56] Serfs were less numerous, maybe, elsewhere, for reasons that are not clear. Reclamations might have acted on the group in a beneficial way: in 1279, the hundred of Stoneleigh, where they had been considerable, counted 50 percent free tenants, 27 percent sokemen, and 23 percent cottagers, while the figures in the older hundred of Kingston were 30 percent, 46 percent, and 24 percent.[57] As frequently, the poor, the serfs might beget few children. Lords granted collective or individual enfranchisements, but serfs continued to exist and were clearly sepa-rate from the rest of the population. Their status did not fundamen-tally change: they were prohibited from leaving the manor, from marrying a stranger, and less commonly, from selling their tenements except to the lord and from bequeathing it to others than relatives of the same condition.[58] This does not support the thesis of a "second servage."[59]

All inhabitants of the village were subject to the same court of the aldermen of the lord. I have not discovered so far any traces of a do-mestic and arbitrary justice of the lord in the late Middle Ages.

*

THE CONSTITUTION of the *seigneurie banale* influenced the unity of the rural community in another way. It led the peasants to react to the action of the lord. And such a reaction could not expect success unless all or nearly all concerned people participated.

What the peasants wanted was the preservation of extant customs, of—as their descendants in fifteenth-century Germany would say— *gutes altes Recht* (good old law or God's law)[60]: no change, either in the regime of the tenements—perpetuity of concession and fixity of rent— or in personal status—no new taxes or, at least, no arbitrariness in their amount and frequency. To enforce their wishes, the peasants resorted to two forms of action, legal and illegal. I use these terms with some approximation—as always when we use modern words for medieval realities.

The common "legal" way of checking the lord's and his officials' *exactiones* was opened by the *placita generalia* (general pleas) from the Carolingian epoch, which survived mainly in northern Europe down to the end of the Ancien Régime. They gathered all the members of a district under the presidence of the mayor and his aldermen. A passage from a Belgian chronicle from the early twelfth century deserves to be quoted here in spite of its length. The *Historia Walciodorensis monasterii* narrates a conflict of about 1050 with the adjacent monasteries of Waulsort and Hastière, next to Dinant:

> Major villicus de Hasteria cum universis officialibus suis et omni potestate ejusdem Hasteria per annum tribus vicibus ad generalem concionem in Walciodoro conveniebat. [Now,] quoniam diebus illis annuatim Walciodorensium omnis circumiacens potestas certis et assignatis temporibus, post Domini natalitium, Pasca et Pentecostem, congregabatur discutiendo, audiendo et respondendo, eadem Hasteriensis potestas de suis judiciis eisdem diebus cum ceteris adveniebat. (The estate headman of Hastière with all his officials and the whole people of the territory subject to the authority of the abbot, convened three times a year in a general assembly at Waulsort. Now, since at that time the entire surrounding *potestas* of the Waulsort people came together annually at assigned dates —after Christmas, Easter, and Pentecost—to discuss, listen, and decide, the aforesaid *potestas* arrived with its judgments on the same day as the others.)

Hence some agitation. Nevertheless, the Abbot of Waulsort decided to gather all the people of Waulsort on the said day, "atque de rebus publicis se tractaturum ibidem disposuit, dicens alicui nullam facere injuriam si in suae potestatis banno et in loco sub sua ditione constituto audiendus, responsurus necnon populus conveniret" (and decided he would treat public business in the same place, saying it would harm no one if the people convened to hear and decide in the *bannum* under his authority).[61]

Here is a second example, extracted from a chronicle of the same region and roughly the same period, the *Cantatorium Sancti Huberti.* About 1070, the *pontenarii* (toll men) of the Count of Chiny harassed the servants who were conveying the tithes of the monastery, "meliores garbas violenter rapientes" (seizing with violence the better crop shares). Then the count

> indicta bannali evocatione totius potestatis, adjuravit antiquiores et meliores, interposito sacramento facte sibi fidelitatis, ut edicerent ei veritatem huius consuetudinis. Illi, locuti cum consilio, responderunt comiti per Rodericum prepositum et Gobertum villicum, sicut erant adjurati, exactiones istas ab iniquis ministris dominorum esse inventas et injuste et fraudulenter impositas et ideo judicio eorum, si justitia servaretur, omnino adnichilandas (The count, having issued a banal summons of the entire *potestas,* adjured the older and better men, by virtue of their oath of fidelity to him, to tell him the truth about this *consuetudo;* they spoke together [or they discussed the matter with an assembly?] and replied to the count via Roderic, his official, and Gobert, his steward, as they had been adjured, that these exactions had been invented by evil servants of the lords and imposed unjustly and fraudulently and, in their judgment, had therefore to be abrogated if justice was to be preserved).[62]

The assemblies, here as elsewhere,[63] offer many common features with another institution that likely also derived from Carolingian administration—*scabini* (aldermen): a convocation by the lord and presided over by him or his officials, gathering the whole community; oaths by the *antiquiores, meliores,* or *jurati;* deliberation by the aldermen, out of the presence of the mayor. And the assemblies interfered in many matters. Their competence was sometimes reduced by the *aldermanate* and more often by a third organism that in certain regions also sank its roots into Carolingian soil—the *universitas ville,* the *comune,* or *le common del ville.* The assembly's independence was probably never complete. Mayor and aldermen were sometimes forced, in the words of the chronicler of Saint Hubert, "exactis violenter judiciis in posterum firmare" (once judgments had been exacted by violence, to confirm them for the future).[64] Their main sphere of activity remained the elaboration of rules for cultivation, pasture, woods, and above all, the defense of custom against seignorial rights. And they succeeded in getting custom written down and recorded yearly in what the texts call, precisely, "records." We shall return to that kind of document and to those assemblies when we discuss the era when all of them took definite shape—the late twelfth and throughout the thirteenth centuries.

Another means of fighting against *exactiones* was for the community to get the assistance of an advowee or of some *potens,* or even of the prince, by paying a yearly rent called *advocatia, soignie,* or, significantly, *sauvement*. The protector would, in the words of a text from 1289, "saveir et wardeir cil de le ville envers lor saingnor et ailleurs que nus tort ne lours soit fait s'il en est requist" (preserve and guard those of the village vis-a-vis their lord and elsewhere, so that no wrong might be done to them, if he [the advowee] be required to by them).[65]

Of course, rural communities could also join together for a collective defense or seek the help of a neighboring town.[66] As a matter of fact, not a few ones were in the late Middle Ages associated with a city, especially in Italy. But did they ask for aid? Or had they been subdued by the urban authority?

On the other hand, the local lord was frequently led by political or financial aims or difficulties to curb his appetite. Sometimes this happened very quickly. When, for instance, he had to contend with another noble or landowner, he might make some concessions to the community in order to gain or maintain his *bannum*. He had also to wrestle with the prince, who was building his "territory," his princedom, by eliminating local powers and placing the vill under his direct authority[67]—or at least subjugating those powers, thanks to feudalism, and becoming the *sire souverain* (sovereign lord), legally qualified and ready to defend his "people."[68] Competition to local lords could also come from cities or boroughs: their *libertates*—the privileges they were endowed with—the protection they provided, and the employment they offered would attract men from villages where status was low and duties were heavy. In a first phase, cities freely welcomed all immigrants, even serfs. Afterward, they limited immigrants under pressure from local lords and to avoid being overwhelmed by vagrants.[69] And of course the lord had to be careful not to kill by his *exactiones* the hen that laid the golden egg.

The optimum result for the rural community was the acquisition of a charter. This is one of the most studied subjects in medieval history, but it is too often studied either with prejudice or without sufficient care. The prevailing prejudice is the theory that the economy of the Middle Ages, as in other times, was the motor of mankind's evolution and, consequently, that concessions of charters were dictated by economic concerns and that the economic centers, the cities, paved the way and set the pattern for "emancipation." Others do not bother to collect all the charters of a region, classify them chronologically, or analyze their entire diplomatic form and elements ("suscriptio, arrenga, narratio, corroboratio, subscriptio") to determine, for instance, whether they had been spontaneously granted by the lords or had been solicited and even wrenched from him by the peasants. So many questions await a satisfactory solution. It is not certain, but it is possible, that documents formulating the rights of the advowee, (*règle-*

ments d'avouerie) were the model for the charters, as has been suggested for Lorraine and Champagne.[70]

It is less and less sure that the earliest charters aimed at economic objectives. Where they have been systematically collected and analyzed, it appears that they were granted exclusively by the prince—or by some *potens* who hoped to escape him or to become himself a prince—for mainly political reasons, in order to build his "territory" by getting a foothold in places pertaining to other princes, to bishops, to monasteries, or to noble families, or in places where his authority was weak or contested. So it was in the Lotharingian duchies and counties in Savoy and in Spain.[71] The most revealing case comes from the Countess Ermesinde of Luxembourg, who contemplated subjugating the old imperial abbey of Echternach: she elaborated a charter of franchises for the men of the district, but in the end she did not dare to promulgate it.[72] The economic goals were not everywhere and completely absent, especially in backward regions, which needed help and stimulus.[73] Economic goals weighed more heavily from the mid-thirteenth century, when boundaries of the *Territorien* (principalities) had been definitively fixed. Political objectives still operated, as in Italy or in southern France,[74] but economic ones now prevailed,[75] and they would weigh more and more with the so-called crisis of the late Middle Ages. And lesser lords now imitated the prince.

A third point is also at issue: did the towns give the impulse to the "emancipation" of the peasantry? No doubt they provoked some grants to the countryside, as urban charters were given to rural communities or, more exactly, adapted to their needs. But many scholars contest that the phenomenon was a general one and that urban charters preceded and produced rural ones. According to them, the movement was twofold, and it started and developed simultaneously in the cities and in the villages.[76] At any rate, it began very early, in the first half of the twelfth century in the old Carolingian principalities, in the century's second half in northern France, and peaked about 1250 in central and southern France and after 1300 in Germany.[77]

The contents of the charters varied greatly. All of them intended to suppress customs that had already rooted or, perhaps, to prevent their establishment. Some were miserly and some were generous, like the famous loi de Beaumont, which established the main lines for eastern Germany's *Landgemeinde*.[78] They helped organize self-government, including the election of heads of the community, the administration of justice, and the levy of troops, as we shall see later.

More important from our present viewpoint is to know that the charters did not always apply to the whole *universitas*. Some charters left untouched the old part of the villa, cases where a *ville neuve* had been founded, or where assarting had taken place and enfranchised fields had been won from the forests. In other cases, some parts of the *universitas* pertained to another entity, where the *villa*, the *districtus*, and the *parochia* did not overlap.[79] Many more were limited to the inhabited portion, delineated by a palisade, an *Etter*, a fence, a road, or a succession of crosses.[80] Many charters excluded serfs, at least the serfs of the lord, but there was no uniformity in that matter.[81] For instance, two charters granted by the Duke of Brabant in 1180 and 1187 to two adjacent villages suppressed the heriot for all people "cujuscumque familie fuerint preter eos qui omnino de familia mea sunt," here, and there, "cujusve familie mee vel alterius fuerint" (whomever they were dependents of, except if they pertained to me [here, and there] "whether they were dependents of me or anybody else").[82] Finally, some people, probably a tenth, especially immigrants, did not attain to the bourgeoisie because they would have had to buy this status or because they were poor and therefore indifferent to privileges mainly concerning taxes on wealth (ibid.).

A tenth was also the likely proportion of villages that received a charter.[83] But one ought to be careful: thirteenth-century polyptychs mention "burghers" in localities that did not enjoy such a document or had lost it.

Beside collective grants, there were individual grants that modified the status of a person—or more often of a family—and might introduce him into or isolate him from the community. For brevity's sake and because they are less significant for our purpose, we simply mention them. In the eleventh century and throughout the twelfth century, most of these charters transformed a serf into a *cerocensualis* (property of a saint).[84] A few, in the late Middle Ages, were bestowed on serfs, bastards, or strangers, especially servants or farmers of the lord, in order to suppress their legal inferiority. Some, on the contrary, affected not persons but groups, because of their activity: clerics, ironworkers, or crossbowmen.[85]

In the princes' Italy, the lords were reluctant to grant charters. However, some communities succeeded in getting more or less free of the lords—for instance, by paying them rent of recognition or by integrating them into their members.[86] Where cities extended their power over the surrounding territory, they liberated the *homines et rustici* of their *contado* from statute labor and the *extorsiones* of the *domini*. Vercelli, Bologna, and Florence are famous examples of that phenomenon.[87] By the thirteenth century, the *extorsiones* had disappeared from Tuscany.[88]

In the customary lands of northern continental Europe, the *lex villae* was generally not determined in a charter but was kept in what the medieval texts call records (*wijsdommen, Weistümer*). That kind of document raises many questions regarding its juridical definition, its origins (initiative of the lord or pressure from the peasants?), its aims, its date, and the circumstances under which it was written down.[89] In any case, it took shape gradually and slowly and assumed its definitive forms only on the threshold of the twelfth century. It was then read every year in the presence of the whole community, which had been summoned for the occasion. The aldermen, with their predecessors' help, and the elders recorded the custom. And the assembly either accepted their declaration, as in 1375 in a fief close to Namur, where "tous les massuiers, mannans et surcéans sur le fief rien ne débatirent au record" (all the inhabitants of the fief in no way contradicted the record)[90]—or alleged that some dispositions were new and would not admit them. In fact, the lord sometimes tried to increase his rights with the complicity of the aldermen.[91] But the community was, or would be by the late Middle Ages, strong enough to counter such attempts.

To counter these innovations, the community might also sue the lord and his officials, especially where superior public courts existed and were willing to hear its charges. Thus in England, the tenants of Halesowen or Battle Abbey appealed to the king's bench, to royal inquests, and even petitioned the king and his council.[92] In southern France, too, lawsuits and transactions led to the alleviation or suppression of many seignorial rights.[93] The plaintiffs, however, did not always get the upper hand: in 1276, some tenants of Leicester Abbey alleged before the king's bench that they were freemen, but they were compelled to confess their *villeinage*.[94]

Amiable agreements, too, were probably reached between the lord and his men, for charters, records, and sentences do not encompass the whole reality. The rentals of the thirteenth century show that, in the greater part of the Continent, most rural communities had obtained a substantial mitigation of the customs. In a word, these were clearly defined in periodicity and amount. Arbitrariness was banned. To assert, as quoted above, that only a tenth of the villages were freed is both true and false and could distort the picture. Only a tenth received a charter of franchise that has been preserved. But the majority stopped and even turned back oppression.

Although this was true over the greater part of the Continent, it was not true everywhere, and was not true in England. In this country, some lords' behavior apparently fluctuated.[95] In the thirteenth century, they retracted the franchises they had earlier bestowed in order to profit from the opportunities offered by the market economy, the increase in corn prices, and the growing scarcity of fields. They enlarged the demesnes, exacted more statute labors, increased entry fines, and so on. However, the movement was neither general nor definitive, and it did not annul all previous concessions. At the end of the thirteenth century, of forty-five villages of northern Warwickshire, statute labor was ignored in eighteen, but was light in twelve, seasonal in thirteen, and heavy (workweeks) in two; for the south, the figures are ten, eight, twenty-two, and eight, respectively.[96] In other countries, like Spain and Portugal, the seignorial rights also weighed more and more heavily in the twelfth and thirteenth centuries. In the Mino valley, they combined with divisions of inheritances to oblige the majority of small free owners to sell their fields and even to enter into dependency. In thirteenth-century Catalonia, where the count could no longer dominate the nobles, the latter obtained from the Cortes a confirmation of the *jus maletractandi* (the right to exact *mal usos*).[97] Or real (territorial) serfdom, based not upon birth but upon residence in a servile locality, appeared and imposed servile burdens on all inhabitants, whatever their personal status.[98] Those phenomena paved the way to a more active "illegal" resistance.

Other developments in the later Middle Ages exerted pressure in the same direction. At this point, it is impossible not to think of the much studied "crisis of feudalism."[99] The matter remains somewhat unclear, and scholars do not agree in their analysis of the situation. What were the causes of the phenomenon? Was it the system in itself: a fundamentally defective organization of the relations between the different factors of production? Was it the excessive burdens imposed by lords, clergy, owners, and state on the peasants' shoulders? Was it lack of investment or inadequacy in the size of the tenements and the labor force? In the long run, the system seized up. However, the data in monographs do not fit this "model" exactly.[100] Here one feature is absent, there another one. And external factors no doubt interfered—for instance, monetary manipulations, which affected prices and therefore the real weight of rents and demographic evolution. Specialists are also at issue as to the intensity of the "crisis" and on its effects for different groups of people. Obviously, the factors involved were many, the variety was great, and any generalization is dangerous. Whatever the theory and its validity, one thing is beyond question: in many countries and places, the seignorial regime became harsher in a number of ways.[101] Hitherto, the tenements, according to the medieval idea that everything is by nature perpetual,[102] had been *ad censum* (without limit of duration), and the tenant might not be evicted as long as he paid the rent. Now, in Germany the *Zeitpacht* tended to replace the *Erbpacht*—a temporary letting replaced the hereditary one.[103] In other regions, too, fields were henceforward frequently

TABLE 3. FROM *TENURE IN BONDAGIO* TO *TENURE AD VOLUNTATEM*, IN KILWORTH HARCOURT

Date	in bondagio	ad voluntatem
1359–69	34	7
1370–79	4	3
1380–89	6	4
1390–99	7	20
1400–1409	0	8
1410–19	4	16
1420–29	5	37
1430–39	2	44
1440–49	0	17

Source: C. Howell, "Peasant Inheritance Customs in the Midlands, 1200–1700" in J. Goody, J. Thirsk, and E. P. Thompson, *Family and Inheritance: Rural Society in Western Europe, 1200–1800* (Cambridge, 1976, p. 133).

given in temporary leases, as in *tenures révocables* in Flanders.[104] Even in England, where in the early fourteenth century many *villeins* had received a copyhold,[105] in the following hundred years, concessions *ad voluntatem domini* (at the lord's will) superseded those *ad censum*.[106] That did not mean that cultivators had to leave their fields unexpectedly or frequently. But there was a risk of dispossession without recourse. In Italy, the *mezzadria*, the *métayage*, introduced in the twelfth century by city dwellers,[107] gained more and more ground.[108] Urban owners who invested in the land and, in the fifteenth century, the *fittabili* to whom they leased it wished to make money from the properties and to keep control of them.[109] Now, peasants always prefer a fixed rent to a fluctuating one. Thus they lost two things they badly wanted: perpetuity of tenure and a fixed rent. These changes touched them more than anything else. Moreover, in the long run, loans by owners of seed, cattle, and money frequently ruined the peasants.[110] In some countries, like Alsace, Castile, and León, the lords also reduced the surface of the commons and the right to hunt, fish, and use the water from the streams.

At the same time, *villeinage* was in some regions extended to free people and not solely by way of "real" serfdom. Personal ties became stricter and personal burdens, heavier. In Germany, people were more closely bound to the manor and were prohibited from leaving it at will and to marry outside of it.[111] Statute labor also increased in Silesia and in Schleswig.[112] In southern Italy and in Spain, compulsory labor and taxes were revived, augmented or even introduced for the first time.[113]

Newer and more prone to raise riots were the attacks against the system itself. Some philosophers, lawyers, and preachers denounced the system as injurious, oppressive, destitute of any justification, or contrary to the natural order. The constitutions of Bologna and Florence had asserted in 1257 and 1289 that "jure naturali omnes homines liberi nascuntur" (according to natural law, all men are born free) and that in Paradise all are equal.[114] The system, on the other hand, was based on violence. "Die Knechtschaft," proclaimed the main German customary of the time, "beruhet nur auf Gewalttat" (serfdom rests on force alone).[115] It was backed by wealth, which Jacob van Maerlant and Jan Boendale, in Flanders, claimed to be the source of all evil.[116] It was useless: peace, justice, and protection were no longer assured by the lords but by the state. Did such ideas and others of similar ilk, like Italy's millenarist conceptions,[117] reach and move the masses? At any rate, they may have incited agitators and upstarts whose economic and social ascension was obstructed by the existing structures of lordship and clergy.

The state we just mentioned often fomented discontent. It actually took care of local order. It frequently supported rural communities against their lords, in order to eliminate the latter or to restrict their power and financial pressure and to establish a direct contact with the people.[118] In the seneschalship of Toulouse, for instance, 166 charters had been conceded before 1271; two centuries later, the number was multiplied by three or four.[119] But its officials were arrogant, harassing, and sometimes iniquitous in justice and finances; and above all they cost a lot. So, too, did diplomacy and war. The royal or princely fisc required and devoured more and more: in Spain, from 1269, by means of the *servicios* granted by the Cortes and the *alcabala* (duty on the transactions); in England, by the demands of the Crown;[120] in Flanders, by the tallage regularly levied from 1358;[121] in southern Germany, where, to increase their income, some princes extended part of the servile taxes to all their subjects. One gets the impression that rebellion and the presence of the state were intimately linked.

More terrifying than wars, famines and epidemics afflicted the fourteenth century and were the main factors behind the "agrarian crisis of the late Middle Ages."[122] This crisis may have been favorable for the lords in southwestern Germany.[123] Elsewhere, it was detrimental to them. *Wüstungen* and *Preisschere* were its two constantly emphasized aspects. *Wüstungen* refers to desertions of villages and fields, provoked by a catastrophic demographic recession and aggravated in some countries by emigration to the towns and by the search for refuge amid internal and international hostilities. *Preisschere* is a scissoring in prices; grain prices fell while those of tools and labor rose. Add a third feature, less stressed by scholars but no less dramatic and more general: a drastic fall in rents and important delays, even failures, in their payment. The situation of the middle-sized lords became difficult. The peasants, on the other hand, profited from falling rents and, if they were capable of profiting from it, an increasing supply of vacant tenements. Moreover, to check depopulation, a new wave of charters was launched, especially ones abolishing the heriot in villages and even in whole territories. In 1431, Philip the Good did so for the county of Namur and, in 1447, for the duchy of Burgundy.[124] But farmers received less for their grain and paid more for their tools. So the large number of delays and failures in rent payments might suggest that the situation of the lower segment of tenants was not as good as might have been expected. The cities were also factors in the deterioration of the economic and social climate, since they attracted people but could be, particularly in Italy, as cavilling and exacting as any king or prince. In Languedoc, some villages united to fight them and gain their own institutions.[125] Twice now we have met the upstarts, the new lords who managed their manors as businesses.[126] That they were strangers made the problems even greater. So, in all sectors there were grounds for the peasants to be dissatisfied and to resist more energetically than ever.

*

FOR THE PEASANTS had always resisted.[127] "Plebs semper in deterius prona est" (the people are always prone to the worst), said the Archbishop of Mainz in 1127, when he heard of peasants refusing to pay the tithe.[128] The documents allude to *violentia, contradictio, rebellio,*[129] words whose meanings are questionable. The records narrate some clashes. Around 1225, the Bishop of Utrecht and the population of Drente clashed, the peasants fearing they would be reduced to dependence, even to serfdom. Several times in the thirteenth and fourteenth centuries, the Abbot of Halesowen, near Birmingham, clashed with his tenants, who succeeded before the Black Death in stopping and even reducing the seignorial exactions.[130] The documents do not report many clashes. But do they offer a true image of their time? The authors probably judged the risings of the common people devoid of interest or so foul that reporting them would soil the parchment. What recourse do we have? Collecting, as historians will, all traces of opposition for large regions and over long periods? Such a method risks distorting reality.

Although resistance was apparently real, if we judge from times and countries for which we have official and complete information, like England in the thirteenth century and Naples in the fourteenth,[131] the peasantry remained essentially passive until the late Middle Ages.[132] Resistance consisted, for instance, of delaying or neglecting to pay the rent or to perform the imposed labor,[133] of refusing to receive a mayor whom the peasants did not want,[134] of preventing a lord's official from inquiring into the conditions of the tenancy,[135] and, more commonly, of trespassing against the customs. Resistance could be more durable and organized, for instance, under the cover of a brotherhood.[136] It could sometimes become violent.[137] The aims were always the same: to hinder any novelty: "rebellious feelings were often generated when custom was broken by the ruling groups."[138] The result was disappointing, except for Switzerland, where the cantons paved the way to independence.[139] The peasants had few and ineffective arms,[140] and they lacked unity.[141]

Things changed in the fourteenth century. "Passive" resistance continued, supported by kings and princes eager to curb the nobles. And it reaped valuable successes, like new charters or better conditions of tenancy.[142] But popular revolts also exploded[143]—in Flanders, France, England, and Spain.[144] The part played by various components of society and the goals of these players have been less controversial. The masses in the countryside were likely involved, especially at the beginning and end of the risings. Numerically, as always happens under such circumstances, they were predominant, but not economically, fundamentally, or structurally.[145] The leaders were not poor fellows but well-to-do farmers or nobles of secondary rank, middle-aged, who had held offices and who had a long commitment to the villages. These were inspired more by personal ambition than concern for the common welfare. They aimed to destroy the old order, the restraints of which hindered their economic and social ascension and especially impeded them from profiting from opportunities opened by depopulation. Resistance was a success only in Spain, where the *pagenses de remensas* were liberated from the *mal usos*.[146] If revolts exploded, it was because the *universitas* no longer was an isolated village but embraced a large region. From our viewpoint, the revolts were less effectual for the consolidation of the rural community than the local assemblies that had survived or emerged in the second millenium. To conclude the study of the legal aspects of country life, it remains to analyze those institutions—their origins, composition, working rules, and

powers, and as a corollary, the position of the lord in the latter part
and at the end of the Middle Ages.

*

OF COURSE, central and regional institutions intervened in the life of
the villages. In their turn, the villages sometimes had a hand in the
nomination of the officials who interfered in their affairs. English boroughs in the late thirteenth century received or bought the right of
choosing the sheriff. The *Gemeinden* of Swabia in the fifteenth century
acquired a *Mitsprachrecht* (right of taking part) in the designation of
the *Schultheiss*.[147] This aspect of the rural community's insertion into
its *terra* will be treated in chapter 5. Here we are dealing with the local
organism.

The majority of these local organisms were born before the eleventh century, but nearly everywhere they were appropriated and
more or less distorted by the lord. Then new ones, entirely or largely
independent of the lord, would arise and compete with them.

We have already encountered the *placita generalia*. The lord took
them over, probably in the eleventh century. The *Cantatorium Sancti
Huberti* (the author of which was an excellent lawyer) narrates two
conflicts that occurred in 1079 and 1081 and reports here *antiquiores
et meliores* and there the sole *villicus* (the mayor) were required by the
abbot to declare the custom. Half a century later, according to the
Historia Walciodorensis monasterii, "villicus et scabini" recorded it.[148]
The mayor, assisted by the aldermen chosen by the lord, presided
over the meeting, just like the reeve in the English hallmoot.[149] The
placita were no longer in charge of justice but of defending the *legiti-
mae consuetudines* (the legal customs).[150] The aldermen played the leading part in this, helped by *antiqui* (elders) or *jurati* (jurors). In Italy,
the *jurati* could be elected jointly by the lord and the community.[151]
And in some parts of Germany, the community superseded the lord
and his officials on the eve of early Modern Times.[152] The pleas also
decided every year upon how to cultivate and graze.

The aldermanate, or the manorial court, likely underwent a similar
evolution. It derived from old "public" institutions and was annexed
and reshaped by the lord.[153] It was presided over by the *villicus* and
composed of *scabini*, all of them chosen by the lord, who sometimes
tolerated or granted to the community by a charter (like the "Loi de
Beaumont" of 1198)[154] the right of electing them.[155] It no longer held
exclusively judicial functions but also gained administrative functions.
First of all, it preserved the lord's goods and rights and collected his
rents and taxes or distributed the taxes when they had been collectively assessed. It recorded the customs in the pleas, and if necessary,

interpreted them with the elders' help.[156] It could take every kind of decision in internal affairs. It exercised justice, even high, criminal justice, if the lord was endowed with it and registered transfers of land ownership and heard suits.

The field of competence and means of the aldermens' action were largely encroached on more or less quickly by concessions gained by or made to the rural community and by the creation of new corporations depending on it, like the *molenpolders* of Holland, who erected mills for draining the water. Such corporations were presided over by the *schout* or *buurschap* (the chief of the village, but which covered only a part of this one).[157] We have alluded to the community's right to intervene in the election of aldermen. Other facts were just as significant in the lord's attitude or latitude. Prior to gaining the community's recognition, he had to take an oath—a capital act in the medieval mind and practice—to *bien atenir le frankise* (rightly maintain the liberties) and, if he refused to do so, the aldermen would no longer administer the justice.[158] He had to get the community's approval, especially in regard to using the commons.

In the same way, the mayor gradually drew closer to the community. He swore to defend not only the lord's but also the peasants' interests: "wardeir les droits du seigneur et des masuiers" (maintain the lord's and the men's rights). In charge of preserving the lord's property and income, he was sometimes accused by him of, jointly with the community, trespassing against him. He was chosen as the community's proxy before notary or court.[159] So he became as much—or more—the leader and champion of the peasants as the lord's agent.

Simultaneously, mainly in the franchises of northern continental Europe, there appeared, beside or in the place of the seignorial college of the aldermen, a college of *jurati, jurés, Heimbürgers,* headed by one or two *bourgmestres,* or *Bauermeister,* whose name is doubly significant: it does not exist, to my knowledge, in Latin,[160] and it means master of the borough or of the peasants. The *jurati* and their presidents were actually elected by the community to protect and administer it. The circumstances of their creation are obscure and debated. Initially, they might have been in charge of maintaining internal peace. Afterward, their powers differed from region to region: managing the finances of the village, elaborating and preserving the *lex statuta,* the *decreta villae* (the village's decrees) as distinct from *lex villae* (the former was probably called *Flurordnung* elsewhere and may be compared with English by-laws) or administering the *Burggericht* or *basse justice.* Their evolution varied, and some were absorbed by the aldermanate.[161]

From the thirteenth century, documents reporting a decision concerning the community say that it was made by "villicus, scabini et universitas villae." The origin of this assembly is based on guesswork. In England, it might have been the hallmoot, used by the king for assessing military and judicial duties.[162] On the Continent, it may have descended from an offspring of the *Hofgenossenschaft* made up of the *familia* (the lord's dependents), who in the eleventh century endeavored by means of the *lex familiae* to counter the advowee's exactions and who generated the *Dorfgenossenschaft* and the *Landgemeinde*.[163] Or else, possibly, it may have sprung from an informal group, the *Burschaft* (a spontaneous association of neighbors formed to meet common needs of the *Einung*), which grew with the associative climate of the eleventh century. Members of the *Burschaft* united by oath and met yearly for ritual libations.[164] At any rate, one ought not to speak of *Landgemeinde* before the twelfth century. In Bavaria, for instance, the *judicium villae* is not mentioned before 1250.[165]

The evidence does not give much more information on the composition, working rules, and powers of such assemblies in northwestern Europe. And one must avoid two temptations: applying to the northwest what holds for the south and for "colonial" Germany, and defining more than did the Middle Ages. Constitutional matters were not as precise as our modern legislation. Practice counted more than coherent and detailed theory, especially in England, where it is difficult to separate *curia manerii* from *communitas villae;* regarding the latter, scholars cannot understand how the *communitas* might meet and act when the *villa* comprised several manors.[166] Taking the words of the charters in their strict sense, the assembly grouped all the inhabitants: "bourgeois, manans et sorséans et toute la communauté."[167] Freeholders and *villeins:* the court rolls mention the "assensus omnium tenentium liberorum et nativorum" to the by-laws.[168] Did the *universitas* encompass all men above fourteen years of age, or each family's eldest, or those of each hearth and widows without a son of age? Did it group only proprietors and tenants of the lord, or residents possessing an *Ehofstaat* (house) or exercising a profession and partaking in the commons?[169] Did it exclude priests and noblemen or knights dwelling in the village or in the district and pertaining to the same lord? Was descent from a local family required, as it was in Piedmont?

It seems that reality was somewhat different. The assembly was dominated by an oligarchy of *probi viri* (honest men), of *meliores* (rich men, landholders),[170] and of *antiquiores* (elders), who were supposed to be experienced in and aware of the customs.

The working rules of such assemblies are practically unknown, except for the evidence provided by a few franchises. How was a meeting convoked? Was it with the leave of the lord or without it? In eastern Germany, meetings were independent of the lord.[171] In England, some were independent—but only with difficulty.[172] Were meetings regular? More probably, a meeting was called when necessity demanded. What percentage of members of the community was required to make a decision valid for all? Was the assembly "representative"? How were decisions determined—by unanimity or by a proportional vote? Apparently, some people might not agree with the decisions and therefore would not be bound by them.[173] Last but not least, were decisions obeyed? Official accounts were likely checked yearly by the community, sometimes jointly with the lord,[174] but in the meantime, who watched over them, and how?

The first duty of the assembly was to maintain the customs and, above all, to decide on the use of the commons—whether the commons were to be alienated or exchanged and to direct their exploitation by designating a host of heralds, foresters, shepherds, and so on.[175] For this, it enjoyed *Gebot und Verbot* (the right of ordaining and prohibiting) in Germany; in England, it gave out by-laws; in eastern Germany, *Willküren*.[176]

The *Landgemeinde* could also assume a juridical function. It administered the *Niedergericht* (low justice) in eastern Germany; in Bavaria, it was even competent in some penal affairs, according to the *Landrecht* (country law) promulgated by the duke in 1346.[177]

To perform its duties, the community elected representatives— proxies—to act in its name. Some were permanent, like the *Vieren* (four) for justice.[178] Some were appointed for a particular problem. The character desired in delegates is instructive. An agreement concluded in 1362 between two little villages of the Sambre-et-Meuse on the maintenance of the parish church was discussed by six "sages homes et honestes maistres" and ratified for the first community by two clerks and churchwardens and several "bonnes gens de la ville"; and for the second by two priests of adjacent parishes, one carpenter, one clerk and procurator, and one churchwarden.[179]

This panoramic view of northern Europe reveals three features. First, there was collaboration between the different institutions. To take two examples from many, by-laws were jointly discussed and promulgated by the lord and his manorial court and the community. Offenders against the by-laws were brought to court. If some ambiguity appeared in the customs, the court chose elders of the community or *jurati inquisitionis* (jurors of inquest) to solve it.[180]

Second, the lord might not act arbitrarily. His rights were fixed in a charter or a "record," and at his taking possession, he swore—in the franchises and likely elsewhere, too—not to alter them. If he tried to do so, he was opposed and, in most cases, defeated. On the other hand, he was endowed with effective power. In many places, he no longer chose the aldermen or even the mayor, all of whom had previously been his representatives and servants. In other localities, he chose the administrators and their president from candidates presented by the community. In the majority of the cases, however, he still appointed them as he wished. The community was bound in "legislative" matters to the will of the lord. Financial measures also required a cooperation of lord and assembly. No special toll, the usual way for the community to raise money, could be assessed without leave of the lord, who exacted a part of the fixed or presumed receipts. Even in questions that essentially concerned only the peasants, the lord intervened. He checked the transfer of his tenures, mainly to prevent their acquisition by strangers whom he did not know. He checked their conveyance to institutions of mortmain, which paid no fines at the changing of tenants because they neither sold nor died. Since he claimed the ownership of unappropriated grounds, he accorded to immigrants, especially religious houses, the right of participating in the uses of the commons.[181] Sometimes he even modified these uses. Yet he could not take action in a sector so important to the peasants without their *laudatio* (approval). Alone or jointly with the community, he chose the officials who would watch over fields, pastures, and forests.[182] And, of course, being the owner of the water and the air, he regulated fishing and hunting.

According to the medieval conception of public authority and its mission—the maintenance of the peace—the lord normally kept the upper hand in justice (internal peace) and the army (external peace). He seldom granted to the community the privilege of doing justice but continued at the least to preside over the courts held by his officials. He allowed some villages to organize their own protection, especially by erecting walls or palisades;[183] but in military as in juridical affairs, he kept control.

To sum up, from the seignorial viewpoint, one would probably not be wrong in distinguishing, at least in the ancient West, two waves and two kinds of franchises. The first had mainly political aims. It granted what may be called private, individual liberties—fundamentally, protection against the *malae consuetudines* (novelties)—but did not grant self-government, because the donor (normally the prince or some of his rivals) wanted to get or to keep "public" authority in places of special interest for building or consolidating a territory. In the second wave, economic goals prevailed, and in order to attract people and trade, some old and even more new settlements of small political and strategic importance were given a large degree of internal autonomy.

Third, present within the community was an upper group of *probi viri*, whom francophone documents call *honestes*, *honorables*, or *sages*.

Figure 14. French Fortified Village. Chauriat, in Auvergne, belonged to the bishop. The two churches were the seat of a Cluniac priory. In 1396, the inhabitants fortified a part of the vill around the churches. In the early 15th century, they built a large rampart, which provoked several conflicts with the bishop between 1430 and 1452. Later, the rampart was removed and replaced by the large boulevard that still circles the town.

Source: G. Fournier (Hélicoptère de la Protection civile).

This group was heterogeneous in its origins and constituent elements: both *déclassés*, who had descended from nobles and knights, and successful peasants. Yet it was coherent in its way of life and as a result of marriages. Most members were farmers who managed their ownership or the lord's or a citizen's possessions and who mimicked the aristocracy by holding a fief, by keeping a piece of military equipment in their closet and even a war-horse in their stable, by surrounding their mansion by a ditch and flanking it with a tower, and by discharging public offices. The foundation of their superiority was obviously wealth [184]—more exactly, landed property. Age, experience, and judgment were other factors of social recognition, as expressed by promotion to social duties; but these factors were less influential. [185]

In southern Europe, assemblies were older and, as a rule, better organized. They maintained greater liberty, without gaining complete independence—except for those in mountainous countries. In the Pyrenees and, at least from the thirteenth century, in the Alps, communities escaped "seignorialization" and kept or gained self-government. [186]

In Spain and Portugal, rural communities, which were coherent prior to 1000, struggled against the lord's grip in several stages and with diverse results. [187] In a first phase, the peasants of Catalonia were supported by the count and obtained from him many charters of franchises. But from the eleventh century, when he gradually retreated before the noblemen, the latter imposed their power and their *mals usos*. Some communities succeeded in keeping partial liberty in a portion of their territory, the *sagrares* around the church, which were the incentive and the model for granting anew more or less generous *fueros*. This second wave of concessions did not suppress *mals usos* or prevent rebellions by the end of the period.

Through these fluctuations, an organization took shape. [188] A *commune consilium,* or *consejo abierto* (open council), grouping all the people, elected a *credentia,* or *concejo cerrado* (permanent, closed council) of a few members who made the decisions. It was headed by an executive chosen by the lord from candidates presented by the community. The lord intervened in the peasants' affairs in another, more peculiar way: he himself entered the council. He also heard the pleas, even some that were internal to the community, in his court, where *probi* or *boni homines* might sit beside his judges. Actually, such *probi* or *boni homines* had the upper hand in collective matters. They succeeded the *maximi* of earlier times and the *infanzones* and the *barones* of the eleventh and twelfth centuries.

In Italy, the Carolingian political crisis opened the door to the *sei-gneury*. The *potentes* (landowners) imposed their *dominatio* on *districtus* (communities) that already enjoyed relative autonomy. After a period of weakness, these communities united and structured their strengths in the eleventh century.[189] Initially, they intended to maintain the *consuetudo praedii*, or *fundi*, and above all to defend their commons. Then, stimulated by the example of *castellani et burgenses*, they enlarged their horizon to government, administration, and justice. In a document of 1116, *consules* replaced *maiores;* another, of 1162, mentions a council elected by the *populus* and drawn from *curiales, maiores,* and *burgenses,* not from *rustici,* that assumed legislative and executive action and designated a *consul* to administer justice. Henceforth, the *universitas*— sometimes there were two, one of *domini* and one of *rustici*—took every power in its hands. In some cases, the lord kept a nominal authority, especially for approving *statuta* elaborated by the council. In other cases, his place was taken by a city. At first hesitant, if not hostile, toward the peasants, the big towns later supported peasants' actions. But eventually they subjugated their *contado*, sent their own *podesta* and *capitano* to rule it, checked that the statutes of the rural councils conformed to their urban laws, and exacted heavy taxes.[190]

Southern France offers, at the end of the Middle Ages, a case of rural communities the wide independence of which was encroached upon not by a city but by the state.[191] In Lauragais, for instance, these communities enjoyed justice and self-administration. In low Languedoc, the lord kept important prerogatives even in the most privileged communities, the *villes de consulat:* judging, convoking the assembly, and remodeling customs.[192] In the region of Beziers, the communal organism (*Parlement de l'université*) made decisions only in the spheres where it still held sway. Elsewhere, an assembly was dominated by an oligarchy that officially delegated the bulk of its powers to a *concilium* composed mainly of elders, or that transferred a part of its functions, especially in financial matters, to *probi viri*, who, in moments of crisis, seized the direction of all business. Hence, assemblies were less and less attended, all the more so since their leaders, the *consuls*, managed at their leisure, chose the members of the *concilium*, met it at their pleasure, and succeeded one another by co-optation. In the fifteenth century, the situation worsened: the king's officials restricted rural autonomy more than the lord had done, by strictly checking the election of the *consuls* and the accounts.

So in Mediterranean countries, two major features emerge from the variety of situations. Rural communities barely got and kept complete independence. In nearly all cases, a lord or a city or a prince kept or acquired important powers. Most often, the lord was the king, the prince, or an urban republic. The state played an even more important part than in the north. As in the north, the community was, from political and administrative viewpoints, internally dominated by *probi viri, consuls, preud'hommes*—whatever the name—who derived their influence mainly from landed property. This coincides with the results reached in the study of economic features.

*

BOTH observations introduce this chapter's conclusions. From the eleventh century, the rural community in western Europe gained consciousness, strength, and shape. In the first stage, this occurred under the exactions of the lords, who had superseded public authorities and who imposed the same obligations upon peasants, *homines*, and *servi*, thereby largely unifying their status. In the second phase, this developed thanks to concessions of liberties by many lords and the pressure of population growth, which led to fixing and normally mitigating seignorial burdens and to creating or reinforcing local bodies: aldermanate, jurors, "universities." The powers of these organisms varied according to many factors. Natural setting might make resistance easier. Local, regional, or "national" political structures played a role in whether the village had one or several lords; whether the lords had descended from native families or were outsiders; whether they dwelled in the village or not; whether there was a hierarchy between them and the state, whether the state generated the *villata* and made them the cells of society, as in England, or placed some villages under its direct sovereignty, like the *Freidörfer, Königsdörfer,* and *Reichsdörfer;*[193] and whether the state supported the efforts of the *rustici* against the noblemen, whom it tried to integrate into its territory and, after succeeding, strictly checked the local administration. Economic factors intervened, too: the concentration or dispersion of settlements, the intensity of commercial life, and the nearness of big cities. At any rate, except in extraordinarily few cases, rural communities did not remain or become entirely independent.

Progress toward emancipation was not constant. In many regions, the movement inverted in the thirteenth, fourteenth, or fifteenth centuries.[194] But the consciousness of being a community continued; at any period, exactions fostered unity.[195] Rural communities were not uniform in all aspects. During the late Middle Ages, an oligarchy took the upper hand in their political and economic life, without going so far as to provoke internal conflict[196] or to destroy or damage their fundamental unity. These results, which paved the way to early Modern Times, were fortified by religious regulations, structures, and actions.

4

PAROCHIA:

RELIGIOUS ASPECTS

*

T HE POLYPTYCHS of the thirteenth century list the lord's rents and rights by parishes. The accounts of the fourteenth and fifteenth centuries order their receipts in the same way. These are signs of the prominence of the parish in rural Middle Ages, from the time when, in a region like Auvergne, the custom of naming new villages after the saint of the local church took root.[1] To quote two well-known French historians: The parish was, for Duby, "l'élément le plus vivant des cadres ruraux" (the most lively element among rural structures); it was, according to Le Goff and Toubert "la structure globalisante de la société" (the globalizing structure of society).[2] Or, to cite a medieval text, one of the first Frisian juridical sources, the "24 Landrechten": "Here is what is a village: where take place baptism, burial and the three pleas."[3]

Why did the religious unit play such a leading role in peasant life? We may divide the diverse reasons into four categories. The parish had clear boundaries and watchfully imposed them on the human reality. Thanks to its organization, it was present and active in all events of both the individual and the collective existence: spiritually (in the broad sense the period gave to the term, including charity and teaching) as well as materially, worldly. It associated its members in its management. It infused cohesion and strength into the group, especially by imposing common duties and obligations.

*

W HAT made the parish a convenient entity for every purpose was its clear-cut limits, which included compact territories and transcended the mosaic of villages and hamlets, freeholds and fiefs, and lordships of every kind. At the outset, it was probably, like every formation in the early Middle Ages (epoch of the *Menschenstaat*), more personal than territorial. It associated all people who had been baptised in its church, all those whom it could reach in order to confer the sacraments. But, as we saw, the introduction of the tithe forced the determination of material boundaries. And the need only increased with land clearing. Every holder of the tithe and every peasant who had to pay it wanted to know exactly the *metae parochiales*.[4] How many conflicts emerged since the eleventh century over the right of collecting the *decimae novales* (the tithes of the assarts)! So much so that Alexander III, the first of a long and brilliant series of canonist popes, demanded in 1179 the definition by deeds and witnesses of the boundaries of every parish.[5]

The determination of the boundaries made it all the more necessary that the faithful comply with other duties: maintaining a part of the church, furnishing many items of religious equipment, making offerings at every stage of life, from birth to death, as well as at the great liturgical feasts.[6] From the eleventh century, the canon was better obeyed than under the Carolingians. In England, most of the parishes had gotten precise limits in the Anglo-Saxon period, but in some regions, like Devon, many acquired them only in the second half of the twelfth century. This was true, too, in the archbishropic of Cologne, and in Portugal.[7]

Delineating parish boundaries was also more and more indispensable because the religious network had become denser and, in some manner, more intricate. New churches were built with or against the wishes or the will of church authorities, who could be inclined either to meet the desires and needs of the Christian people or, on the contrary, to maintain the traditional framework and to restrain the lords' interference in ecclesiastical affairs.[8] In the archdeaconry of Xanten (Cologne), eight churches are mentioned before 900, twelve in the tenth and eleventh centuries, twenty-eight in the twelfth, and forty-three in the thirteenth.[9] These foundations aimed at adapting the religious organization to the changes in population distribution. Old settlements declined, others grew, and new ones emerged. People moved for economic and political reasons but also to abide *ad sanctos* (close to the relics of a saint), to live under his or her protection, and, not infrequently, to be able to use the church—which in some regions was fortified or erected on an easily defensible plot[10]—and its cemetery as a shelter and an asylum. They wanted, too, to fulfill their spiritual duties within walking distance of home ("intuitu locorum distantiae").[11] In regions where the seignorial system was weak or absent, like the Pyrenees and Frisia, the faithful themselves constructed and endowed the sanctuaries.[12]

But that was the exception. As a rule, the initiative came from the lords: in the bishopric of Bamberg, of all the twelfth-century church foundations, none was due to kings or princes, eight were surely or probably due to the bishop, four to chapters and monasteries, seventeen to noblemen, and one to a *ministerialis* (a knight of servile origin). For the thirteenth century, the figures are just as eloquent: two, five, two, ten, and nine.[13] The lords were anxious no doubt to get their own place of worship "in proprio territorio" (in their own territory), as one of them said in 1223.[14] They were also probably eager to meet the desires of their men, even perhaps to master or to control their religious life, whose implications were heavy in every field. Did their creations derive from the appearance of the *seigneurie banale* or of castles, as has been asserted? The *seigneurie banale* was normally linked with the church. The latter had usually been built by a noble on his *allodium* (freehold), and the possession or exploitation of the *bannum* gave him the opportunity not necessarily of creating a new parish but of extending the territory of "his" church to a compact and delimited block inhabited by "his" men. As for castles, which offered protection to a people longing for peace, in some regions, like Latium, they provoked a new gathering of people and deeply reshaped the religious map.[15] In other countries, they did not.[16] To complete and complicate the situation, especially from the thirteenth century on, a host of chapels were created in priories, convents, mansions, hospitals, and lepers' houses.[17]

Private sanctuaries did not all become independent and obtain parochial status. To prevent confusion in the muddle and conflicts between old and new religious centers, canon law forged a hierarchy of churches: *mater ecclesia* (a term first attested in 908 in Italy, where the phenomenon has been carefully studied),[18] *media ecclesia,* and *quarta capella.* The *mater ecclesia* scarcely kept full authority over her "daughters" but only over some disciplinarian and financial rights. In Italy, precisely, the archpresbyter oversaw the priests of his *pieve* (parish); in most countries, inhabitants of the *mediae* and *quartae capellae* were obliged to make a procession to the *mater,* to attend mass and make offerings there several times a year—nine times, for instance, in Châtillon-sur-Indre.[19] In different ways, new religious centers in southern England, in Italy, and elsewhere[20] first received a part of the tithe. Afterward, they got the privilege of baptizing, marrying, and burying, and of possessing properties, receiving revenues, and appointing wardens. The latest centers, especially during the thirteenth century, remained oratories for private use, mainly castle chapels for the lord and his *familia.*

Religious organization was not always successful in keeping the parish in touch with village and *seigneury.* The parish might not follow all the modifications in the structure and boundaries of the *villa* and the manor that resulted from reclamations, new settlements, partitions due to inheritance or to the owners' financial difficulties, donations to churches or vassals, and so on. Clearings were normally opened at the boundary of two localities and sometimes had to be divided between two parishes. In Sambre-et-Meuse, Sart-Eustache, whose name is significant in etymology (assart), has a chapel dedicated to Saint Eustache (the French language is proof of a recent creation) that belonged partly to the old parish of Biesme and partly to the equally ancient parish of Gerpinnes.[21] A charter of 1358 concerns "le communateit del ville de Florifoul" (in the county of Namur) "demorans en le paroiche de Malone" (in the principality of Liège), or, the community of the village of Florifoul dwelling in the parish of Malone.[22] In some regions, especially in Italy, southern England, and central France,[23] new churches were built or, more often, private chapels received parochial rank and powers and maintained full contact with other geographical, economic, and legal entities. Elsewhere, these new churches and chapels remained part of earlier parishes: the faithful were allowed to discharge their usual duties, particularly to attend mass, in them—but nothing more.

Two concrete examples will illustrate this process. In 1198, the church of Moignelée, on the lower Sambre, had jurisdiction over Moignelée, Oignies, Aiseau, Le Roux, and Menory. Between 1198 and 1233, the church suffered a *deminutio capitis:* it remained *mater ecclesia* and seat of the local synod but retained jurisdiction only over Moignelée. A young rival, the chapel of the priory of Oignies, the establishment of which had made this village a success, obtained the parochial altar and authority over the other four localities. Finally, about 1300, a chapel was laid out in the castle of Aiseau and another one in Le Roux, both served by the same vicar.[24] In the mid-fifteenth century, the parish of Frizet, apparently deriving from a fisc of the Frankish era, comprised six very small *villes*, 100 hearths in all! Each of them had its own chapel, the patrons of which—Médard, Nicolas, Remy, Catherine, Notre Dame—suggest ancient origins, but none had a cemetery or a brotherhood. Their inhabitants were "paroichiens de le paroiche de Frisey," and Frizet parochial boundaries remained those of the manor of the early Middle Ages and of the franchise of the twelfth or thirteenth century.[25]

In Germany, mainly in Saxony, many parishes covered several villages.[26] In Holland, small villages joined together to create a parish, which remained common to them. But in adjacent Frisia, village and parish coincided.[27] In some parts of England, the need and wishes of the faithful were not met in a satisfactory way—many peasants had still to walk a long way to get to church, and the Winchester statutes, decreeing that chapels with graveyards should be built in all villages that were more than two miles from their parish church, remained an ideal not always achieved in practice.[28] Clearly the solution to the problems arising from demographic, economic, and political development varied from place to place.

All in all, in most cases, the coincidence between the religious center and secular entities subsisted or was to some extent, and with some delay, restored.[29] At any rate, the church maintained intact and even tightened its contact with human realities and collectivities,[30] all the more so since the parish's flock was small: ninety-seven communicants in the bishopric of Chartres in the second half of the thirteenth century; in central Italy, twenty hearths; in England, 300 people.[31]

The parish constituted the most frequently mentioned community in virtually all matters. In the diocese of Tuy, for instance, it occurred as the basic structure of reference in all kinds of business four times in the twelfth century, twelve in the first half of the thirteenth, and thirty-one in the second half.[32]

*

CONTACT was close, first of all, in spiritual matters. Since the Carolingian period, the church had required the faithful to receive the sacraments, attend mass on Sunday and feast days, and be buried in the parish. One may doubt that these rules were strictly obeyed, for they had to be repeated until the Fourth Lateran Council enforced them. Its canons tied every Christian to his parochial church: "spectat ad ecclesiam" (he belongs to it).[33] He should be baptized, married, and normally buried there,[34] confess his sins, receive the eucharist at least once yearly from his curate or vicar, and hear mass weekly on the spot. Indeed, some synodal statutes in Brittany demanded that, before celebrating mass, the priest check whether any strangers be present and, if so, turn them away to their parishes; "cum a sanctis patribus sit constitutum et synodali judicio interdictum ne sacerdos recipiat parochianos alterius ecclesie" (since it has been established by the holy fathers and prohibited by synodal judgment that a priest receive parishioners of another church).[35]

Such decrees certainly aimed at instructing the people, but with questionable success. The rector was obliged to preach on Sundays. But did he do so?[36] Opinions vary.[37] What did he say? Theoretically, according to some episcopal constitutions of 1240, he expounded the Ten Commandments, the deadly sins, and some points of doctrine. Practically, he commented on the day's readings or the life of the saint of the day.[38] And did the audience listen to him? In thirteenth-century England, the men used to leave church during the sermon. And surprisingly enough for us, catechizing the children was left entirely up to the parents. What exactly the laity knew of church doctrine remains problematic.[39] A partial solution might come from an attentive study of the images, if any, carved or painted on parish churches, but not the art of cathedrals and monasteries.

At any rate, the canons imposing what the Germans, who may forge words at will, expressively call the *Pfarrzwang* were also intended to watch the faithful by binding them to the local religious authority. About 1240, an archbishop of Rouen demanded that the curate draw up a list of his flock.[40] And canons contributed powerfully to making the rural community effective and perceptible. Parishioners met every week in their church or chapel and several times a year in the *mater ecclesia*, where they experienced the major events of their existence, mainly with the attendance of the whole community.

And their decease bound them to their parish no less. The cemetery adjoined the church, and the living and the dead were in communion[41]—especially since Cluny and the growth of the cult for the departed. From the twelfth century onward, the practice spread of founding obits, or liturgical anniversaries, of the deceased.[42] In some villages in northern France and Belgium in the fourteenth and fifteenth centuries, a third of the families in every generation contributed money for the yearly celebration of an anniversary mass for their relatives.[43] Less common were the Sunday recommendations, which commemorated a deceased person and requested prayers for him from the audience.[44]

The synod which we have already met and, later, the visitation, also regularly gathered the *plena parochia* (the whole parish)[45] or its main members and surveyed the morality of all. Until the twelfth century—and in Germany and on the borders of northern France in the thirteenth century and sometimes later—the synod was in theory held annually, in fact, every second or third year, under the presidency of the bishop, the archdeacon, or the dean, and exceptionally, the rector.[46] The *scabini* of that *placitum christianitatis* and the *testes synodales* were appointed by the religious authorities but often were chosen or proposed by the community. They were still in charge of identifying and punishing what the Carolingian texts had named *crimina ecclesiastica*, a wide and ill-defined field wherein, in 1130, the Bishop of Liège included even *homicidia*.[47] Church law was so wide, in fact, that a few scholars claimed that, in post-Carolingian times, it superseded the inefficient civil judges. Actually, in the twelfth and thirteenth centuries, these church judges reported or took testimony on sexual trespasses, usury, and attacks against the clergy and their properties.[48] But they also paid increasing attention to material affairs, like maintenance of church buildings and payment of the tithe. Regarding moral behavior, they were gradually confined to collecting accusations, while the *officialis* (episcopal delegate) actually judged. In the late Middle Ages, the synod was replaced by the *visitatio*[49] organized within the framework of the deanery or parish, when the archdeacon's or dean's superintendence slackened. The program remained the same: the emphasis was still on administration rather than on behavior.[50]

The church also played a part in what one might call mixed matters, which united, and to some extent confused, spiritual and worldly problems. It provided the protection of God, of a patron saint, and of saints specialized against the devil and harmful natural forces. It formulated and distributed benedictions for nearly every conceivable occasion. It staged processions to insure the fertility of the fields. And the list could easily be lengthened.

Charity was another of the church's cares. From its origins, it had devoted a large part of its income to help those whom canon law would call *miserabiles personae*. From the beginning of the Middle Ages, when the state was obliterated, it alone provided for the poor, the sick, widows, orphans, and abandoned children. One example: in 1263, an inquiry in Romanesque Brabant stated that "les parroches doient nourrir" (the parishes were obliged to foster) foundlings. Thus in 1264, the Lord of Jauche forced *li ville* to nurse a baby found at the door of the local abbey.[51] The victims of fate and men were many. To quantify is very difficult because of the shortcomings of documentation. Moreover, poverty is a relative concept. In a well-documented parish in the region of Namur at the end of the Middle Ages, 42 percent of the population received some help. But 14 percent got from sixty-one to seventy-two liters of wheat or half a cubic meter of wood or a pair of shoes; 19 percent were given from eleven to thirty heaumes, that is to say the salary of a mason's laborer for two or six days; 9 percent were totally impoverished.[52] One might risk asserting that, on average, the poor formed at least 15 percent, more probably 25 to 30 percent, of inhabitants.[53] To deal with such a situation, organization was indispensable. From the twelfth century, the *mensae pauperum* or *mensae Spiritus Sancti* multiplied. By the thirteenth century, there was one in every village.[54]

Many contemporary villages also had *hospitalia pauperum* (hospitals for poor people) and lazarets. Like the *mensae*, they too owed their existence to piety, but they were mostly foundations of religious institutions, particularly of regular canons[55] and of private persons, rather than of the parish. In the late Middle Ages, as a result of financial difficulties and a general trend toward laicization, some may have passed under the authority or the control of the churchwardens, but that remains to be proved.[56] Moreover, they had originally been intended—and increasingly effectively were functioning—to shelter travelers, not to provide relief for the local inhabitants.

From the early Middle Ages, especially in the ninth century, canons and statutes urged the clergy to create rural schools, essentially, to be sure, to train their own successors. Such prescriptions were not much observed before the twelfth century. Then, according to Lesne, there was "un pullulement d'écoles véritables" (a multiplication of real schools), mainly however in the boroughs and in parishes pertaining to an abbey.[57] The phrase may be exaggerated.[58]

The vicar and the church were also deeply involved in profane matters. The former was a local VIP. Besides his dreadful power over minds and souls and their eternity, he was relatively learned—at any rate, far more so than his flock. The level of his instruction, low in the eleventh century, improved in the thirteenth, especially in England.[59] Did he understand the Latin books intended for his education? Probably not, if we judge from the gross and countless faults in his few lines in that language.[60] But he was able to read, reckon, write, and, not infrequently, to draw up a deed like a *publicus notarius* or take the inventory of landed properties and rents. In 1362, Nicole du Jardin, "prestre curés de le églize de Tringne et puble notaire del autoriteit impérial" attested an agreement between the community of his village and the adjacent one; in 1415, Sire Lambert, *vesti* (rector) of the church of Boneffe, composed the register of his parish's properties.[61]

The vicar was also richer than most of his parishioners. The church possessed several sources of wealth: the *dos ecclesie* (dowry of the church), constituted at the creation of the parish, increased by gifts and wills, and which, in a middle-sized village of the county of Namur, amounted in 1414 to sixty acres of yard, meadows, and fields;[62] annual rents, especially for the obits—which in another parish of the same region produced in 1450 the equivalent of the hire of 112 acres;[63] the offerings at Sunday masses, on the major feasts, and the casual fees paid for celebrating ceremonies, like baptism and above all funerals; in a third parish, in 1422, the collections at the displays of the relics probably formed 15 percent of yearly receipts.[64] Some parishes were poor. Between 1390 and 1404, in the eastern part of the diocese of Reims, 33 percent of the parishes could not afford to pay their tax arrears, and 12 percent of them could not maintain a priest. But this situation might have been caused by the troubles of the time.[65] More generally, a big portion of the revenues went to the patron; the local officiant got only what canon law qualified as *portio congruens* (appropriate part) and what the French translated as *portion congrue* (modest part). In 1230, the archdeacons of the bishopric of Lincoln included in their inquiries the question: "are there any clergy who do not have enough to live on?"[66] But normally the product of the casual duties—which, as we have seen, was by no means negligible—went to the vicar and made him better off than the faithful.[67] To fully appreciate the position of the clergy, we ought never to forget the distinction between rector and vicar—not to mention the countless chaplains and altarists—and between urban and rural parishes.

Finally, the origins, if not always the behavior, of the vicar gave him more contact with and influence on his flock than has been recently asserted.[68] In most cases, he was the son of a yeoman or small landowner or peasant[69] and very close to his parishioners. And his conduct was less reprehensible than suggested by the normative sources, which were anxious to prevent all possible excesses, and by literary works, which, to attract and entertain readers, ceaselessly blamed and mocked him.[70] Since the twelfth century, the clergy had been regimented and watched over by religious authorities: visitations of the bishop, the archdeacon, or the dean were not always in every time and region regular and earnest, but they became increasingly so, especially at the very end of the Middle Ages.[71] And the charters prove that, except perhaps in England, the curate or vicar enjoyed a real respect from the community. He was sometimes at issue with it, mainly over financial matters, first of all over the tithe. Money is never an indifferent matter for peasants, nor for priests, some of whom did not make a rich living.[72] But he was also repeatedly solicited by the community for his advice, to discuss and decide with its leaders, and what is more significant still, to represent and defend it in every critical situation.[73] In Frisia, he belonged to the college that dominated the aldermen, took part in writing up the customs, and sat on the court of appeals in civil matters.[74] More astonishing still, according to a charter of 1296, the rector of a small village of Hainault was mayor ex officio.[75] The title with which society decorated its priests is suggestive, a title it otherwise awarded only to knights: *messire*, not *sire*.[76]

On the other hand, the church was used for many secular affairs. The community met in or in front of its nave, which served as a town hall. After the Sunday mass, the community heard information of

Figure 15. Church and Shelter. The steeple of the parish church of Wierde, near Namur, was the lord's property and the peasants' refuge.

Source: L. F. Genicot, *Les églises mosanes du XIe siècle*, Louvain-la-Neuve, 1972, 209.

every kind, like statutes promulgated by the lord or by itself, punishments inflicted by the court, announcements of tours of inspection of roads and ditches, or sales by auction.[77] When some danger threatened, it sought protection for people, cattle, and goods in the steeple or cemetery. The Nineteenth Canon of the Fourth Lateran Council prohibited warehousing profane things in the churches "except in case of hostile attacks, of sudden fire and of other emergency situation."[78] The community was allowed to take shelter there, provided it paid for the maintenance of the upper part of the tower and of the walls of the churchyard. Markets, balls, and pageants took place in the cemetery, even sometimes inside the church.[79]

To perform all that was expected of it, the parish needed the help of some institutions, which we shall meet in examining and measuring the part played by the peasants in the matters we have rapidly sketched.

*

For the peasants, one thing was essential: the choice of the priest who assumed the *cura animarum* (charge of their souls) and who occupied such a prominent place in every sector of rural life.

Theoretically, the priest was appointed by the bishop. But the bishop did not act alone and freely. The Gregorian Reform had fought against the laity's interference in the recruitment of Christian ministers. It could not suppress patronage—that is to say, the right of a church's owner, normally a descendant of the founder, to designate the rector, who was in that way his "man," as explained by the Capitulary of Pitres in 869. In the Piedmont and Lombardy regions of Italy, the *communia* succeeded in eliminating the lord and it inherited his privilege. Here, it directly chose the *plebanus*, there it delegated power to representatives (*concilium* or *consules*).[80] The situation was the same in Frisia, which partially escaped the seignorial and feudal society: the parishioners elected their pastor.[81] So, too, in northern Switzerland.[82] In the Pyrenean valleys, patronage was also attributed to and exercised by the communities, which presented their candidate to the bishop.[83] In central Italy, the *plebanus* had since the thirteenth century been *prelectus a plebe*, and he was still proposed to the ecclesiastical superiors by the clergy and the faithful or accepted by the faithful.[84] Elsewhere, especially in northern Europe, patronage receded from the mid-tenth century,[85] and some lords restituted their churches to the ecclesiastical authorities. The movement accelerated with the Gregorian reform. But many parishes remained in the hands of noble families or, most frequently, passed into the control of chapters, monasteries, or other religious institutions, not of the community. Here are, for instance, the figures in percentages for the diocese of Amiens in the thirteenth century: [86]

PATRON	CHURCH	CHAPEL
Bishop	17	21
Cathedral chapter	24	30
Monastery	53	17
Lord	6	32

But in adjacent Normandy, the majority of parishes still belonged to laymen at the end of the Middle Ages.[87] And in Swabia, on the eve of the *Bauernkrieg*, the communities still claimed in the first "Article of Rapperweil" the right of choosing the priest "who would preach them God's word." [88]

The sexton was the rector's permanent auxiliary. He often was a cleric, which might mean nothing more than having received and kept the tonsure, not wearing bicolored garments, and not practicing an "inhonestum mercimonium" (an indecent business). But not infrequently, especially in parishes of some importance, it might also apply to a man with a better education than the common people. The community participated in his designation—or at least pretended to participate in it. In 1305, for instance, a conflict opposed the *vestit* (rector) of a small chapel located on the low Sambre and the "maire, escevins et li commons de le ville" (mayor, aldermen, and the common of the village) about the right of "mettre et estaulir le marlier" (choosing and establishing the sexton).[89]

Some institutions assisted the priest. We have already met the *mensa pauperum*. Here now are the *luminare* and the *fabrica* (luminary and churchwardens). The *luminare* provided wax and, so, light—the light so intimately associated with the liturgy, symbolic of Christ, *lux vera* (the true light: John, 1, 5) and gateway to paradise; *locum refrigerii, lucis, et pacis* (place of refreshment, light, and peace: memento of the Latin mass); the light that defeats darkness and its *fantasmata* (spectres: as the hymn *Te lucis ante terminum*) and kindles joy; the light without which there is no celebration; the light we cannot, now in our time and civilization, imagine the momentousness of. Alms and gifts in money and rents were collected for it by a special office, administered by two or more wardens.

The *fabrica* was in charge of expenditures for liturgical furniture and clothing and, the much heavier ones, for the maintenance of the building or some parts of it: the roof and, in most cases, the tower or its floors.[90] For a long time, the parishioners had been invited—and sometimes required, as in the legal texts of the diocese of Modena in the Carolingian period,[91]—to meet this expenditure. But it had been done informally. When needs increased, a structure became indispensable. In the twelfth century, the *fabrica* took shape.[92] In the thirteenth century, a bull of Honorius III gave it an official existence, with its own tasks and income and its own administration by laymen. At that time, churchwardens appeared in England and, later, the first preserved accounts were submitted to the community.[93]

The faithful wanted to be associated with the management of parochial institutions, especially in their financial affairs. And the question arises: how were the decisions made and the operations checked? The answer is not everywhere clear and rarely totally explicit. The administration was entrusted to *mamburni* (wardens). They were here, certainly—there, probably—elected by the parishioners.[94] The latter also oversaw the church's management; they attended to drawing up and checking the inventory of the parochial properties and to establishing the yearly statement of receipts and expenditures. In 1415, the list of the goods of the church—that is to say, the *fabrique*—of the luminary, and of the table for the poor in the parish of Boneffe was composed by the rector and the two *manbours*, read "en présence de tout le ville" (once again we observe the identity of parish and village), and posted up three Sundays on the sanctuary's gateway.[95] Since the thirteenth century, the accounts of religious institutions in a small village of Hainault were submitted to the lord, the clerics, and the people.[96] The people are mentioned only in theory. As a matter of fact, the checking was frequently done only by a few influential persons.

This observation leads to a problem of primary importance: what was the parochial community exactly? Was it dominated and manipulated by a minority? To respond to this twofold question, we ought to broaden the horizon in two directions, first, by considering a late religious organism, the brotherhood; and second, by taking into account the civil officers: mayor, aldermen, members of the council.

Brotherhoods had flourished in the early Middle Ages.[97] After an eclipse, at least in northern Europe, caused by the distrust of the ecclesiastical authorities toward any kind of association that might degenerate into emancipation of the laity or into social and political struggles, they rose again. According to a French scholar, who does not substantiate the figure, 40 percent of the parishes in thirteenth-century France had one or more brotherhoods.[98] They have been much studied, and traditional views are now enshrined about them—views that recent monographs for Italy and Belgium do not confirm, suggesting that major questions on the matter remain open, especially about their founders' purposes and about their members and leaders.

The brotherhoods are frequently, if not classically, supposed to have been less religious than social or political: a framework for imprisoning the population; a means for the notables to subdue the common people; a ladder for social ascension; a means for the common people to gain esteem by associating with notables; a mask to disguise antiseignorial action; a means for the common people to sap the lord's and the clergy's power.[99] None of these contentions have been firmly demonstrated. On the contrary, the latest research tends largely to invalidate them.[100] No doubt the confraternities played a social role, mainly by supporting their ill, injured, or impoverished members, widows, and orphans, but these activities were basically dictated by piety. It happened, too, that they favored a political movement, like that which in La Sauve-Majeure, near Bordeaux, in 1247 militated for a charter of franchise.[101] They were possibly used by dissidents where they were the sole organized body that comprised all the men or, at least, as in La Sauve-Majeure, all the *caps d'ostau* (heads of households). But their inspiration and intention were fundamentally Christian: to perform in common some acts of devotion, especially to promote the cult of the Virgin, and above all, in a time attentive to death and the departed, to hold wakes, pay for a decent funeral, stage the funeral cortege, and attend mass for the deceased.[102] So it seems unlikely they were created or used against the institutional church, to undermine or escape clerical authority. In central Italy, 90 percent of them were created with the approbation and frequently with the help of the parish priest.[103]

To measure the individual and collective impact of the brotherhoods, one ought to know the number and the wealth of their wardens. La Sauve-Majeure was no normal case. The brotherhoods were usually open to any man of "good reputation." The entry fee and the yearly assessment were relatively light, except for the poor.[104] In some towns, there were two brotherhoods, one for the rich, one for the common people. This was not so in the villages. About 40 percent of the rural population was enrolled,[105] not all the inhabitants. Neither all the well-to-do belonged nor always the wealthiest of them. A majority of the members came from the middle class, and not a few were poor men.[106] Their wardens were elected by the brethren for their wealth, their wisdom, their experience, or their honesty.

Under such conditions, it is not easy to determine whether the brotherhoods helped unify or divide the community. If they represented the bulk of the population, they might favor solidarity.[107] On the contrary, if they did not do so, and if they were led exclusively by rich men, they might oppose members to nonmembers, higher and middle classes to lower class,[108] and strengthen the pressure of the notables on the community. The alternatives cannot be resolved without viewing the brotherhoods in the whole context of the parochial and even of the civil organisms and their heads.

There was no partition between the different religious organisms or between them and secular ones. To be sure, they were specialized, but they often intervened in fields other than their own. The Table of the Poor frequently enlivened religious feasts and ceremonies by paying for minstrels or a friar who would deliver a special sermon. Or it granted a loan to people in financial difficulties. In the same spirit, the parishioners did not isolate the institutions in their minds and deeds: in their wills, rich men made gifts to all of them. Church, *fabrica*, Table, hospital, lazar house, brotherhood all lived in symbiosis.

This was also true of civil organisms. For instance, the Table of the Poor might lend money to the aldermen and the village to perform some public work, like building a bridge.[109] In the early fourteenth century, a suit against the chapter of Notre Dame in Namur on the obligations of the tithe was prosecuted by the *vestitus*, the *mamburni* of the luminary and the *fabrica*, and "villicus, scabini et incolae totius universitatis parrochie" (vicar, churchwardens, mayor, aldermen, and inhabitants of the whole university of the parish).[110] It would be a mistake to conceive the rural community as divided by walls separating its diverse institutions.

*

IT WOULD also be wrong to set apart their leaders. Here, we have to broaden our horizon in the second direction. First, we must take into account the civil officers: mayor, aldermen, and members of the council, and draw up a list of all the people who exerted some function as well as of all the data about each of them: family, wealth, profession, title (like "master"), and qualification (like *probus* [wise], "honorable," "sire") in order to get the profile of every single one. Afterward, we must confront all elements of that prosopography so as to abstract a general portrait.

The results are clear. The same men generally appear at the head of the different bodies, active in every sector: churchwardens, administrators of relief institutions, guardians of the brotherhood, and mayors, aldermen, and delegates of the community. Sometimes they were chosen by religious authorities, like the *testes synodales* or *juratores*, who witnessed in the synod,[111] or the *probi viri* consulted by the clergy on the utility of creating a new parish in 1249.[112] More often, they were elected by the *universitas parochianorum*[113] or by the *universitas villae* because of their riches and also their birth, age, experience, and wisdom. The structures of rural society display parallelisms from all viewpoints—economic, political, and religious—but no strict identity. The poor seem to have been less rare among leading persons in the religious institutions.

The prosopographical analysis of the latter and the study of canonical regulations underscore an important phenomenon, which is certain in Belgium and northern France, and probable elsewhere: the nobles did not pertain to the parish. They attended mass—if they were rich enough, in their own chapel or, if they were not, in the choir or in the front part of the nave. A synodal statute from about 1300 for the diocese of Cambrai prohibited "ne laici una cum clericis in choro seu cancello interesse presumant dum ibidem divina celebrantur nisi nobiles existant" (let laymen not dare to stay in the choir or the chancel during the office if they are not noble).[114] They were buried by the dean, not by the curate or vicar, and inside the church. Other people might be interred there, but they had to ask for that *licentia*. Nobles were not subject to the archdeacon's synodal jurisdiction but answered directly to the bishop.[115]

One might wonder whether these arrangements were marks of respect or proofs of independence from the parish. The second interpretation is nearer to the basic claim and ambition of the aristocracy: to escape all structures that imprisoned the common people: *seigneury*, principality, and realm, with their laws, courts, and taxes. As we have seen, being free from seignorial rights was the very sign of nobility. Did this status also bring exemption from the by-laws, the decrees of the rural assembly, especially in matters of cultivation? Apparently not, in some places.[116] In other places, nobles and knights and their descendants enjoyed or pretended to enjoy the privilege of owning their own flock and of reserving to it alone the grazing of their fields and pastures.[117]

Sometimes, landowners and their farmers obtained the same advantage and, in that way, partially got out of the community.[118] Or, as in Saxony, those who did not possess a plot of a *verhuftes Land* (*masuirs*, in French documents)—handicraftmen, day laborers, and so on— were not admitted in the *Gemeinde*.

*

To SUM UP and conclude, the parish was an important, probably the most important, factor in the birth or maturation of the rural community. In some regions, like old Catalonia or Portugal, building a church or engaging a priest to serve in it was the first collective enterprise.[119] In others, the church clustered and rooted the population. Everywhere, it was the center of practically all individual and collective events. Significantly enough, at the end of the Middle Ages, in 1374, a

⁊ Dyonisij · de Warsoulh et Margarete uxoris
sue pro quibz hem[us] · vj · d · supra ortum iuxta
cimiteriu[m] de Tirley · fc[t]a tenet co

Nathalie del aris et agnetis es[t] vr pro quibz hen[t]
vj · d · sup[er] tenariam eo[rum] in moue qua tenet
Iohes mariett co[m]par[is]

Beatricis vx michael michou pro qua hem[us] xviij d
sup bur[?] tornale tr[e] prope le spmete le moue et
p[er] de cell maria sur torrit · dim mychons de desoul

margnete dele monge et lamber eiq pls[?] sup quibz habemus
tres pprnes[?] p[er]sti sp ead tenuia in moue a cedris q dicu[r]
le bloketii[n] del cursse iuxte sup pr[a]d a pr[a]d iuxete ad pel[a]u pr[a]d
s[??] ꝑ anni[ver]sario marie ꝑ ꝑ[er]ores p[r]dn[?] argngrete del cursse
biui sup[er]i[?] ꝯsuile spte sup ꝑdtam tenuria del cursse
et ꝑdtu ꝑdta[m] tenuria a sup[er]i[?] l[er]o ad pr[a]d de Hulgraiu[?]

⁊ Iohis de helbe et Elizabeth uxoris sue pro
quibz hemus · vj · d · sup terram eo[rum] v[er]s[us]
le katise q[ua]m tenet lt hynelbies · de sam mar

Iohann[us] dechampilhous laterina uxoris eius ⁊ eius
pue[ro]r eciam p[er]quo habent iij d moieti eua[rn]e[rn]s
supra tenuelam aconboie q[ue] fuit mabili douen
scl maria dona xij d ibidem

Figure 16. The Parish: A Community of the Living and the Dead. This is the folio 52 verso of the Obituary of the rural parish of Frizet (see plate n.13). It lists Masses to be read on the 13th, 14th, and 15th of November: six notices from hands 1, 2, 5, 13, 17, and 9. The text of the first one is: *Commemoratio Dyonisii de Warisoulh et Margarete uxoris sue pro quibus habemus VI denarios supra ortum juxta cimiterium de Frisey: ecclesia tenet.* Translation: Commemoration of Denis de Warisoulh (a hamlet of Frizet) and Margaret his wife for whom we [the vicar] have six pence on the garden close to the cemetery, which is not rented but is in the church's hands. Half of the families founded an anniversary. The dead were a real part of the community.

Source: Namur, Archives de l'Évêché. Photo Piron, Namur. See L. Genicot, *Une source mal connue* (50), p. 201–202.

sentence of the Parlement of Paris judged that the presence of clergy or of a lazar house attested the reality of a political entity.[120] The parish was thus considered the base and the proof of the existence of a rural community.

This was quite normal, even if we take away its direct religious or charitable action. Its members were subject to the same material obligations that infused cohesion into their group. They had to pay for the tithe, for the maintenance of the church, for obits, for the use of land belonging to the church or parochial institution, and for rents constituted by gifts or in some other way by their ancestors. In the well-documented parish of Floreffe, near Namur, the number of rents amounted in the mid-fifteenth century to 353 for 180 families. Under such conditions, writing that the parish was "une collectivité sans autre lien que le juridique" (a collectivity whose only tie was juridical)[121] seems implausible.

Nothing is more illustrative of the place occupied by the parish in the rural community than the role of its steeple bell. It was rung at noon, at vespers, and at compline, dividing the day and giving rhythm to work. It summoned to collective labor, warned against danger, turned aside the storm, called for the pursuit of a criminal, sounded during capital executions, tolled for the dead, chimed for the feasts, and introduced a new lord.[122] In a word, it participated in every event. The chronicler who, in the sixteenth century, wanted to describe the county of Namur, began by giving the number of the "villages à clocher" (villages with a steeple bell).

Moreover, the power of excommunication, the supreme and terrific arm of the church, could theoretically exclude a person from the community, and therefore from the whole region, of which village, lordship, and parish were a part. Abuse of this power weakened the church.

5

IN TERRA:

EXTERNAL ASPECTS

*

"MANY THREADS led outward from the village, to the locality, to the region, to the state, not only economic, but ideological and cultural as well."[1] Separating the village from the regional, even national, reality would be an error. To gain a true image of it, we have to insert it into a broad economic, political, and religious context. Not all relations of the rural community with adjacent ones, with the towns, with the prince and his institutions, or with the ecclesiastical authorities are of interest to us, but those relations that were established primarily by the collectivity—secondarily by some of its members—that fostered the conscience of being a distinct entity are essential to our study.

Rural communities might be connected to others without their will but not necessarily against it. They pertained to the same old institutions, like the *échevinages territoriaux* (territorial aldermanate), which in the region of scattered settlement of Flanders and west Brabant extended their jurisdiction over several villages.[2] Or they answered to the same lord, who possessed a lot of manors, went from one to another with his retinue, and managed the whole with the same officials or bodies. Around Beziers, the "Parlement de l'université" comprised the inhabitants not only of the village but also of the castle's whole district.[3] And in Germany, the *Frongemeinden* performed their *corvées* (forced labor) together.[4]

Some villages spontaneously joined forces to unite their fate, especially to forge and defend a more or less complete autonomy and to administer themselves together, as in the mountainous countries, the *valles* in the Douro region, with their *anteiglesias* meeting the free men of a valley in the front of the church, and their *juntas*, or, in the matter of justice, their *merindades*, the *universitates vallis* of southern France, the *Talschaften* or *Groszgemeinden* in the empire.[5] Or to confront limited but vital needs that exceeded the boundaries or the ability of a single village: determining the ownership and the use of the commons, achieving important, expensive, and permanent works, like maintaining the highways, draining, damming up, particularly in Holland,[6] or in minor cases, pursuing criminals,[7] and, as in late medieval Navarra, organizing the defense of one fortified place, which became the shelter for the surroundings.[8] But all that enhanced the solidarity and the means of the group more than each component's feeling that it constituted a discrete unity.

*

IN THE LATE Middle Ages, when the main roads had been firmly laid out, they converged on the towns. Clearly, from the tenth or eleventh century, the towns increasingly played the leading role in the west. The countryside did not escape their attraction.

Some rural communities, namely in Holland, concluded *verbondsoorkonden* (agreements) with towns. Many more, especially in Italy and Spain, were absorbed into the *contado* or the *communidad de villa y tierra* of the neighboring city.[9] A still greater number, in any country, were integrated into a *banlieue*.[10] Or if they did not entirely lose their liberty, they were subject to or checked by its officials, decrees, and taxes.[11] Finally, a great many villages, too distant to be integrated, had received town franchises and become subject to its courts for their interpretation.[12]

Relations between city and countryside also multiplied in individual and informal ways. Rich citizens purchased land and, like the *caballeros-villanos* who dominated the urban *concejos* in Spain, could exert some pressure on rural assemblies, especially in the matter of the commons and their use.[13] On the other hand, peasants entered into more frequent, diverse, and perhaps influential contacts with the towns. For the towns and, at a lower level, the boroughs, the *Minderstädte* which apparently spread particularly in the thirteenth century,[14] were the focus of trade, employment, and money.

They were, as F. Lot wrote, "permanent markets." The cultivators had to sell at least a small part of their production, to get the pennies due for rents and taxes and the things they did not make themselves. There were *mercatores bladorum* who wandered and bargained for corn and other merchants who trafficked in wool, leather, flax, dye plants, and so on.[15] The accounts of a chandler and green grocer of Douai for 1368–70 show that he acquired wax and vegetables within a radius of thirteen miles.[16] But urban authorities were hostile to such transactions between producers and *recoupeurs* (intermediaries), which raised prices. And, anxious to secure their supply of food and stuff, they went

TABLE 4. NUMBER AND PROFESSION OF INHABITANTS
IN THE COUNTRYSIDE OF NAMUR WHOSE MAIN OCCUPATION
IS NOT CULTIVATION, 1265

Profession	Number	Percentage of Tenants of the Count of Namur
Iron metalworker, farrier, cutler	32	1.25
Leather shoemaker, harness maker, tanner	26	1

Textile
    cloth   16
    linen   5
	21	0.8

Building, "other jobs" [1]	49	1.9

Auxiliary crafts of the industries
    (e.g., digger, charcoal burner,
        miner)
	9	0.35

Food butcher, baker, brewer	23	0.9
Innkeeper, cook	10	0.4
Money	4	0.1
Trade (general)	5	0.2
Farmer, farmhand	8	0.3
Shepherd, swineherd	9	0.35
Falconer, master of the wolfhunt, huntsman, fisher	9	0.35

Source: M. Soumoy, *Les métiers dans les campagne namuroises (fin du XIIIe siècle)* (Louvain Université Catholique) unpublished dissertation, 1974.

[1] M. Soumoy did not, unfortunately, distinguish building (carpenter, bricklayer, tiller) from "other crafts" (e.g., joiner, cartwright, turner, vatmaker, solderer, potter, basket maker).

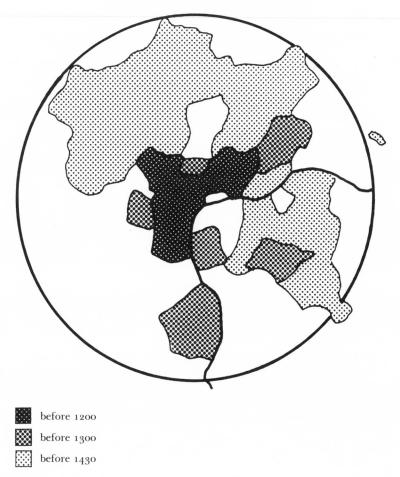

before 1200

before 1300

before 1430

Figure 17. Town and Countryside: Theory and Reality. The circle indicates the radius of one league (9730 meters) around Namur, over which the town's authority. in the form of its *banlieue,* theoretically extended. Shaded sections show the actual progressive extension of Namur's *banlieue* over surrounding villages between the 12th and 15th centuries.

Source: Genicot (47), 199.

so far as to establish an *estaple* to compel the peasantry to bring goods to their markets. Even a modest borough like Couvin, in Sambre-et-Meuse, recorded in 1377 that "ceux de la chatellenie ne peuvent aller au marché en divers autres lieux voisins hors du pays pour y mainer et vendre grains, pourceaux, boeur, fromage, poissons et autres vitailles si premièrement ils ne sont staper au marché et halle de Cou-

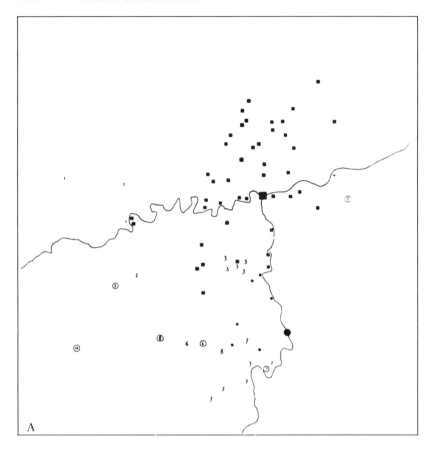

A

vin" (the inhabitants of the castelry [some ten villages around the castle] are prohibited from going to market outside the country, for bringing there and selling corn, cattle, red wools, sheep, oxen, cows, pigs, butter, cheese, fish, and other food if they did not previously offer it on the marketplace of Couvin).[17] At any rate, the towns were the best places for trade. They needed food and they had concentrated the bulk of industry within their walls.

Some branches of industry, like mines and metallurgy, were tied to the subsoil and consequently to the countryside. They were not part of the peasants' collectivity: they had their own working-rules, their privileges, their courts, and their masters.[18] Other sectors manipulated agricultural products like flax, wool, woad, and saffron. The linen drapery industry remained partially rural.[19] The woolen drapery industry became essentially urban in order to improve the quality

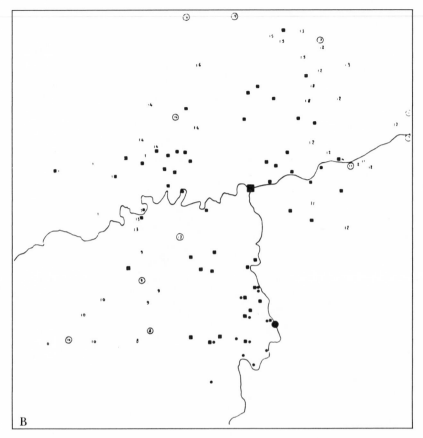

■ Measure of Namur
● Measure of Dinant

Figure 18. Economic Structure of a Medieval Principality. Numbers (1–18) identify measures originating in other places within the county (2,3,4,5,6,7,8,10,11,17,18) or in foreign cities (1, Nivelles; 4, Inden, Germany; 12, Huy; 13, Fosses; 14, Gembloux; 15, Louvain; and 16, Wavre). Measure standards used in local grain markets can reveal their integration into a larger economy. Classifying the grain markets in the County of Namur according to the measures used in the grain trade uncovers changing patterns in the principality's economic structure. Measures used in the grain trade in 11th and 12th centuries are shown in A, and B shows the same in the 13th and 14th centuries. Even though the number of local grain markets slightly increased, the proportion of markets using the measures of the capital, Namur, and of another important town, Dinant, also increased, along with the area over which these two measures extended their influence.

Source: L. Genicot, Études historiques à la mémoire de Nóél Didier, Paris, 1960, p. 163.

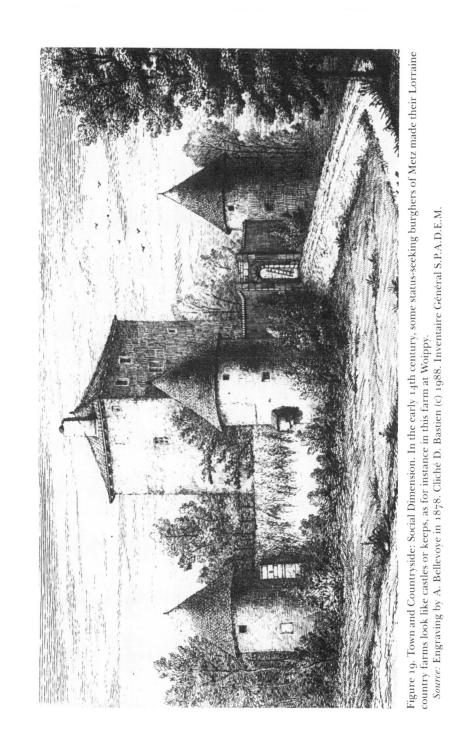

Figure 19. Town and Countryside: Social Dimension. In the early 14th century, some status-seeking burghers of Metz made their Lorraine country farms look like castles or keeps, as for instance in this farm at Woippy.

Source: Engraving by A. Bellevoye in 1878. Cliché D. Bastien (c) 1988. Inventaire Général S.P.A.D.E.M.

and quantity of its cloth by using the best material and reaching cus-
tomers in remote places.[20] There were still weavers in the villages,[21]
especially after the fulling mill came into use in the thirteenth century
and was erected on a stream.[22] But village weavers were not numerous
and they made common cloth for local needs or half-finished cloth.
Quite a variety of handicraftsmen also lived in the countryside: millers,
bakers, brewers, cartwrights, farriers, shoemakers, tailors, masons,
carpenters, and thatchers.[23] All together, with traders, innkeepers,
and shepherds, members of the tertiary sector amounted to at most
15 percent of the population. Even then, they spent a part of their
time tilling some patch, and sometimes several acres, of land. In the
region of Namur, this sector constituted 8 percent of the population
at the end of the thirteenth century and between 10 and 15 percent in
the mid-fifteenth century. The figure for Florence in the same period
is 14 percent. Does this suggest an increase in the late period? The
figures are based on anthroponomy, the interpretation of which is
dangerous[24] and isolated. They do not therefore justify general conclusions. Among these men, a few were rich but the majority were of
modest condition.

So the peasants had not only to sell but also to buy. They needed or
wanted many things: spices, of course, at least salt; special or valuable
products like agricultural tools (local handicraftsmen apparently re-
paired tools rather than make them);[25] pieces of furniture, particularly chests, and even quite common household goods. Excavations in
medieval villages have uncovered imported ironware and earthen-
ware.[26] In 1289, in the little market of Fleurus in the county of Namur,
one could find corn, linen, thread, wool, fabrics, furs, new and used
garments, fat, skins, raw and wrought iron, vessels, cauldrons, sauce-
pans, spices, and cattle.[27]

The town also provided employment. Urban immigration has been
much studied in recent decades, but because of the shortcomings of
the evidence,[28] firm views cannot be reached before the thirteenth
century—that is to say, before the appearance of the registers of new
burghers and of fifteenth-century censuses.[29] Let us take the case of
Douai, a well-documented city.[30] Annual immigration amounted to
2.25 percent of the population. Was this enough to compensate for
the high mortality rate?[31] Most new arrivals came from less than
twenty kilometers away and from 526 villages and 117 agglomerations
of 2,000 inhabitants or more. Two-thirds had been born in the countryside. The majority were infrasalaried (people without professional
qualification); others were artisans. Those who worked with hard materials came from the towns and boroughs, while those who worked

with timber and thatch and those who were locksmiths, and cloth-makers left the villages, a fact that reflects the place the iron and textile industries held in the countryside. Many studies confirm these figures. In France, the areas of recruitment covered the same-sized territory.[32] In the big cities of Germany, it was larger because urban authorities restricted immigration, and until the Black Death, the bulk of new arrivals were servants, artisans, or officials without any link with agriculture.[33] In Italy, immigrants were mostly poor people but also included some members of the middle class.[34] On the other hand, craftsmen did not abandon their birthplaces definitively; some were hired for only a few years, especially for public works: masons, carpenters, and their servants who were engaged in 1282–83 to build the royal castles of Chester and Bristol came from twenty-five counties.[35]

All these people did not cut their ties with their villages, even if they had left them for remote countries. In the second half of the thirteenth century, a man living *ultra mare* managed to transfer to his brothers his part of a modest tenement in the small locality of Hinderclay, in Suffolk; and a son and a daughter were informed of the death of their father *in partibus extraneis*.[36] Thanks to the immigrants, the peasants became more familiar with the urban way of life and more conscious of the specificity of their own life experiences, a development which was bound to strengthen community feeling.

Third, and finally, city dwellers had money and could use it in different ways. They could lend it to the peasants at short term until the next harvest or at long term by acquiring perpetual rents on landed properties.[37] They could bargain for a *bail à cheptel* (cattle on lease): they leased the beasts, the peasants bred them, and the offsprings were shared half and half.[38] They could buy fields, farms, and lord-

TABLE 5. BIRTHPLACE OF IMMIGRANTS WHO ACQUIRED
BURGHERSHIP IN DOUAI IN THE FIFTEENTH CENTURY

Birthplace (distance from Douai in kilometers)	Percentage
less than 20	48.4
20–39	30.5
40–124	17.5
more than 125	3.6

Source: Y. Minet, "Les inscriptions des registres aux bourgeois de Douai au XVe siècle (1399–1506)" (Louvain Université Catholique) unpublished dissertation, 1973.

TABLE 6. PROFESSIONS OF IMMIGRANTS IN DOUAI
IN THE FIFTEENTH CENTURY

Profession	Percentage
Cloth trade	17.6
Leather trade	12.2
Commerce	11
Food trade	10.6
Building	9.8
Garment	7.9
Timber trade	6.2
Iron trade	5.8
Linen, drapery	5.2
Public and private services	5.1
Agriculture	4.2

Source: Y. Minet, "Les inscriptions des registres aux bourgeois de Douai au XVe sièle (1399–1506)" (Louvain Université Catholique) unpublished dissertation, 1973.

ships. Here, too, relations were frequent between town and village and the differences perceptible in their activities, interests, and mentalities.

Individuals and communities of the countryside also played a role in public institutions. They were integrated into regional districts, the organizations of which mainly administered justice and finance. And some of them were involved in the nomination of regional officials. Along the middle Rhine, the *Heimbürgers* sat in the court of the *Schultheisz,* outside of their villages, but in that case, they did not act as delegates of it.[39] In England, the *villata* had been inserted into the state as the latter's basic unit[40] and, in the late thirteenth century, some boroughs received or bought the right of choosing their sheriff. In fifteenth-century Swabia, *Gemeinden* took part in nominating the *Schultheisz.*[41] More interesting, the *Landsgemeinde,* distinct from the *Landgemeinde,* was a personal association of lords and free landed peasants, living under the law of the *Land,* not subordinate to the prince and debating with him about the affairs of the *Land.*[42] In not a few countries, rural collectivities participated in the parliaments: in Norway and Sweden, in the Tyrol in Vorarlberg, where in 1406 a princely constitution promised that the *Landvolk* would henceforward form a *Landstand,* in Switzerland, where they made up the majority in

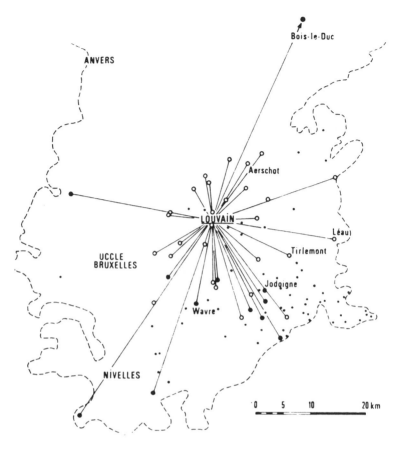

● Localities certainly following the "law" of Louvain in the 13th century
○ Localities certainly following the "law" of Louvain in the 14th and 15th centuries, and probably earlier
· Localities certainly following Louvain "law" in the 14th and 15th centuries, and less probably earlier.

Figure 20. Town and Countryside: Legal Dimension, Louvain law. Louvain, the capital of the duchy of Brabant—the boundaries of which are drawn in dotted lines on this map—did not, like the Italian cities, absorb its *contado*. Rather, it gave its "law," its customs to many localities. The same was true, although to a lesser extent, of Uccle-Brussels and Nivelles.

Source: Genicot (51), 124.

the cantonal assemblies, and in the Comtat.[43] But they had no representatives in neighboring Languedoc,[44] in Belgian and Dutch principalities, and in most parts of Germany, where the influence of the
peasants nevertheless became perceptible in the *Landschaften* and
Landtagen in the late fifteenth century.[45]

During the same period, local priests more and more bound the village to higher religious authorities and districts. After the Carolingian
era, to answer the needs of both clergy and laity, the parishes were inserted into a net of archdiaconates and deaneries.[46] From the time of
the Gregorian reform, vicars were increasingly directed and watched
over by the bishop and his regional delegates. Ordination, appointment and installation, visitations, synods, confirmations, delivery of
the holy oil on Maundy Thursday: the contacts grew narrower and
narrower between them and the bishop, and they became, especially
from the thirteenth century forward, the latter's representatives.[47]
From this viewpoint, too, the village was, by the late Middle Ages, part
of a larger world. Indeed, some rural churches symbolized the general phenomenon of the growing relations between the countryside
and the towns, the state, and the diocese: they modestly imitated urban buildings.[48]

CONCLUSIONS

Partial conclusions have been given at the end of each chapter of this volume, so these final conclusions will be concise—all the more so in that, because of a puzzling diversity resulting from the complexity of rural life, the medieval countryside did not offer many really general features and movements definitely common to the whole western world.

Diversity was the countryside's main characteristic in all things and at all times. To give a final example, the rearing of cattle differed from one peasant to another, from one village to another, and from one region to another. At Taunton in 1348–49, 40 percent of the *villeins* did not possess a beast, but in southern Wiltshire, nearly all the inhabitants had a cow, a calf, or a sheep. At the end of the fourteenth century in Flanders, some peasants tilling less than 2.5 acres bred up to seventy sheep, but cattle were not important; on the other hand, in Cuxham, most *villeins* had a cow, and there were few sheep. Between 1485 and 1496, on the edge of Champagne, the percentage of hearths without a cow fluctuated from one to four in one village and from six to fifteen in another, and the percentage of hearths without a horse was from twenty-five to thirty-six in one village and from fifty-four to sixty-three in an adjacent one.[1] In such circumstances, some scholars conclude that it is nearly impossible to build up a pattern of the medieval lordship. "Die angedeutete Vielfalt der Erscheinungsweisen von 'Grundherrschaft' und die grosze Zahl von offenen Fragen lassen Konstruktion eines Typus der Grundherrschaft im westlichen Mitteleuropa für das späte Mittelalter als wenig tragfähig erscheinen";[2] and "La recherche systématique de schémas généraux et élémentaires est contraire à la connaissance du passé médiéval."[3]

Diversity was a result of complexity. In an *Essai d'interprétation comparative* written to explain the Flemish situation, a specialist recently listed seventeen natural and social factors that could theoretically play a role in the village's life.[4] Personal differences also influenced the position and decisions of each peasant. Not all of them were always operative, and none was indispensable.[5] Moreover, the factors acted jointly in variable combinations and with variable intensity. Hence, the difficulty of establishing causal connections between them. The lack of chronological precision is inherent to collective phenomena, as is the problem of gauging the respective importance of each of them.

For instance, economics and politics operated together, or more exactly interfered with each other, in different ways. Sometimes economic factors prevailed, sometimes political aims and ambitions took control. In Portugal during a first phase, the king dominated the noblemen and restrained them from imposing new duties on the peasants; at a later date, he could no longer control the nobles, and seignorialization went on at the expense of the common people. In fourteenth-century Flanders, the count skillfully set lords and towns against each other and simultaneously protected his "men" (from the late Middle Ages, he called them his "subjects") from seignorial abuses and urban pressure and submitted them to his "sovereignty."

These difficulties are very real. Nevertheless, they should not prevent us from cautiously describing some general features and trends.

Everywhere, the essential phenomenon was the enclosure of the peasants into geographical, economic, political, legal, and religious frameworks, which formed them into local entities conscious of being distinct from each other. Despite the relative continuity of the *villae* and *vici* of classical antiquity, which was probably stronger in post-Roman Britain than on the Continent, the bulk of the rural population in the early Middle Ages lived scattered in small settlements and on isolated farmsteads. From the ninth century in England[6] and from the tenth century on the Continent, people gathered together in villages and hamlets because of economic progress,[7] demographic expansion, the need for new fields and more food, and the search for security. This concentration was directed or stimulated by the landowners' desire to dominate people[8] or as a defense against the latter's "exactions."

Landowners who held property inherited from their ancestors or as a result of royal grants and also those who held offices possessed, received, or usurped the "bannum et justitia" (right of commanding and judging). Caused or facilitated by the weakening of public authority, if not by a hypothetical change in the nobles' mentality, who henceforth thought of profit more than of warfare and pillage, seignorialization started in or progressed from the late tenth century. It was slower or later in regions where the mountains helped the peasants to preserve a total or partial independence and where the king or prince retained his power. But nearly everywhere, sooner or later, the *seigneurie banale* took root. It created *novae, malae consuetudines* (new, bad burdens). And by imposing them on all people, whatever their juridical conditions, it largely unified their status. It also compelled them to act collectively in order to escape, limit, reduce, or at least fix the lord's rights and his mens' duties. This, too, gave impetus to legal uniformity. The charters of franchises and the customs defined by

Weistümer or other documents of this kind applied to all except the very poor.

The third force—which in many, perhaps most, cases was the first to give people a spiritual and material unity and a consciousness of it—was the parish, within definite boundaries, around a church, where the main events of personal and collective life took place, with the same duties imposed on the faithful, especially those of paying the tithe and maintaining the steeple.[9]

This threefold movement was not continuous. In some countries and at some periods, it was stopped, or was divided into two—or was even reversed. The demographic flood led to the settlement of new small hamlets and farmsteads on the edge of the village, as did growing business activity, especially in the Italian *contado*, where the *tecta dispersa* (the scattered houses) multiplied at the end of the period. Economic evolution also incited some lords, instead of or after conceding franchises, to increase their demands from the thirteenth century on. As a result, revolts exploded, mainly against the seignorial system and also against the state, which renewed its power and protected its subjects but burdened them with taxes. The risings were initiated and led not by the mass of the peasantry but by upstarts anxious to profit by the economic possibilities. To meet the needs and wishes of the faithful, parishes were in some cases divided. More often, they were provided with *mediae ecclesiae* and *quartae capellae*, where mass could be heard and some sacraments received, but which remained more or less dependent on their *mater*. In all respects, the unity of the community persisted.

Unity was not complete, particularly during the second part of the Middle Ages. A group of *probi viri* played a growing role in village life. Its influence was based on birth, age, and wisdom, but first of all on wealth. From the eleventh century, the texts mention *laboratores* and *manuoperarii*, people who tilled with plough and oxen or horses and those who cultivated with hands and spade. Between the two groups, the gap became broader and broader. The increasing mobility of the land market gave to officials, skillful peasants, and urban citizens the opportunity of adding field to field and building not seignories but estates. These men and the farmers who managed or leased the properties of others tried to escape the common regulations, especially those prohibiting enclosure. This was made possible by the fact that these men held official posts and led the local assemblies. On the other hand, they benefited from the franchises that granted more to rich men than to poor ones. However, the community did not suffer violent internal clashes between inhabitants. Its first object was always to preserve the peace. Relations with the lord were sometimes difficult, but "l'anachronisme serait de concevoir la seigneurie en terme d'oppression" (it would be anachronistic to think of the seignory in terms of oppression).[10] It is likely that they became not exactly worse but less personal in the last stage of the Middle Ages, when the seignory was acquired by new owners who had not been born in the village and did not dwell in it. With the rector or the vicar, relations were better than has been asserted by some scholars. Moreover, the same "honest men" were in charge of religious and secular functions. Within the community and between members, leaders, and civil and ecclesiastical superiors, an equilibrium was reached, which was synonymous neither with equality nor with oppression.

To push the analysis further, especially in order to distinguish several large areas of development, would in the present stage of knowledge largely be to pile up truisms or to engage in guesswork. Some differences are obvious. The more striking ones are ascribable to nature. A chain of mountains, such as the Pyrenees or the Alps, helped people to gain or to keep independence. Sea, lakes, and marshes demanded collective efforts to provide water defenses, especially with regard to the North Sea, and thus promoted unity. Fertile soil attracted people and supported technological improvements, as in Flanders, with its progressive agriculture. Historical survivals produced other features. One immediately thinks of the classical distinction, which is constantly referred to, between Mediterranean countries and northern Europe. Roman concepts and structures remained alive in the south—hence the survival of central and local institutions, which in Spain and in southern France preserved communities for a long time against seignorialization. Hence in Italy, survivals in the economic field, especially commerce, were attested by the meanings of *lavoro* (any kind of labor, in Italian) and of *labour* (tillage, in French). As a consequence of the vigor of trade, the precocious and powerful urban revival made cities able to extend their protection and authority to their surroundings and, in most cases, to absorb them. There was also a contrast between older and newer regions, between west and east, between the west and the less populated regions of the east where a liberal regime, imported indeed from the west, drew immigrants to larger holdings but where, at the same time, the seignory established firm roots and prepared the manorial reaction of the *Gutsherrschaft* on the eve of modern times. As for England, it demonstrated a particular evolution, as original here as any and as amazing for the Continental historian.

To say more would require new investigations.[11] Many views that seemed true have been rendered doubtful by recent researches, like the almost universal adoption of the three field system from the eleventh, twelfth, or thirteenth century. Many problems have not been dealt with, or not properly dealt with. Many questions are still doubtful or have recently become so. Answers can only come from new inquiries—inquiries into unwritten sources, particularly in the fields of archaeology and earth sciences, which have proved to be rich sources of information. Systematic examinations, both qualitative and quantitative, are needed on the use of neglected types of documents like genealogies and liturgies. A closer examination, especially with the aid of computers, of charters of franchises might uncover information about dates, motives, aims, rhythms, diffusion, and other characteristics, which have been too rapidly and too rashly judged in the past. We might discover the force of attraction on people, the weight of suppressed or reduced rights, and their interest for different groups. We need inquiries into the social and juridical vocabulary for words that had or could have had a technical meaning—*mancipium* and *servitus,* for example. We need monographs inquiring into concrete cases, for after all, only the concrete is true. To summarize is always to eliminate, to simplify, and to impoverish.

At this point, the reader might well ask whether there was in the Middle Ages a rural "class"—if the term is not anachronistic—with the same features for all peasants in dress and food, in behavior and mentality, in belief and culture. Here, too, before answering, one would have to conduct research on words like *rusticus* and define such frequently used expressions as "popular religion" and "popular art" with greater precision than has been done so far. Moreover, this is a matter that concerned country life in general everywhere and did not make each community distinct from others and conscious of its unity and specificity.

One thing is certain: the Middle Ages created, regenerated, or shaped the rural community and thus formed country life for centuries to come, down to the last few decades. This was an achievement of primary importance.

APPENDIX:

OUTLINE FOR AN INQUIRY INTO THE

ORIGINS OF A RURAL COMMUNITY

IN THE MEDIEVAL WEST

I. Nature
   A. Relief
      1. Flat, open country, terrace, steep slope
         a. fit for dwelling and cultivating
         b. not fit for dwelling and cultivation
      2. Natural refuge
         a. against water
         b. against men
      3. Orography
   B. Presence of water
      1. Wells
      2. Meadows rearing
      3. Small streams
      4. Fish ponds
      5. Mills and other "factories"
      6. Rivers
         a. navigability
         b. fords
   C. Soil
      1. Composition and quality
         a. pedological coefficient: global or according to zones
         b. orientation of fields
      2. Meadows (see above)
      3. Forest
         a. composition
         b. localization
         c. extent
   D. Subsoil
      1. Materials fit for industry
      2. Localization: spots that may attract scattered dwellings

II. Human dwellings
   A. Evidence dated and localized on dwellings and their modes
      1. Archaeological remains
         a. buildings, their layout and importance: castle, farmstead, house, religious buildings, cemetery, tombs
         b. artifacts
         c. industrial sites: iron dross
         d. roads
      2. Aerial photography
         a. buildings
         b. working of the soil: ridges, strips
      3. Palinology
         a. evolution of vegetation: forest, waste, meadows, fields
         b. progress or recession of food crops
      4. Toponymy
         a. macrotoponymy: name of the village and its dependences; ethnic origins; meaning; designation (*vicus, villa, locus,* etc.)
         b. microtoponymy: places, fields
      5. Anthroponymy
         a. evidence of occupation of the ground
         b. evidence of isolate
      6. Ancient maps
         a. dwellings
         b. fields, furrows
      7. Land registers, detailed surveys
   B. Data, classified and combined
      1. Site
         a. continuity from period to period from the origins or not
         b. appearance, disappearance, changes of location
         c. nomadism or sedentarity
      2. Structure
         a. successive plans, planned or disordered
         b. fixed places: castle, church, natural refuge
         c. common spots and buildings: green, mill, washing house
         d. passing points
      3. Lines of communication, internal or with outside world
         a. roads and ways, their kind, their relations with parcels of land, their utilization[1]
         b. streams

4. Forms of fields
   a. possible differences in different sectors of the village
   b. evidence of collective rotation
5. Fundamental movements
   a. concentration of previously scattered dwellings
   b. sprouting, dependencies
      • date
      • author (lord, religious institution, private persons, groups, individuals)
      • significance of name
      • form: farmstead or hamlet
      • localization with regard to the nucleus
      • importance
      • relative autonomy; proper uses and organisms (distinct rotation, proper uses, chapel, aldermanate)
      • houses [2] (site, number, size and plan revealing the structure of the family and the structure of accommodation, farmstead or hamlet clustered for defense)

III. Human organization
   A. Power and property: lordship
      1. Property of soil and air
         a. coincidence of both or not
         b. coincidence of lordship and community; lordship going beyond the village or inversely, covering only a part of it
         c. causes of noncoincidence
            • disruptions
            • partitions
            • grants
         d. limits
            • *seigneurie banale*
            • *seigneurie foncière*
         e. juridical nature: freehold or fief
         f. marks of oldness
            • *culturae,*
            • *quarterii,*
            • organization of the village, planned or not
         g. persons
            • nobles
            • knights

    h. castle, seignorial building
- site: in the very center or on the margin of the village
- date: before or after the village
- form
- appellation

    i. other fortified buildings
- owners
- with a chapel?
- in a hamlet?

B. Management and administration
  1. Aldermanate
    a. appearance
    b. way of appointment
    c. functions
- juridical
- administrative

  2. *Jurati* (jurors): same questions as above
  3. Assemblies of the community
    a. appearance
    b. composition
    c. power
    d. rules of procedure (see economic and social life)

  4. Other officials: crop watcher, shepherd, forester, etc.

C. Spiritual life
  1. Church
    a. rank
    b. area of the tithe
    c. title
    d. owner
    e. patron
    f. site
    g. size
    h. enlargings
- dates
- importance

  2. Cemetery
    a. site
    b. changes of location; dates
    c. tithe
- limits
- owners

3. Adaptation to the evolution of dwelling
   a. "daughter" churches
   b. castle chapels
4. Religious houses
5. Staff
   a. vicar
   b. warden
   c. alms institutions
6. Synod: participation of the faithful active?

D. Economic and social life
1. Unity
   a. persons: *omnes habitatores, rustici, vicini*; who escaped the group?
   b. collectivity: *universitas, communitas*
      • collective conscience
      • moral person
      • demonstrations of unity (see assemblies of the collectivity)
2. Factors of coherence
   a. commons and use of them
      • covering the whole village
      • covering only a part of it
      • going beyond
   b. collective coercions: break or fields
   c. rights, duties, privileges
      • charters
      • unwritten enfranchisement: customs' records, their origins, whether lord or peasants; their rules of procedure, whether initiative, convocation; the aldermen's part
3. Finances
   a. receipts
   b. expenses
   c. management
   d. check
4. Demonstrations of coherence
   a. leaders' actions
      • distinct from the aldermen?
      • appointed by the community?
   b. suits and community's proxies
      • mayor
      • vicar

- aldermen
- ancients
- *probi viri*
- jurors
  c. general pleas
  d. other meetings?
  e. meeting place
  - green
  - town hall or private building
  - presbytery
  - castle's outbuildings

IV. Conclusion
    A. Chronology of the components
        1. Priority of dwelling
            a. lordship
            b. parish
            c. community?
    B. Relations between the components
        1. Coincidence of the boundaries
        2. Presence of the same persons
        3. Relations between public organisms

NOTES

INTRODUCTION: SUBJECT AND METHODS

1. Miller and Hatcher (103), p. 5; Herlihy and Klapisch-Zuber (120), pp. 219–21, who consider as urban centers the agglomerations of more than 800 inhabitants; J. C. Russell, *Medieval Regions and Their Cities* (Bloomington, Ind., 1972), p. 235, gives 26 percent; W. Prevenier, "La démographie des villes du comté de Flandre aux XIVe et XVe siècles," *Revue du Nord* 65 (1983): 255–75.

2. Sinatti d'Amico (11), p. 87.

3. A. Settia, "Stabilità e dinamismi di un'area alpina; strutture insediative nelle diocesi di Trento," in *Atti dell'Accademia roveretana degli Agiati*, 1985 series 4, vol. 25A, esp. pp. 256 and 261.

4. P. George, ed., *Dictionnaire de la géographie*, 2d ed. (Paris, 1974).

5. P. Fénelon, *Vocabulaire de géographie agraire* (Gap, 1970), p. 646; M. Derruau, *Précis de géographie humaine* (Paris, 1967), p. 325.

6. H. van der Haegen, M. Pattyn, and S. Rousseau, "Dispersion et relations de niveau élémentaire des noyaux d'habitat en Belgique. Situation en 1980," *Bulletin de Statistique* (1981): 265.

7. Bader (77) distinguishes *Genossenschaft* and *Gemeinde* in the title of vol. 2 and in vol. 1, p. 52. On *Gemeinschaft, Genossenschaft,* and *Gemeinde* in German history, see Wunder (12), p. 15.

8. So again, Bader (77) in the title of his *Studien.* On p. 275 of vol. 2, he speaks of "people who live and reside in the village and have part or want to have part in the *Mark* and in the *Allmende*" (the commons). So he agrees with Bloch (59), p. 173, who defines the village as "un terroir sujet à diverses règles d'exploitation commune et surtout à des servitudes collectives au profit du groupe des habitants."

9. Tits-Dieuaide, "Grands domaines, grandes et petites exploitations en Gaule mérovingienne: Remarques et suggestions," in (24), p. 29, recommends that we should distrust diminutives, which may be used as a form of true or false humility, as an affectation of style, or for some other reason.

10. A few lines from Ourliac (22), p. 15, deserve to be quoted: "Il y a des solidarités volontaires et des solidarités subies, des solidarités d'intérêts ou de défense, des solidarités virtuelles et des solidarités organiques, des solidarités de famille ou de voisinage, des solidarités de villages ou, dans les pays de montagnes, de vallées, des solidarités larges et des solidarités étroites, répondant à un besoin précis ou, au contraire, provenant d'une tendance ou d'un esprit inclinant à l'association."

11. For Mayer (29), p. 467, the concentration of people does not create a *Gemeinde;* a *Gemeinde* must possess a *zwingende Gewalt*, a coercive power; Kurze (37), p. 236, also speaks of *Zwangsgewalt*. On the same subject, see H. Kreutzer, "Kommunalwesen," in *Staat und Politik*, ed. K. D. Bradcher and others (Frankfurt, 1964).

12. S. Reynolds, *Kingdoms and Communities in Western Europe 900–1300* (Oxford, 1984), p. 2.

*The number in parentheses following an author's name refers to that numbered entry in the Bibliography.

13. Settia (41), p. 493; for Spain, Gilbert (12); pp. 272–74.
14. Brooke (41), p. 691.
15. L. Genicot, "Sur le domaine de Saint-Bertin à l'époque carolingienne," *Revue d'histoire ecclésiastique* 71 (1976): 71.
16. A good example of a systematic collection of all references to a term—here *villa*—is in Jimenez (133), pp. 115–33. This proves that computers are not absolutely necessary; but they make research and tabulation easier, quicker, and more reliable, and they frequently disclose unexpected connections between data, facts, and ideas.
17. All the aspects that may be illuminated by archaeology are systematically listed in *L'archéologie du village médiéval* (2) and *25 Years of Medieval Archaeology*, ed. D. A. Hinton (Sheffield, 1983). Among the best monographs are Beresford and Hurst (27), pp. 114–44; Demians (62); and *Brucato* (113).
18. J. Mertens, "Tombes mérovingiennes et églises chrétiennes," *Archeologica Belgica* 187 (1976): 6–13. In Belgium, nearly all rural churches were built in the late seventh or in the eighth century on an already existing cemetery, frequently on a particularly revered tomb. A. Dierkens, "La tombe privilégiée (IVe–VIIIe siècle) d'apres les trouvailles de la Belgique actuelle," in *L'inhumation privilégiée du IVe au VIIIe siècle en Occident: Actes du Colloque de Créteil 1984*, ed. Y. Duval and J. Ch. Picard (Créteil, 1984), pp. 48–49: at the same time, in many cemeteries, a place was reserved in the center or on the margin for a special tomb.
19. A. Matthys, *La céramique*, vol. 7, *Typologie des sources du moyen âge occidental* (Turnhout, 1973).
20. J. M. Pesez, "Histoire de la culture matérielle," in *La nouvelle histoire* (Paris, 1978), pp. 98–130.
21. The *Typologie des sources du moyen âge occidental*, which has published R. Noël, *Les dépôts de polens fossiles* (on palinology), vol. 5 (1972), brought up to date in 1985, and A. Munaut, *Les cernes de croissance des arbres* (*La dendrochronologie*), vol. 52 (1988), is preparing other volumes on all the earth sciences, namely on *La pédologie* and *Le paysage*. A review is devoted to *Landscape History*.
22. M. D. Hooper, "Hedges and Local History," in *Hedges in Local History* (London, 1971), pp. 6–15.
23. M. L. Parry, "Agriculture, settlement and climatic changes," in *Sources de la géographie historique en Belgique: Actes du Colloque de Bruxelles 1979* (Brussels, 1980), pp. 498–522; H. E. Hallam, "The Climate of Eastern England, 1250–1350," *Agricultural History Review* 32 (1984): 124–32: "We ought to distrust all documents, especially the so-called narrative sources."
24. *Brucato* (113), p. 789.
25. P. Donat and H. Ulrich, "Einwonerzahlen und Siedlungsgrösse der Merowingerzeit," *Zeitschrift für Archäologie* 5 (1971): 234–65.
26. On these changes, see Bader (77), vol. 1, p. 31 and several essays in *Le Paysage rural* (28).
27. The possible instability of place-names is noted by Jones (27), p. 40. On the way in which toponomy can mislead, see D. P. Blok, *Ortsnamen*, vol. 54, *Typologie des sources du moyen âge occidental* (Turnhout, 1988). One instance of such a trap is the fact that persistence of place-name does not prove continuity of settlement, as is shown by Brogliolo (41), p. 286.
28. Taylor (111), p. 126.
29. Brogliolo (41), pp. 288–303; Lusuardi Siena (41), pp. 303–35.
30. Settia (128), p. 492.
31. Brooke (41), pp. 686–711.

32. Mayer, (29), p. 465.

33. S. Reynolds, *Kingdoms and Communities in Western Europe 900−1300* (Oxford, 1984), p. 138.

1. VILLA: ORIGINS DOWN TO THE TENTH CENTURY

1. Slicher van Bath (131), p. 40.

2. The respective importance of water and soil on rural settlement is debated. French scholars, like A. Demangeon and R. Dion, give more importance to the composition of the soil. On the other side, contrary to the traditional opinion that heavy soil was not tilled before the Middle Ages because of the inefficiency of technical implements, Taylor (111) shows that 22 percent of prehistoric sites were located on heavy soil and that the exploitation of this type of soil substantially increased in the Roman period.

3. On all aspects—technical, economic, and social—of houses in the early Middle Ages, see Chapelot and Fossier (20). On the fragility of rural buildings, see Bigmore (88), pp. 173−74.

4. Bigmore (88), p. 158.

5. On the connections between nature and village, see W. S. Cooter, "Ecological Dimensions of Medieval Agrarian Systems," *Agricultural History* 52 (1978): 456−77, with the observations of R. S. Loomis, pp. 478−83, and J. A. Raftis, pp. 484−87.

6. J. Goody, *The Development of the Family and Marriage in Europe* (Cambridge, 1984); Th. Schuler, "Familien im Mittelalter," in *Die Familie in der Geschichte*, ed. H. Reiff (Göttingen, 1982), pp. 26−60; *Famille et Parenté dans l'Occident médiéval: Actes du Colloque de Paris 1974*, ed. G. Duby and J. Le Goff (Paris, 1982).

7. Y. Bessmertny, "Les structures de la famille paysanne dans les villages de la Francie au IXe siècle: Analyse anthroponymique du Polyptyque de l'Abbaye de Saint-Germain des Prés." *Le Moyen Âge* 90 (1984): 165−93.

8. Toubert (25); and Cuvillier (25), pp. 318−26.

9. Miller and Hatcher (103): "the stem family consisting of a husband, his wife and their children is the norm"; and "more usually a dead man's land went to a single heir"; but "the holding was regarded as in some sense the support of a more extended family than inheritance customs suggest" (pp. 134−37).

10. Valence: Bonassie and Guichard (22), p. 97. Auvergne: Ourliac (22), p. 23. German villages: Mortensen, "Fragen der nordwestdeutschen Siedlungs-und Flurforschung im Lichte der Ostforschung," in (26).

11. Hanawalt (24 bis); and Cuvillier (25), p. 317, who refers to the *Lex Salica*, which laid down that, if a dead body was found between two *villae*, the inhabitants of both were bound to declare on oath that they were not guilty.

12. M. Rheinhard, A. Armengaud, and J. Dupaquier, *Histoire de la population*, 3d ed. (Paris, 1968), pp. 61−65. For England, which seems to have been very crowded under the Romans, the population decreased in the early Saxon period and grew again after the eighth century, as shown by Taylor (111), pp. 63 and 121; and Klingelhofer (99), p. 422.

13. Fossier (7), pp. 97−100. But in R. Fossier, *Le Moyen Âge*, vol. 1 (Paris, 1982), p. 474, M. Rouche defends a largely different position.

14. R. Doehard, *Le haut moyen âge occidental (La Nouvelle Clio)*, 2d ed. (Paris, 1982): Merovingian debility was succeeded by Carolingian progress; Stoermer (84): the clearings went on in Bavaria in the eighth and ninth centuries, mainly under impulse of the magnates; Jones (121), pp. 193 and 273: in Lombardy, after a decline,

a renewal started in the seventh century, attested by the obligation inscribed in many contracts of *melioratio* (improving), but the phenomenon took on real strength only in the tenth century and more so in the eleventh; G. Rossetti, *Società e istituzioni nel contado lombardo durante il medio evo* (Milan, 1968): assarting under the Lombards could not cope with demographic progress; A. Settia, "Stabilità e dinamismi," in *Atti dell'Accademia roveretana degli Agiati*, vol. 25 A, 4th series (1985), p. 257: reclamation of land went on in the eighth century in the Po valley.

15. J. C. Russell, "Late Ancient and Medieval Population," *Transactions of the American Philosophical Society* 3, new series 48 (1958): 36−37.

16. L. White, *Medieval Technology and Social Change* (Oxford, 1962), believes in an "agricultural revolution" launched in "Francia" in the late Merovingian period, which climatic conditions hindered in southern Europe. This was the key factor of a demographic and economic expansion that transferred the center of medieval civilization from the south to the north. This theory has been forcibly criticized by many scholars, especially by R. H. Hilton, in *Past and Present* (April 1963), p. 95ff.

17. For example, J. Boussard, "Essai sur le peuplement de la Touraine du Ier au Xe siècle," *Le Moyen Âge* 60 (1954): 261ff, notes the appearance in the early Middle Ages of newly built-up areas but asks whether this is a sign of a renewal leading to the Renaissance of the tenth century or a compensation, even though insufficient, for the loss of old settlements.

18. *Villages* (15). On the predominance of hamlets, see Roesener (13), p. 50; Chapelot and Fossier (20), p. 67; Beresford and Hurst (27), pp. 52−85 (Roman settlement was already one of scattered farms and small nucleations, associated with a landscape of small enclosed fields); Fournier (41), p. 524; Fumagalli (119); Bange (58), p. 551. That predominance excluded neither the existence of villages as soon as in the Merovingian period, as in the Trier region, as noted by Gringmuth (11), p. 168, nor the beginning of the *Verdorfung*, the reunion of hamlets in villages, a phenomenon mentioned by Mayer (29), pp. 465−67, and studied for the Neckar valley by Jaenichen, "Markung und Allmende und die mittelalterlichen Wüstungsvorgänge im nördlichem Schwaben," in (29), pp. 163−222.

19. Slicher van Bath (131); Kramer (82), pp. 5−30; Ourliac (22), p. 24.

20. Chiappa Mauri (116), p. 281: the community of Valera was, in the twelfth century, governed by a consul who, with the aid of *vicini*, managed the estates of the parish and the commons, especially the *nemus vicinorum* (the neighbor's wood).

21. Hilton (22), p. 119, mentions groups of *vicini* who appeared in the court rolls to complain, solicit, or agree.

22. So in Valais and southern France, according to Ourliac (22), p. 23.

23. Hilton (22), p. 119.

24. *Historisch* (26) contains a selection of articles showing the main lines of the evolution of German historiography in that area.

25. Mayer (29), p. 477.

26. According to G. P. Bognetti, *Studi sulle origini del comune rurale*, ed. F. Sinatti d'Amico (Milan, 1978), communities of *vicini* linked by fiscal solidarity and the common use of woods and pastures existed before Rome in the Ligurian and Celtic *vici* (boroughs).

27. Jones (121), p. 262, says that the right of commons was no innovation of the early Middle Ages; F. Schneider, *Die Entstehung von Burg und Landgemeinde in Italien* (Berlin, 1924), dates the rural community from the Lombards.

28. J. P. Devroey, *Le polyptyque et les listes de biens de l'abbaye de Saint-Pierre de Lobbes (IXe–XIe siècle)* (Brussels, 1986), p. 112, refers to rents for using the forests. According to Klingelhofer (99), p. 447, common rights were exerted at least by the

eighth century and were the result of a later development. For other countries, see Déléage (61), pp. 394 and 403, where he presents his and A. Dopsch's positions: commons were seignorial concessions.

29. Bonassie and Guichard (22), p. 81; E. Magnou-Nortier, "A propos du temporel de l'abbaye de Lagrasse: étude sur la structure du terroir et sur les taxes foncières du IXe au XIIe siècle," *Sous la Règle de saint Benoît: structures monastiques et société en France du moyen âge à l'époque moderne* (1982): 235–65; on common rights and the beginning of their regulation, see A. Thieme, *Die Waldnutzung in Nordwestdeutschland im Spiegel der Weistümer* (Cologne and Graz, 1960).

30. On the theory and its value, see G. Tabacco, "Problemi di insediamento e di popolamento nell'alto medioevo," *Rivista storica italiana* 79 (1967): 67–110.

31. Janssen (4), col. 1268.

32. F. Staab, *Untersuchungen zur Gesellschaft am Mittelrhein in der Karolingerzeit* (Wiesbaden, 1975), p. 280.

33. Dollinger (79), p. 3; Verhulst (12), p. 224.

34. Sinatti d'Amico (11), pp. 185–87.

35. Bourin and Bonassie (11), pp. 185–87.

36. R. Pastor, *Structures féodales et féodalisme dans l'Occident médiéval (Xe–XIIIe siècle)* (Rome, 1980), pp. 193–216.

37. A. Bequet, "La villa romaine de Ronchinne et sa brasserie," *Annales de la Société archéologique de Namur* 21 (1895): 178.

38. ———. "Les grands domaines et les villas de l'Entre-Sambre-et-Meuse sous l'Empire romain," *Annales de la Société* 20 (1893).

39. J. Zimmer and L. Bakker, *Ausgrabungen in Echternach* (Luxemburg, 1981), pp. 19–20.

40. Jones (121), p. 227.

41. P. van Ossel, "Les établissements ruraux au Bas-Empire entre le Rhin et la Seine," Ph.D. diss., Catholic University of Louvain at Louvain la Neuve, 1986, vol. 3, pp. 16ff.

42. R. Guadaginin, Ph.D. diss., University of Paris, quoted in ibid., p. 89.

43. Bequet, "Les grandes domaines."

44. Jones, "Multiple Estates and Early Settlements," in (27), pp. 15–40.

45. On the continuity in the rural settlement, see D. Hooke, *Anglo-Saxon Landscape of the West Midlands: The Charter Evidence* (Oxford, 1981); and for the continent, *Villa-Curtis* (28).

46. Bange (58), p. 564.

47. Ibid., p. 533; Steane (110), p. 151; W. Janssen, "Mittelalterliche Dorfsiedlungen als archäologisches Problem," *Frühmittelalterliche Studien* 2 (1968): 305–66.

48. P. J. Fowler, "Continuity in the Landscape," in *Recent Work in Rural Archaeology* (Ottawa, 1975), p. 135.

49. Brogliolo (41), p. 291.

50. A. Castagnetti, "Il potere sui contadini: Dalla signoria fondiaria alla signoria territoriale: Comunità rurali e comuni citadini," in *Le Campagne italiane prima e dopo il mille: Una società in trasformazione*, ed. B. Andreolli, V. Fumagalli, and M. Montanari (Bologna, 1985), pp. 229–30 and 340–41.

51. Brogliolo (41), p. 291.

52. Klingelhofer (99), p. 72.

53. Laffi (41), "Discussione."

54. García de Cortázar (4), col. 1293; García de Cortázar and Ruiz de Aguire, "Espacio y pobniamento en la Viscaya altomedieval: de la comarca al caserio en los siglos XI al XIII," *Estudios in memoria del Profesor D. S. de Moxo* 1 (1982): 349–65.

55. Fournier (66), p. 124.
56. Mayer (29), p. 481.
57. T. H. Aston, "The Origins of the Manor in England," with "A Postscript," in *Social Relations and Ideas: Essays in Honour of R. H. Hilton* (Cambridge, 1983), p. 33. The author does not agree on some points with Sawyer (27), pp. 8ff, who asserts that the boundaries and structure of the manors did not substantially change from the sixth or seventh century down to the late Anglo-Saxon period.
58. Jones (121), p. 266.
59. Dierkens (36), p. 40.
60. The elements of the theories and of the discussions are found in Genicot (49). Among the flood of more recent publications, one may point to F. Cardini, *Alle radici della cavalleria medievale* (Florence, 1981); J. Flori, *Préhistoire de la chevalerie;* and *L'idéologie du glaive* (Geneva, 1983; 1986); and K. F. Werner, "Du nouveau sur un vieux thème: Les origines de la 'noblesse' et de la 'chevalerie,'" *Académie des Inscriptions et Belles-Lettres, Comptes rendus* (1985): 186–200.
61. Bonassie and Guichard (22), p. 81.
62. Tits-Dieuaide (24), pp. 35ff.
63. *Le grand domaine* (24); for Saint-Bertin, see Genicot, "Sur le domaine de Saint-Bertin à l'époque carolingienne," *Revue d'histoire ecclésiastique* 71 (1976); for Italy, see Montanari (125), pp. 87–89 (the *livello* played a large part in the constitution of big estates by absorption of little properties under the Carolingians); for England, see Ford, *Some Settlement Patterns in the Central Region of the Warwickshire Avon,* in (27), p. 286 (many large Anglo-Saxon estates were made up of subdomaines).
64. E. Mueller-Mertens, *Karl der Grosze, Ludwig der Fromme und die Freien* (Berlin, 1963).
65. On the positions of A. Dopsch, O. Brunner, or K. S. Bader, who defend this theory with some variations, see Mayer (29), p. 478; Bader (77), 2, pp. 88, for instance, puts forth that the *Hausgenossenschaft* was in most cases the personal substruction of the *Dorfgenossenschaft.*
66. Gringmuth-Dalmer (11), p. 164. The *innerer Landesausbau* consists in enlarging extant entities.
67. According to Jones (121), p. 267, the system of labor payments by tenants not only existed but was already mature in southern Italy when the ancient world collapsed; afterward, it spread to the north of Italy.
68. L. Genicot, *Les actes publics,* fasc. 3, *Typologie des sources du moyen âge occidental* (Turnhout, 1972), p. 39; mise à jour, 1985, p. 8; Tits-Dieuaide (24), p. 29ff.
69. *Villa-Curtis* (28); *Le grand domaine* (24).
70. The word *mansus,* which initially meant the house with its toft, was also used for independent holdings; in 790, for example, Folrad made to Saint-Germain des Prés the modest gift of one and a quarter *mansus* with four *mancipia,* or slaves (R. Poupardin, *Recueil des chartes de l'abbaye de Saint-Germain des Prés, des origines au XIIIe siècle,* vol. 1 (Paris, 1909), p. 34.
71. Gringmuth-Dalmer (11) gives some instances for the regions of Trier and Marburg and for Bavaria (pp. 168, 169, 172). But in Brehières, in northern France, accurately studied by P. Demolon, *Le village mérovingien de Brehières, Ve–VIIe siècle* (Arras, 1972), settlement was still clearly scattered. Gringmuth-Dalmer dates the *Verdorfungprozesz* from the Carolingian period (p. 175).
72. C. Taylor, "Polyfocal settlement and the English Medieval Village," *Medieval Archaeology* 21 (1977): 189–93.
73. Taylor (111), p. 116: at Brixworth there were thirty to forty settlements scattered over the parish without coherent arrangement; nucleated villages were very few before 1000.

74. C. Despy and C. Billen, "Le peuplement rural dans la région de Couvin pendant le haut moyen âge," *Au pays des rièzes et des sarts* (1982): 21; J. Halkin and C. G. Roland, *Recueil des chartes de l'abbaye de Stavelot-Malmedy* (Brussels, 1909), pp. 1, 90; the diploma of 862 and another one of 873 mention three loci and seven places without qualification; two of the seven places possessed a *capella*.

75. A. I. Njeussychin, *Die Entstehung der abhängigen Bauernschaft als Klasse der frühfeudalen Gesellschaft in Westeuropa vom VI. bis VIII. Jahrhundert* (Berlin, 1961), p. 149; for the other *Leges Barbarorum*, see H. Doelling, *Haus und Hof in westgermanischen Völkerrechten* (Berlin, 1958); for the whole written evidence, see Schreiner, "'Grundherrschaft,' Entstehung und Bedeutungwandel," in (81), 1, pp. 22.

76. J. F. Niermeyer, *Lexikon minus*, sub verbo *Villa* with references to Gregory of Tours. But for Bange (58), p. 533, *villa* meant not "a domanial unity" but "a territorial cell in which landed properties are located." E. Magnou-Nortier, "La terre, la rente et le pouvoir dans les pays du Languedoc pendant le haut moyen âge." Part 1. "La villa: une nouvelle problématique," *Francia* 9 (1981): 79-115, also sees in the *villa* a district, but a fiscal one, derived from the Roman administration.

77. Pallares Mendez and Portela Silva (133), pp. 95-113: *villa* normally means "great manor" but also, and increasingly, "village." See also Fournier (65), p. 213; Tits-Dieuaide (24), p. 26.

78. Déléage (61), p. 223: the coincidence is exceptional; see also A. Verhust, "Le paysage rural en Flandre intérieure: son évolution entre le IXe et le XIIIe siècle," in (28), pp. 11-33.

79. On the method of depicting the parochial network, see Fournier (41), p. 497; Aubrun (56), pp. 223-35, 294, 297. On the connections between Roman roads and *pievi*, mainly in the coastal and mountainous regions, see Lusuardi Siena (41), p. 305.

80. On the existence of parishes before the Middle Ages in *villae* and in some minor localities, see Brogliolo (41), p. 209; and Taylor (111), p. 120.

81. Bonassie and Guichard (22), p. 81. On the choice of the curate or vicar, see p. 100.

82. For Normandy, see Jacqueline (11), p. 412.

83. Settia (41), p. 448: many private churches were the fruit of individual devotion; hence the lack of correlation between the building of churches and demographic movement. It is worthwhile noting that, following Wisniowski (11), p. 568, in Poland, the parish churches were not located in the center but to one side and even on the boundary of the built-up area, because landowners built them close to their mansions, without paying attention to the needs or wants of the population. Stoermer (84): in Bavaria the ancestors' tomb was, in the eighth and ninth centuries, replaced by the domestic church.

84. M. Chaume, "Le mode de constitution et de délimitation des paroisses rurales aux époques mérovingienne et carolingienne," *Revue Mabillon* 27 (1927): 61-70.

85. Fournier (41), p. 522.

86. Aubrun (56), p. 341.

87. *Monumenta Germaniae Historica, Capitularia*, vol. 1, p. 36.

88. D. Krauss, *Die mittelalterliche Pfarrorganisation in der Ortenau* (Baden, 1970).

89. É. de Moreau, *Histoire de l'Église en Belgique*, vol. 1, 2d ed. (Brussels, 1945), p. 298.

90. On the religious work of the Carolingians, see Semmler (41), pp. 862ff.

91. Dierkens (36), p. 38.

92. Castagnetti (114), p. 337.

93. Aubrun (56), pp. 233, 197, 305.

94. Ibid., p. 233.

95. J. Chelini, "Les laïcs dans la société ecclésiastique carolingienne," in *I laici nella*

"Societas christiana": Atti della terza settimana internationale di studio (Milan, 1968), p. 43.

96. *Monumenta Germaniae Historica, Capitularia*, vol. 2, p. 81; Avril (64), pp. 1, 349.
97. Settia (41), p. 453ff; Dierkens (36), p. 35.
98. Aubrun (56), p. 306.
99. Toubert (25), p. 353ff.
100. D. Lambrecht, "De kerkelijke wroegingsprocedure in de Frankisch tijd: Genese en eerste ontwikkeling," *Tijdschrift voor Rechtsgeschiedenis* 49 (1982): 47–100.
101. Folz, "La pénitence publique à Langres au IXe siècle," in (64), p. 331, notes the attempt to restore the public penance under the Carolingians.
102. B. Botte, *Le Canon de la Messe romaine* (Louvain, 1935), p. 79.
103. *Monumenta Germaniae Historica, Capitularia*, vol. 1, p. 178. U. Stutz, "Zur Herkunft von Zwing und Bann," *Zeitschrift der Savigny Stiftung, Germanistische Abteilung* 58 (1937): 345, says the result of that decision fixed parish boundaries. J. Semmler, "Zehntgebot und Pfarrtermination in karolingischer Zeit," *Aus Kirche und Reich: Studien zur Theologie, Politik und Recht im Mittelalter: Festschrift für F. Kempf* (1983): 33–44. Whether the parish at that time was personal (or juridical) or territorial is a debated matter. All aspects probably combined: the parish went as far as people dwelled and tilled.
104. For Scandinavia, Saxony, and Friesland; see Feine, "Kirche und Gemeinde," in (29), pp. 57–62.
105. Fournier (41), p. 530.
106. Taylor (111), p. 120, puts forward the theory that, in Anglo-Saxon England, the boundaries already tended to be relatively stable; people certainly moved, but they moved within the confines of a delimited territory.
107. For Castagnetti (114), p. 343, the parish in Italy did not generate the rural community either territorially or institutionally. In Hampshire, studied by Klingelhofer (99), p. 301, it covered several small estates.
108. From the diversity of specific situations, where only the concrete situation is historical, comes the value of the monograph. Such monographs are particularly desirable for villages that were not ruled by a church. To encourage young scholars to elaborate such specific historical incidents, I have outlined the monograph of a rural medieval community. See Appendix.
109. Bourin (11), p. 350.
110. Bonassie (75), p. 47.

2. UNIVERSITAS: ECONOMIC ASPECTS

1. P. Michaud-Quantin, "Universitas: Expression du mouvement communautaire dans le moyen âge latin," *L'Église et l'État au moyen âge* 13 (1970).
2. H. Foerster, ed., *Liber diurnus* (Berne, 1958), p. 121, n. 63.
3. P. S. Leicht, *I diplomi regi ed imperiali a favore della città nei secoli X–XI ed il sorgere dell'universitas civium: Studi in onore di A. Solmi* (Milan, 1940). The expression does not include the notion of juridical personality, according to O. Banti, "'Civitas' e 'commune' nelle fonti italiane dei secoli XI e XII," *Critica storica* 9 (1972).
4. D. Brouwers, "Chartes et règlements," in *Documents publiés par ordre de la Députation permanente du Conseil provincial de Namur*, vol. 1 (Namur, 1913), p. 27.
5. Bader (77), vol. 2, p. 25.
6. Nikolay-Panter (83), p. 183. The document alludes to the *Weistum*, described on p. 75.

7. Ganghofer (11), p. 437.
8. For our field, see R. Koselleck, "Begriffsgeschichte und Sozialgeschichte," in *Vergangene Zukunft: Zur Semantik geschichtlicher Zeiten* (1970). K. Bosl, "Potens und Pauper: Begriffliche Studien zur gesellschaftlichen Differenzierung im frühen Hochmittelalter," in *Alteuropa und die moderne Gesellschaft. Festschrift für Otto Brunner* (1963), p. 64, affirms the possibility of passing from concepts to realities.
9. See Michaud-Quantin (126). This theory would explain why *communitas* appeared sooner and was current from the twelfth century. This theory must be checked. Wunder (85), p. 12, did not find *communitas* before the Sachsenspiegel, in 1220–30.
10. Genicot (51), pp. 49–60, 311–18.
11. Miller and Hatcher (103), p. 4.
12. Pallares Mendez and Portela Silva (133).
13. H. H. Lamb, "The Early Medieval Warm Epoch and Its Sequel," *Palaeography, Palaeoclimatology, Palaeoecology* 1 (1965): 13–37.
14. Taylor (111), p. 169.
15. For figures on life expectancy and mortality rate, see Genicot (51), pp. 51–52; Portela Silva (139), p. 58.
16. P. Feuchère, "La noblesse du Nord de la France," *Annales, Économies, Sociétés, Civilisations* 6 (1951): 315–18; Genicot (47), vol. 1, p. 67. I join issue with Duby on the family policy of the nobility; for him only the eldest sons married and begot children; according to my and my pupils' researches, on the contrary, these sons generated few children and the name of the lineage had frequently to be preserved by collateral branches.
17. Stoermer (84) puts forward the theory that before 1000 noblemen sacked, but after 1000 they conformed to some laws of the war and to the code of chivalry. In a parallel way, Duby's basic thesis in this area is that, after 1000, the lords changed from warriors to landowners and were permeated by the idea of profit. The reality or at least the revolutionary character of that change needs to be substantiated.
18. Miller and Hatcher (103), p. 4. Genicot (45) lays stress on the frequently underestimated effect of political events on economic matters.
19. Raftis (106) places the peak of the movement a little before 1250.
20. Russell (108); these figures are contested by Postan (3), pp. 561–65, who asserts that the population grew from two to seven million.
21. In the Piedmont, Comba (117), p. 88, calculates that the *mansi* (hides), and afterward the pieces of land, were severely fragmented from the third quarter of the twelfth century to the mid-thirteenth century; the average size of the pieces of land dropped from 7.5 or 8 acres to 2 or 2.5; the phenomenon slowly continued on until the end of the thirteenth century. For England, Raftis (106) observes that the reclamations continued for a century after 1250; Klingelhofer (99), p. 235, states that in Micheldever and the surrounding region, where pastures and woods still covered most of the land in the central Middle Ages, assarting took place from the late twelfth century to the fourteenth. For Belgium, Genicot (46), pp. 121–38, sees the cessation of reclamations around 1300; R. Noël, "Sciences naturelles et histoire des campagnes au Moyen Âge," *Études rurales*, no. 20 (1966): 95, shows, thanks to the palinology, that agricultural expansion continued after 1300 in the adjacent Ardennes; A. Verhulst, "Historio-geografische studie over het oudste domein der Sint-Baafsabdij te Gent," *Tijdschrift van de Belgische Vereniging voor Aardrijkskundige Studies* 22 (1953): 356, writes that the grey soils were cultivated early in the Middle Ages, and the brown ones from the thirteenth century.
22. Clarke (81), pp. 22–23.
23. Miller and Hatcher (103), p. 3.

24. On this phenomenon and the explanations given by scholars, see Genicot (51), pp. 315–16. Also see J. Z. Titow, "Some Differences Between Manors and Their Effects on the Conditions of the Peasant in the Thirteenth Century," *Agricultural History Review* 10 (1962): 1–13. Postan (3) calls that "a counter-point in the marriage." Bresc (25), pp. 400–01, estimates that the difference in age between spouses was fifteen years in the twelfth and thirteenth centuries, six to seven years with the Black Death, and twelve years with the demographic revival around 1400.

25. R. Delatouche, "La crise du XIVe siècle en Europe occidentale," *Les Études Sociales*, nos. 2, 3 (1959): 11.

26. L. R. Poos, "Population of Essex in the Later Middle Ages," *Economic History Review* 38 (1985): 529, states that the high mortality of 1315–17 caused by the famine was more influential on demographic fluctuations than were the epidemics.

27. *Brucato* (113), p. 784.

28. Steane (110), p. 155, places the beginning of the process in Germany in the mid-Saxon period. Klingelhofer (99), pp. 275–315, dates from the eighth and ninth centuries, thanks to grants and to the fragmentation of large estates, the establishment of the classical manor, the cell of the rural community. But D. Hooke, *The Anglo-Saxon Landscape: The Kingdom of the Hwicce* (Manchester, 1985), states that the majority of the nucleated villages in West Midlands are later than the Norman Conquest. Martinez Diaz (4), col. 1294, and Durand (135), p. 206, find rural communities in the ninth century in northern Spain and Portugal; of course, *rural community* and *nucleated village* are not synonymous. For Gringmuth-Dallmer (11), p. 168, the region of Trier contained many villages as early as the eighth century, and from this time onward, the movement started in the fertile plain around Marburg. As J. M. Pesez says, the village is "a medieval creation." Also see Roesener and Pesez (4), cols. 1272, 1274; Schroeder (29), vol. 1, pp. 11–28; Jones (121), pp. 258–59.

29. Bader (77), p. 55.

30. Klingelhofer (99), p. 111.

31. Fournier (66), p. 319.

32. Fortified villages existed, for instance, in Spain and Italy, as shown by Comba (117), p. 74.

33. Of particular interest in this connection is *La maison forte au moyen âge* (32), a collection of reports delivered at a congress held in 1984 at Pont-à-Mousson by medievalists from Belgium, France, Great Britain, Italy, and the Netherlands. *La maison forte* is in theory a single type of fortified building, excluding castles, but the congress often went beyond. See also—mainly for France—*Châteaux* (21), and for Italy, Comba (117), pp. 135–37, 153–57. D. J. C. King, *Castellarium Anglicanum: An Index and Bibliography of the Castles of England, Wales, and the Islands* (New York, 1983) does not raise the problem of *incastellamento* in his later *The Castle in England and Wales: An Interpretative History* (London and Sydney, 1988).

34. In fact, the distinction is not very clear between these types, especially the latest ones. In *La maison forte*, J. Brunouf and B. Metz write, p. 162, that "les sources alsaciennes ne livrent aucune définition de la maison forte et la castellologie française en livre plusieurs contradictoires," and, in the conclusion, p. 331, J. M. Pesez admits that "rien n'est moins sûr que la possibilité de définir la maison forte de manière à satisfaire tous ceux qui font usage de ce nom."

35. H. E. J. Le Patourel and B. K. Roberts, "The significance of moated sites," in *Medieval Moated Sites*, ed. F. A. Alberg (London, 1978); Genicot (47), vol. 2, p. 281; for Lorraine, Champagne, and Franche-Comté, M. Bur in *La maison forte*, p. 11, gives the following figures, which include some castles: thirteenth century, twenty-four;

fourteenth century, thirty-four; fifteenth century, twenty-three; and sixteenth century, six.

36. Castagnetti (115), p. 342.

37. See the contributions of Fournier and Charbonnier, Guiliato, Louise, de Waha, and Pesez in *La maison forte*, pp. 283, 172, 31, 108, 333. Practical conclusion: someone ought to draw up lists of the fortified sites, as did Bur, p. 11.

38. Genicot (47), vol. 3, p. 18.

39. For France, see G. Fournier, *Le château dans la France médiévale* (Paris, 1978), pp. 168−72; for Italy, Jones (121), p. 231, quotes agreements between lords and peasants for the construction of castles; for England, see Taylor (111), p. 146. See also Fourquin (69), vol. 1, p. 388; Castagnetti (114), p. 244; W. Podehi, *Burg und Herrschaft in der Mark Brandenburg* (Cologne and Vienna, 1975); R. Schumann, *Authority and the Commune: Parma 833−1133* (Parma, 1973).

40. G. Rossetti, *Società e istituzioni nel contado lombardo durante il medio evo: Cologno Monzense*, vol. 1 (Milan, 1968), pp. 153−83; Comba (117), pp. 131− 61; Durand (135), p. 208.

41. As Klingelhofer (99), pp. 181 and 184, stresses, some old settlements also moved to better sites. So not everywhere was there continuity from ancient to medieval villages.

42. Fournier (67), pp. 190 and 226, shows on the evidence of plans and aerial views that these new (total or partial) foundations were far more numerous in Auvergne than appears from the texts; this may be true for other regions; see C. Higounet, *Paysages et villages neufs du moyen âge* (Bordeaux, 1975), pp. 245−54 and 347−53.

43. On the controversy about the reasons for founding the *bastides*, fortified villas, in southwestern France, see Genicot (51), p. 311.

44. This is Fossier's thesis (22), p. 40.

45. García de Cortázar (22), pp. 70−71.

46. Toubert (130), p. 210; Lagos Trinidade and Gaspar, "A utilizaçao agraria do solo em torno de Lisboa na Idade Media," in (133), pp. 89−94; Genicot (51), p. 74.

47. Ourliac (22), p. 17.

48. Miller and Hatcher (103), p. 85. The situation was the same in the Netherlands, as is stated by Slicher van Bath (132), vol. 1, p. 30.

49. Abel (16), p. 11, gives an average of eleven and twelve houses with some seventy-two inhabitants. The figures calculated by Russell (108), p. 310, are somewhat different, but they do not distinguish between villages and boroughs:

	In Bucks		In Oxon	
Inhabitants	1086	1377	1086	1377
1 to 25	33	0	40	20
26 to 50	38	3	43	46
51 to 100	58	8	52	92
101 to 200	52	10	58	90
201 to 400	13	15	16	31
401 to 800	2	5	8	9

50. Comba (117), p. 74, and García de Cortázar (4), col. 1295, observe the same phenomenon in Piedmont and in northern Spain. In this last country, *alquerias, barriades, caserios* (small settlements) frequently join into *valles, anteiglesias, merindades, juntas*.

51. B. Tonglet, *L'habitat seigneurial fortifié dans le comté de Namur, Xe–XVe siècle* (Namur, 1985).

52. J. Roland, "Les Coutumes de Biesme-la-Colonoise," *Anciens Pays et Assemblées d'États* 38 (1966): 102.

53. Comba (117), pp. 153–67.

54. Jones (121), pp. 422–25; Herlihy and Klapisch-Zuber (120), p. 232.

55. The *Wüstungen* (desertions) seem to have been less general than has been written. Noël, "Les villages disparus de Gaume à la fin du moyen âge," in (2), pp. 133–39; Arnould (for Hainault) (12), p. 288; H. J. Gilomer, *Die Grundherrschaft des Basler Cluniazenser Priorates St Alban im Mittelalter* (Basle, 1977), p. 115; and Rotelli (127), p. 123, state they were "extremely scarce," to use Rotelli's expression. For this author, there were many more changes in the way of cultivation than real abandonments. On desertions, see Abel (16); and A. Settia, "Insediamenti abbandonati, mentalità popolare e fantasie erudite," *Bollettino storico bibliografico subalpino* 62 (1974): 611–32, who criticizes severely the "fantasies" of some scholars. For regional researches, see W. Janssen, "Research on Medieval Settlements Sites of the Rhineland," in Annual Report of the Medieval Village Research Group, vol. 29, pp. 36–40; K. Wanner, *Siedlungen, Kontinuität und Wüstungen im nördlichen Kanton Zurich (9–15 Jh.)* (Bern, 1984); Portela Silva (139), p. 279, who found no instance of a deserted village before 1300 (four from 1300 to 1348, and fifty-three from 1348 to 1400); Taylor (111), p. 166, who writes that "about three thousand deserted villages have been identified and many more remain to be discovered"; Miller and Hatcher (103), p. 61, who distinguish periods (maximum intensity in the 1440s) and regions (5,600 acres in Sussex; 48,700 in Cambridgeshire); and Clarke (89), pp. 17–22, whose views are temperate and who speaks of "shrinkage" during two centuries. The reasons for desertions varied greatly. In Navarre, Berthe (75), p. 50, observes that the peasant moved when the parish was no longer served.

56. *Bulletin de la Commission royale d'histoire de Belgique*, 5th series (1900): 84.

57. Ibid., p. 33.

58. J. David, "De techniek van de middeleeuwse ontginningen," in *Sources de la géographie historique en Belgique* (Brussels, 1980), pp. 317–29.

59. G. Franz, *Quellen zur Geschichte des deutschen Bauernstandes im Mittelalter* (Darmstadt, 1967), p. 192.

60. Miller and Hatcher (103), p. 40.

61. Genicot (47), vol. 3, pp. 271–73.

62. Genicot (48), p. 9.

63. R. A. Donkins, "The English Cistercians and Assarting, c. 1128–c. 1350," *Analecta Sacri Ordinis Cisterciensis* 20 (1964): 49–75. C. Hoffman Berman, "Medieval Agriculture, the Southern France Countryside, and the Early Cistercians: A Study of Forty-Three Monasteries," *Transactions of the American Philosophical Society* 76, pt. 5 (1986), confirms the conclusions developed by R. Fossier and C. Higounet, *L'économie cistercienne: Géographie-Mutations du Moyen Âge aux Temps modernes, Troisièmes journées internationales d'histoire du Centre culturel de Flaran* (Auch, 1983): the *grangiae* were created by purchases and expropriations.

64. On the part played by the lords, see Gringmuth-Dallmer (11), p. 175; W. Schlesinger, *Kirchengeschichte Sachsens im Mittelalter*, vol. 2 (Cologne and Graz, 1962), p. 24.

65. C. Dyer, *Lords and Peasants in a Changing Society: The Estates of the Bishopric of Worcester, 680–1450*, Past and Present Publications (1980).

66. W. Blockmans and W. Prevenier, "Armoede in de Nederlanden van de 14e tot het midden van de 16e eeuw," *Tijdschrift voor Geschiedenis* 88 (1975): 504. For a farm in Mecklenburg in the nineteenth century, Abel (76), p. 106, gives a still lower figure: 53.5 percent.

67. Genicot (47), vol. 3, pp. 288–93; Miller and Hatcher (103), p. 154, give for Minety, then in Gloucestershire, 14 sheep per person, 1.4 cows, 1.4 oxen, and, for most tenants, 1 horse. The number of sheep is especially impressive, at least from the thirteenth century; see some figures in Genicot (51), p. 89, n. 4, and Genicot (47), vol. 3, p. 291. Horses were also, at the end of the Middle Ages, more numerous than expected: L. Genicot, "Cherruiers et Manouvriers dans le Namurois à la fin du moyen âge," in *Hommage à la Wallonie: Mélanges offerts à M. A. Arnould et P. Ruelle* (Brussels, 1981), p. 181.

68. *Acta Sanctorum Oct. 13*, chap. 16, p. 421; *Bulletin de la Commission royale d'histoire de Belgique*, 5th, s. 4, p. 12. Whether the lords had conceded common rights, as Déléage (61), p. 403, suggests, is questionable. Or did they claim they had done so? This is one of the many theories on the origins of commons.

69. Castagnetti (114), p. 230.

70. The relative importance of arable land and pasture and its evolution in the late Middle Ages is a matter of controversy. For Postan (104b), pp. 219–49, pasture diminished in the thirteenth century. For the majority of the scholars, especially Duby (5), p. 615, it increased. This seems to be beyond question for the late Middle Ages; about 1300, the chamberlain of the Count of Namur, whose operations are detailed by Genicot (47), vol. 2, p. 245, obtained from his master the right to breed sixteen horses and fifty-one "large cattle" in the two farmsteads he had put together piece by piece; R. H. Bautier, "Les mutations agricoles et les progrès de l'élevage," *Bulletin philologique et historique (jusqu'en 1610)* (1967): 1–27, claims that there was a constant increase in rents, expressed in terms of oats; in the region of Lyon studied by Lorcin (71), p. 402, the percentage of meadows in landed property rose from 15 in 1388 to 21 in 1493; between 1471 and 1484, the popes unsuccessfully tried to stop the reduction of corn cultivation around Rome and in Apulia, and the number of sheep grew from 600,000 in 1463 to 1,048,000 in 1536, according to Jones (121), p. 226. On the way to resolve the problem, see Genicot (51), p. 341.

71. Miller and Hatcher (103), p. 39.

72. Bader (77), p. 144.

73. In some villages, the charters of the late Middle Ages show the rights to the commons as limited to a part of the population, the *masuirs*, the holders of a portion of the oldest fields, the *mansi;* see Genicot (51), p. 84, and (47), vol. 3, pp. 66 and 294. Did such a custom date from the end of the period? And did it provoke conflicts within the community? See ibid., p. 56.

74. Durand (135), p. 209.

75. Comba (117), p. 114.

76. R. Pastor de Togneri, "Ganadaria y precios," *Cuadernos de Historia de España* 35–36 (1962): 37–55; and D. L. Farmer, "Grain Price Movements in Thirteenth Century England," *Economic History Review* 10 (1957): 207–20, give methods for evaluating cattle and grain prices, which can be misleading.

77. L. Genicot, "Le droit de restor," *Namurcum* 14 (1937): 28.

78. In the late thirteenth century, some lords and big landowners already excluded the peasants' cattle from their fields, meadows, and woods, as observed by Schneider (74), p. 403; Stolz (42), p. 118. For England and the famous enclosures,

see Hilton (97), pp. 117−36. In Galicia, Martino-Veiras (22), p. 233, states that from the mid-fourteenth century, a great many collectively owned properties were, under the influence of Roman law, converted into individual ownerships.

79. Archives de l'État à Namur, Échevinage d'Assesse, 1674−78, 130. To the same effect, see a decision of a court in 1405, in Séminaire de Namur, no. 30, f. 148.

80. Genicot (47), p. 255. Having a proper flock was possibly a privilege of the *hommes de loy* (descendants of knights, up to the seventh generation), who were exempt from the *herdage* paid to the *herdier* (the common shepherd).

81. The struggle against water could be led by individuals or by small groups financially supported by the community, as shown by Verhulst (12), p. 246, and Van der Linden (12), p. 479.

82. Archives de l'État à Namur, Commune d'Ohey, no. 2.

83. V. Barbier, *Histoire de l'abbaye de Géronsart* (Namur, 1885), p. 295; Duby (5), p. 267.

84. Bader (77), vol. 2, p. 376; and vol. 3, p. 4. What engaged the attention of the peasants was less opposition to the lord than the struggle between individual and collective utilization of the land; see Homans (98), p. 330; R. S. Hoyt, "The Farms of the Manor and the Community of the Vill," *Speculum* 30 (1955): 147−69; Ault (87), p. 68. The community also leased quarries and minerals, for instance in the Pyrenees, as Poumarède (11), p. 393, observes.

85. Jones (121), p. 214, and Verhulst (12), p. 227, note that most parts of the commons were wrecked in the late Middle Ages.

86. A detailed description of agricultural operations is given by Ault (87), pp. 20−50. See also B. M. S. Campbell, "Agricultural Progress in Medieval England: Some Evidence from Eastern Norfolk," *Economic History Review* 36, 2d series (1983): 26−46; M. Mate, "Medieval Agrarian Practices: The Determining Factors?," *Agricultural History Review* 33 (1985): 22−31; Thoen (52), p. 784.

87. *Monumenta Germaniae Historica, Scriptores*, vol. 16, p. 670.

88. Miller and Hatcher (103), p. 13.

89. J. Langdon, *Horses, Oxen and Technological Innovation: The Use of Draught Animals in English Farming from 1066 to 1500* (Cambridge, 1986), gives figures on the growing use of horses in Essex: 10 percent of the draft animals in the Domesday Book, 50 percent at the end of the thirteenth century.

90. "Photothèque d'histoire rurale," of the *Centre belge d'histoire rurale: Belgisch Centrum voor landelijke Geschiedenis*, located in the Catholic University at Louvain la Neuve, provides rich material on the agricultural tools of the late Middle Ages, as illustrated by Belgian iconography, and on the ways of using them. Ample documentation and illustration are also given by Bentzien (18). Interesting observations are also found in J. David, "Het middeleeuws gereedschap. Enkele problemen," *Handelingen van het Genootschap voor Geschiedenis te Brugge* 116 (1971): 5−26; and in Thoen (52), p. 776.

91. W. Abel, *Agrarkrisen und Agrarkonjunktur*, 2d ed. (Hamburg, 1966), p. 22.

92. Whether sowing ticker is more profitable is a question still debated by theorists and peasants, as discussed by M. J. Tits-Dieuaide, *La formation des prix céréaliers en Brabant et en Flandre au XVe siècle* (Brussels, 1975), p. 99.

93. Archives de l'État à Namur, Souverain Bailliage, no. 516, f. 57, and no. 519, f. 14.

94. Jones (122), p. 323.

95. Searle (109), p. 275; A. Verhulst, "Bronnen en problemen betreffende de vlaamse landbouw in de late middeleeuwen," in *Ceres en Clio* (Wageningen, 1964), pp. 215−16; B. Slicher van Bath, *The Rise of Intensive Husbandry in the Low Countries, Britain, and Netherlands* (London, 1960), pp. 133−34.

96. Titow (112), pp. 41−42.

97. Tits-Dieuaide (53), p. 598; A. Derville, "Dîmes, rendements et 'révolution agricole' dans le Nord de la France au moyen âge," *Annales, Économies, Sociétés, Civilisation* 42e année (1987): 1424.

98. A. Plaisse, *La baronnie de Neufbourg* (Paris, 1961), p. 144.

99. Jones (121), p. 217.

100. Ault (87), p. 18. Among the latest statements on the problem for England is A. Dodgshon, "The Landholding Foundations of the Open-Fields System," *Past and Present* 67 (1975): 3-20; R. T. Rowley, *The Origins of Open Field Agriculture* (London, 1981), with a contribution by D. N. Hall, "The Origins of Open-Field Agriculture: The Archaeological Fieldwork Evidence," pp. 22-38; and as provocative as the title, H. S. A. Fox, "The Alleged Transformation from Two-field to Three-field Systems in Medieval England," *Economic History Review* 39 (1986): 536-48. For Europe, see R. Hoffmann, "Medieval Origins of the Common Fields," in *European Peasants and Their Markets*, ed. W. N. Parker and E. L. Jones (Princeton, 1975), pp. 23-71. At a symposium on Property Rights, Organisation Forms and Economic Behaviour held at Upsalla University in 1986, S. Fenoalta dismissed en masse the "popular, ecumenically accepted" theories; he developed his views in "Transaction Costs, Whig History, and the Common Fields," which he kindly submitted to me.

101. H. Mortensen, "Fragen der nordwestdeutschen Siedlungs- und Flurforschung im Lichte der Ostforschung," in (26); A. Krenzlin, "Die Entwicklung der Gewannflur als Spiegel kulturlandschaftlicher Vorgänge," in (26); K. H. Schroeder, "Die Gewannflur in Süddeutschland," in (29), pp. 11-20, summarizes the German scholars' theses.

102. J. P. Devroey, *Le polyptyque et les listes de biens de l'abbaye Saint-Pierre de Lobbes (IXe–XIe siècles)* (Brussels, 1986).

103. Miller and Hatcher (103), p. 15, observe that, in Charlton in 956, peasants' fields joined. B. Schwinekoeper, "Zu der Pertinenzformeln der Herrscherurkunden bis zur Zeit Ottos I," *Festschrift für Helmut Beumann* (Sigmaringen, 1977), p. 54, suggests that the addition of "*et inviae*" in Lewis the German's diplomas indicates tracks grafted onto the roads to give access to the strips and proves that the layout was already in the form of open fields. In Portugal, open fields, called *agros*, existed at least from the early eleventh century, as shown in the recension of Portela Silva (139) in *Revue d'histoire ecclésiastique* 74 (1979): 78. But open fields and three field rotation are not necessarily connected.

104. Hall, "The Origins of Open-Field Agriculture," asserts that archaeological and physical data attest that the medieval strip fields were laid out on a large scale before the Norman Conquest, with a subsequent subdivision of the long strips and a remanagement. According to Fox, "Alleged Transformation," the three-field system developed "during a filling up of the landscape in the last three centuries of Saxon England, as ploughlands of existing settlements expanded at the expenses of pastures and wastes."

105. Fossier (22), p. 41.

106. Klingelhofer (99), p. 234.

107. Postan (102), p. 55; J. Thirsk, "The Common Fields," *Past and Present* (1964): 3-25; and Fox, "Alleged Transformation," insist on the coexistence of both systems.

108. García de Cortázar (22), pp. 70-71; Collantes de Teran (133), pp. 135-54; Fox, "Alleged Transformation"; van Lennep and Verhulst (12), pp. 228, 231, and 486; Thoen (52), p. 772.

109. D. Faucher, "L'assolement triennal en France," *Études rurales* 1 (1961): 7-17.

110. Fox, "Some Ecological Dimensions of Medieval Field-systems," in (1), p. 140.
111. These words and others, like *Vergetreidung* and *Verdorfung*, were coined by W. Mueller-Wille, "Langstreifenflur und Drubble: Ein Beitrag zur Siedlungsgeographie Westgermaniens," *Deutsches Archiv für Landes- und Volksforschung* 8 (1984): 8–44, esp. 41.
112. For Spain, see A. Barrios García, *Estructuras agrarias y de poder en Castilla: el ejemplo de Ávila (1085–1320)* (Salamanca, 1983–84).
113. M. Harvey, "Planned Field Systems in Eastern Yorkshire: Some Thoughts on Their Origin," *Agricultural History Review* 31 (1983): 91.
114. B. M. S. Campbell, "The Regional Uniqueness of English Field Systems: Some Evidence from Eastern Norfolk," *Agricultural History Review* 29 (1981): 16–28.
115. D. Brouwers, *Cens et rentes du comte de Namur*, vol. 2 (Namur, 1911), p. 350.
116. Jacqueline (11), p. 417.
117. Jones (121), p. 243. Olland (73), p. 252.
118. Scholars do not agree on the evolution of the yield ratio in the late Middle Ages. B. A. Slicher van Bath, "Yield-ratios 800–1820," *A.A.G. Bydragen* 10 (1963), who collected the most data, calculates that in France it moved from 3 to 1 prior to 1200 to an average of 4.7 for the fourteenth and fifteenth centuries; and in England from 3.7 between 1200 and 1249 to 4.7 between 1250 and 1499. Bois (19) also thinks, for other reasons, that there was an increase, not as a result of technological improvements but because of an increase in the size of holdings, which enabled tenants to exploit their labor forces more intensively. According to van der Wee and van Cauwenberghe (54), p. 3, there are good grounds for believing that there was a stabilization at the high level reached in the mid-fourteenth century. But E. Miller, "The English Economy in the Thirteenth Century: Implications of Recent Researches," *Past and Present*, no. 28 (1984): 38, claims that the yield ratio was lowered from the late thirteenth century. In fact, Harvey (91), p. 57, states that from 1289 and 1299 to about 1350, it fell from 8.3 to 4.3. R. Delatouche, "L'économie céréalière médiévale: L'exemple de la Flandre et du Brabant au XVe siècle," *Académie d'Agriculture de France: Procès-verbaux des séances* (1977): 51–66, puts forth that there was a lowering of productivity caused by the reduction in labor forces. H. Neveux, "Dîme et production céréalière. L'exemple du Cambrésis, fin 14e-début 17e siècle," *Annales, Économies, Sociétés, Civilisations* 28 (1973): 58, concludes that there was a decline of at least 15 percent from 1370 to 1450. Other figures for Belgium are in Genicot (47), vol. 3, p. 294, who lists the factors that must be taken into account when considering this difficult matter—and that make any generalization hazardous. Thoen (52), pp. 817–22, also invites prudence.
119. Herlihy and Klapisch-Zuber (120), p. 278; Genicot (47), vol. I, p. 293, analyzes the terms of the leases on that point.
120. Titow (112), p. 232, estimates that most of the lords invested less than 5 percent of their gross income. M. M. Postan, "Investment in Medieval Agriculture," *Journal of Economic History* 27 (1967): 576–87; and Fourquin (69), p. 581, defend the same view. No doubt many citizens invested in the countryside, especially from the late thirteenth century, first by buying rents, as noted by R. Maertens, *Wertorientierungen und wirtschaftliches Erfolgsstreben mittelalterlicher Grosskaufleute: Das Beispiel Gent im 13. Jahrhundert* (Cologne and Vienna, 1976), p. 284; and afterward were stimulated, at least in Italy, by an opposite development of the commercial and agricultural returns, calculated by Jones (121), p. 197, to purchase pieces of land. In the first stage, they sometimes cleared, dammed, and drained, as in examples reported by D. M. Nicholas, *Town and Countryside: Social, Economic and Political Tension in Fourteenth-Century Flanders* (Bruges, 1971), p. 131; in the second

stage, they developed the rearing of animals. But did they improve the methods of cultivation?

121. Schneider (74), p. 401; Duby (5), vol. 1, p. 248.

122. P. Andrieu-Guitancourt, *L'archevêque Eudes Rigaud* (Paris, 1938), p. 375. Other examples are in R. W. Emery, *The Jews of Perpignan in the 13th Century* (New York, 1959), pp. 64–65; and E. Sapori, *Studi di storia economica. Secoli 13-14-15*, vol. I, 3d ed. (Florence, 1955), p. 183.

123. S. Mestdagh, "511 chirographes tournaisiens de 1314 à 1320: Contribution à l'étude du papier de crédit au moyen âge." Ph.D. diss., University of Louvain, 1980. Clark, "Debt litigation in a late Medieval English vill," in (10), pp. 247–79, confirms her observation thanks to the court rolls of a large village in Essex, which lived by culture, rearing, and in some measure, commerce: between 1382 and 1429, actions formed from 8 to 24 percent of the suits; 39 percent of the liabilities dated from one to three years before; they were concerned with payment by installments, implements and grain, and payment for work.

124. M. Mollat, "Les réactions des pauvres à la pauvreté en France au bas moyen âge," in *Aspects of Poverty in Early Modern Europe*, ed. T. Riis (Odense, 1986), pp. 78–80.

125. A. Stella, *Politica ed economia nel territorio trentinotirolese dal 13 al 17 secolo* (Padua, 1958), p. 74.

126. Taylor (111), p. 159, notes the abundance of market grants between 1100 and 1300, allowing the lords to hold weekly markets in their villages. So do Miller and Hatcher (103), p. 162. Other contributions on this point lack chronological precision. Moreover, such grants might have resulted from political aims.

127. L. Genicot, "La structure économique d'une principauté médiévale," *Études N. Didier* (1960): 163–71, reprinted in *Études sur les principautés lotharingiennes* (Louvain, 1975).

128. E. King, *Peterborough Abbey 1086–1310* (Cambridge, 1973), pp. 8–9, speaks of an "intensive land market."

129. One of the first registers of this kind, begun in 1210, has been published by M. Gysseling and A. Verhulst, *Het oudste goederenregister van de Sint-Baafsabdij te Gent* (Bruges, 1964). Of course, registers were also the result, like the flood of rentals and accounts in the thirteenth century, of better management and of the growing use of written records.

130. Genicot (44), p. 130.

131. Jones (121), p. 407.

132. Harvey (92).

133. Genicot (44).

134. Raftis (107), pp. 68, 74, 77, 90; Hilton (96), p. 161.

135. On the rent, strictly speaking—as distinct from the census—and on its successive forms, see Genicot (51), p. 82.

136. C. Howell, "Peasant Inheritance Customs in the Midlands 1200–1700," in *Family and Inheritance*, ed. J. Goody, J. Thirsk, and E. P. Thompson (Cambridge, 1976), p. 133.

137. Slicher van Bath (14), p. 44.

138. Lennard (101), pp. 340–44.

139. R. Le Jan-Hennebique, "'Pauperes' et 'paupertas' aux IXe et Xe siècles," *Revue du Nord* 50 (1968): 170–74.

140. Déléage (61), p. 249; Jones (121), p. 244.

141. J. Yver, "Remarques sur l'évolution de quelques prix en Normandie aux XIVe–XVe et au XVIe siècles," *Revue historique de droit francais et étranger* 36, 4th series (1959): 145.

142. G. Sivery, "Herchies, un village du Hainaut (1267–1314)," *Revue du Nord* 52 (1970): 319.
143. Genicot (47), vol. 2, p. 271.
144. Archives de l'État à Namur Chartrier du Chapitre d'Andenne.
145. Levett (102), p. 190.
146. Schneider (74), p. 374; L. Genicot, "Aspects de la vie rurale aux environs de Gand dans la première moitié du XIIIe siècle," *Études rurales*, no. 21 (1966): 123.
147. Genicot (44), p. 130.
148. Lennard (101), pp. 340–44.
149. Kosminsky (100), pp. 212–13. C. N. L. Brooke and M. M. Postan, "Cartae nativorum," *Northamptonshire Record Society* 20 (1960): 38–66, support the opposite thesis. P. R. Hyams, "The Origins of a Peasant Land Market in England," *Economic History Review* 28 (1970): 18–31, argues that none of those authors give solid proofs. And at the same time, Titow (112), p. 73, speaks of "evidence that the rural population had become largely one of smallholders"; and Miller and Hatcher (103), p. 145, speak of a "tendency for smallholdings to multiply in most places." For northwestern Spain, Portela Silva (139), p. 134, deduces from the growing fragmentation of the *casales* a reduction of the size of the peasants' holdings. On a general level, Duby (5), p. 531, believes in such a reduction; so does B. A. Slicher van Bath, "Les problèmes fondamentaux de la société préindustrielle en Europe occidentale: Une orientation et un programme," *A. A. G. Bydragen* 12 (1965): 8.
150. On social advancement through mounted service, see Genicot (51), p. 87.
151. Kosminsky (100), pp. 221–23. For other figures giving the same stratification for Flanders, Hainault, Picardy, and Normandy, see Genicot (48), pp. 22–23; Sivery, *Herchies*, p. 313; Fossier (65), p. 637; Bois (19), p. 149.
152. Genicot (47), vol. 3, pp. 279–302, shows how complex the problem is and how elementary most of the solutions are.
153. Genicot (45) summarizes the causes, dimensions, aspects, and results of the phenomenon. He proves there the decisive influence of public disorders on agricultural prices and on the reduction of rents.
154. D. Herlihy, "Population, Plague and Social Change in Rural Pistoia, 1201–1430," *Economic History Review* 18, 2d series, (1965): 225–44; Neveux (69), vol. 2, p. 77; Jones (121), p. 242.
155. Chiappa Mauri (116), p. 263.
156. Many examples are in Genicot (47), vol. 3, pp. 328–37; the table of farms at the end of the Middle Ages, vol. 2, p. 274, speaks for itself.
157. Bois (19), p. 139.
158. Dewindt (90), p. 161; Hilton (93), p. 149, calls the century after the Black Death "possibly the golden age of the middle peasantry."
159. Genicot (47), vol. 3, p. 335.
160. Lorcin (71), p. 242. The interpretation of the figures on the poor derived from fiscal sources is difficult. At any rate, in Flandre wallonne, people in the countryside considered poor by the administration constituted 22, 27, and 37 percent of the population in 1432, 1449, and 1485 (see W. Blocmans and W. Prevenier, "Armoede," *Tijdschrift voor Geschiedenis* 88 (1975): 516. In Brabant, according to a census of 1437, they formed one-third of the inhabitants; that figure, given by R. Van Uytven and W. Blocmans, "De noodzaak van een geintegreerde sociale geschiedenis," *Tijdschrift voor Geschiedenis* 84 (1971): 277, is contested by M. J. Tits-Dieuaide, "L'assistance aux pauvres à Louvain au XVIe siècle," in *Hommage P. Bonenfant* (Brussels, 1965), p. 437.
161. Van der Wee and van Cauwenberghe (54), pp. 151–56.

162. Jones (121), p. 241.
163. On purchases of seignorial rights in the north of Germany, mainly by merchants of Lübeck, see K. Fritze, "Bürger und Bauern zur Hansezeit: Studien zu den Stadt-Land Beziehungen an der südwestlichen Ostseeküste" vom 13. bis zum 16. Jahrhundert, Zeitschrift für Bayerische Landesgeschichte 39 (1976), p. 83; and for southwestern Germany, see W. Leiser, "Territorien süddeutscher Reichstädte: Ein Strukturvergleich," *Ibid.* 38 (1975): 967–81.
164. Hilton (95), p. 27.
165. Genicot (50), p. 80.
166. *Stranger* is an ambiguous term, as emphasized by M. Boulet-Sautel, "L'aubain dans la France coutumière du moyen âge," in *Recueils Jean Bodin*, vol. 10, *L'étranger* (Brussels, 1958), pt. 2, p. 668; one may be a stranger to the village, the district, the principality, or the kingdom. For that subject, see also N. Guglielmi, "Modos de marginalidad en la Edad Media: Extranjeros, Pobreza, Enfermedad," *Anales de historia antigua y medieval* (1971).
167. Sinatti d'Amico (11), p. 191.
168. Verhulst (12), p. 233.
169. Aureggi (22), p. 208.
170. Ourliac (22), p. 23.
171. Genicot (47), vol. 3, p. 142. Particularly dangerous were the acquisitions by the Cistercians, who tried to build their *grangiae* to the prejudice of the inhabitants, not infrequently by expelling them; following many studies, M. Schaab, "Die Grundherrschaft der südwestdeutschen Zisterzienserklöster nach der Krise der Eigenwirtschaft," in (81), vol. 2, p. 53.
172. In Uri and Schwyz, as noted by J. C. Gemperle, *Belgische und Schweizerische Stadt-verfassungsgeschichte im Mittelalter* (Louvain, 1941), p. 125, one had to take an oath to obtain any plot of land.
173. So in the Pyrenees, as noted by Poumarède (11), p. 395.
174. Aureggi (11), pp. 216 and 220, observes that, in the period of the commune, local ascendency and residence became essential to be a member of the *universitas*.
175. H. E. Hallam, "Some Thirteenth Century Censuses," *Economic History Review* 10 (1957/58): 356. Weston was an extreme case: it lacked holdings.
176. Herlihy and Klapisch-Zuber (120), p. 315.
177. Dewindt (90), p. 151.
178. Haverkamp (81), vol. 2, p. 341.
179. L. Verriest, "La bourgeoisie foraine à Ath," *Annales du Cercle archéologique d'Ath* 26 (1940): 232–33. Also, P. Godding, "La bourgeoisie foraine de Bruxelles du XIVe au XVIe siècle," *Cahiers bruxellois* 7 (1962): 1–64. On the *bourgeois du prince* or *du roi*, see A. M. Patault, "Hommes et femmes de corps en Champagne méridionale à la fin du moyen âge," *Annales de l'Est*, Mémoire no. 58 (1978): 35.
180. R. Petit, "L'extension du droit de bourgeoise de Laroche au XVe siècle" in *Album C. Wyffels* (Brussels, 1987), pp. 383–94.
181. Genicot (47), vol. 2, pp. 293–301.
182. Ibid., vol. 3, pp. 66 and 294; Ganghofer (11), p. 435.
183. Slicher van Bath (132), vol. 2, pp. 67, 193–94.
184. Wunder (85), p. 9.
185. Bentzien (18), p. 97.
186. Fried, "Grundherrschaft und Dorfgericht im spätmittelalterlichen Herzogtum Bayern," in (81), vol. 2, p. 307.
187. Grava (22), p. 194.
188. Klapisch-Zuber, "Structures démographiques et familiales," in (129), p. 12.

189. M. Montanari, "Strutture familiari e forme di conduzione fondiaria durante il medio evo: Spunti per una storia della società contadina nelle Romagne dei secoli 10–13," in *Problemi di storia demografica nell' Italia medievale* (Sienna, 1983), pp. 69–80; Ruiz Domenec (133), pp. 61–68.

190. Clarke (89), pp. 33–40; Chapelot and Fossier (20): the houses are smaller, with hall, bedroom, and store.

191. Fossier (25), p. 367.

192. Genicot (51), p. 62.

193. E. Le Roy Ladurie, *Les paysans du Languedoc* (Paris, 1966), p. 165.

194. Herlihy and Klapisch-Zuber (120): in the countryside, one out of five households was multiple.

195. Tabacco (118), p. 208.

196. Hanawalt (24 bis) estimates that the neighbors were even more important than the extended family.

197. Ourliac (22), p. 23.

198. Kramer (82), pp. 5–30; for the lower Rhine, see Wunder (85), p. 69.

199. Genicot (47), vol. 3, p. 130; Cauchies (30), p. 192.

200. Hilton (96), pp. 248–61.

201. Charter of Brogne, forged at the end of the twelfth century: see Genicot (47), vol. 3, p. 374.

202. A. Delcourt, *La vengeance de la commune* (Lille, 1930). Compare, for Languedoc, Ourliac (22), p. 21.

203. Cauchies (30), p. 193, refers to a charter of Hainault that allowed the aldermen to disobey the lord if he did not restore damage he had caused to a member of the community.

204. L. Verriest, "La fameuse charte-loi de Prisches," *Revue belge de philologie et d'histoire* 2 (1923): 340 and 344. Bonassie (75), p. 47, points to the example of Catalonia and the revolt of the *pagenses de remensas* against the *mal usos*. Frisia and the Swiss Alps succeeded in this way in remaining independent of any authority. On the peasants' rebellions, see ch. 3.

205. Rucquoy, "Molinos et acenas au coeur de la Castille septentrionale (XI–XVe siècles," in (140), p. 115, notes that the mills along the Duero and in Portugal were frequently built by the rural communities and ignored the banalities.

206. Raftis (107), p. 111.

207. See n. 80: this work was sometimes assumed by groups of different sizes, larger or smaller than the village.

208. Ault (87), p. 71.

209. Genicot (47), vol. 3, p. 110.

210. Haverkamp (81), p. 2.

211. Wunder (85), p. 46.

212. Miller and Hatcher (103), p. 156.

213. Schubert, "Entwicklungsstufen der Grundherrschaft im Lichte der Namenforschung," in (81), vol. 1, p. 95.

214. Arnould (44), p. 297, lists not a few villages of Hainault that possessed a seal from the fourteenth, even thirteenth centuries.

215. Ibid.

3. BANNUM: LEGAL ASPECTS

1. I use the French vocabulary, which is clear: *banal* means founded on the *bannum*, and *foncier*, founded on the *fundus*, the ground. The English *manor*, like the

seigneurie foncière, frequently did not cover the whole village nor include more than landed property, especially jurisdiction. Kosminsky (100), p. 73, calculates that, in Cambridgeshire, 11 percent of the villages, and in Oxfordshire, 63 percent coincided with the manors. Klingelhofer (99), pp. 373–74, observes that the lords wished "to hold jurisdiction as they held property." The German *Grundherrschaft* is particularly awkward: it suggests an institution based on the ground; so German scholars often use another word: *Leibherrschaft*, lordship of the bodies. French-language medieval documents use *seigneurie hautaine*, because *bannum* and *alta justitia*, high justice for the "major" cases, were connected; for the same reason, the jurists of modern times speak of *seigneurie justicière*. In my opinion, the old adjective *hautain* made it unnecessary to invent a new one: *banal*. For the sake of conciseness, I shall in this chapter call the *seigneurie banale* the lordship.

2. Compare with the English situation mentioned in n. 1 and with the German one analyzed by Mayer (29), p. 480, where several *Herren* shared the property of the ground of the village but only one had the *Obrigkeit* on the whole.

3. In 1173, a family of Lodi sold the "onores et districtus et condiciones cum amiseribus et albergariis" in Valera; another document also quoted by Chiappa Mauri (116), pp. 279 and 294, says the *dominatus*.

4. Genicot (49).

5. Klingelhofer (99), p. 439.

6. Bonassie and Guichard (22), p. 99; S. de Moxo, "Los señorios," in (133), pp. 163–73.

7. Genicot (47), vol. 2, p. 13.

8. *Vita Wicberti*, written between 1071 and 1099, in *Monumenta Germaniae Historica Scriptores*, vol. 8, p. 509. Wicbert founded the monastery of Gembloux, ten miles from Namur.

9. *Miracula sancti Foillani*, dating from 1102–12, in the same *Scriptores*, vol. 15, pp. 418 and 421. Foillan contributed to the foundation of the *monasterium Scottorum* of Fosses, also near Namur.

10. Genicot (47), vol. 3, p. 7.

11. Text of 1265 for the Forez quoted by E. Perroy, *La terre et les paysans en France aux 12e et 13e siècles: Explication de textes* (Paris, 1973), p. 212. On the "protective" function of the lordship, see Tabacco (118), p. 200.

12. On the social position of the first *advocati* and the distinction to be made between them and the *defensores*, see L. Genicot, "Sur le vocabulaire et les modalités de l'avouerie avant l'an mil dans la Belgique actuelle," *Publications de la Section historique de l'Institut Grand-Ducal de Luxembourg* 118 (1984): 9–32.

13. Many German scholars, like Bader, see the core of the lordship in the *Vogtei*, the charge of the *advocatus*.

14. On that matter, Perrin (33), pt. 5, remains essential; Bur (60), p. 392, is right in establishing a parallel, even a link, between those *règlements d'avouerie* and the charters of franchise.

15. One wishes to have available for all countries lists such as D. J. C. King, *Castellarium Anglicanum: An Index and Bibliography of the Castles of England, Wales and the Islands* (New York, 1983); and C. L. Salch, *Dictionnaire des châteaux et des fortifications du Moyen Âge en France* (Strasbourg, 1979).

16. *Châteaux* (21); *Die Burgen im deutschen Sprachraum: Ihre Rechts—und verfassungsgeschichtliche Bedeutung*, ed. H. Patze, in *Vorträge und Forschungen* 19 (1976).

17. Typical is B. F. Porschnew, "Das Problem des Klassenkampfes in der Epoche des Feudalismus," *Sowjetwissenschaft: Gesellschaftswissenschaftliche Abteilung* 3 (1952): 460–82.

18. J. Halkin and C. G. Roland, *Recueil des chartes de l'abbaye de Stavelot-Malmedy*

(Brussels, 1909), vol. 1, p. 339. On this problem, I refer to texts of the same region, to avoid drawing a composite picture. R. Aubenas, "Les châteaux-forts des Xe et XIe siècles: Contribution à l'étude de la féodalité," *Revue d'histoire du droit français et étranger* 63 (1938): 548–86, convincingly emphasizes that the castle was an instrument of *tuitio*, or protection.

19. Quotation from the *Cantatorium Sancti Huberti*. Genicot (47), vol. 3, pp. 8–9, gives the list of the *violentiae*, which according to the chronicler, who was especially interested in juridical questions, afflicted the monastery, located in the Ardennes, from 1048 to 1103.

20. Fourquin (69), vol. 1, p. 388; Castagnetti (114), p. 244; W. Podehi, *Burg und Herrschaft in der Mark Brandenburg* (Cologne and Vienna, 1975); R. Schumann, *Authority and the Commune: Parma, 833–1133* (Parma, 1973).

21. Lennard (101), p. 365, did not observe such a reduction of statute labor in eleventh-century England. And, as we shall see, M. M. Postan stresses the increase of it in the thirteenth century.

22. Genicot (47), vol. 1, pp. 113, 356.

23. Ibid., p. 244.

24. W. Janssen (81), vol. 1, pp. 313–42, estimates as negligible the product of landed property for building a *territorium*, or principality.

25. J. F. Fino, *Forteresses de la France Médiévale*, 2d ed. (Paris, 1970), pp. 156–58.

26. Genicot (51), pp. 95–96, and on the main factors—individual, physical, demographic, economic, juridical, political, social—that influenced the lords' behavior, pp. 97–98.

27. Duby (6), p. 203.

28. J. F. Fino, *Forteresses*, p. 133, and C. Gaier, "Les armes," *Typologie des sources du moyen âge occidental* 34 (1979; updated 1982).

29. The origins of the classical banalities have been the theme of many discussions, which may be summed up as follows: normally, the lord built a mill and the peasants used it; but whether the use was compulsory is not established. G. Roehme, *Das Recht der Muhlen bis zum Ende der Karolingerzeit* (Breslau, 1904), did not find any evidence prior to the mid-tenth century, in spite of the assertion of L. Verriest, *Institutions médiévales* (Mons and Frameries, 1946), p. 54.

30. R. Sanfaçon, *Défrichements, peuplement et institutions seigneuriales en Haut-Poitou du Xe au XIIIe siècle* (Québec, 1967), p. 17; J. F. Lemarignier, "La dislocation du "pagus" et le problème des 'consuetudines' (Xe–XIe siècles)," in *Mélanges Louis Halphen* (Paris, 1951), pp. 403–10; E. Magnou-Nortier, "Les mauvaises coutumes en Auvergne, Bourgogne méridionale, Languedoc et Provence, au XIe siècle. Un moyen d'analyse sociale," in *Structures féodales et féodalisme dans l'Occident méditérranéen (Xe–XIIIe siècles)* (Rome, 1980), p. 155; Bur (60), p. 392. On a general level, Duby (6), p. 255, distinguishes the same stages. Schneider (31), p. 70, describes another evolution.

31. J. P. Devroey, "Recherches sur l'histoire rurale du haut Moyen Âge. Les polyptyques de Saint Rémi de Reims et de Saint-Pierre de Lobbes," Ph.D. diss., Brussels, 1982, p. 308, calculates the monetary dues at Lobbes, eight to twelve pennies, at Prüm, fifteen, at Saint-Germain des Prés, seventeen, and at Montierender, eighteen.

32. Several historians, like G. Stephenson, "The Origin and Nature of the Tallia," *Revue belge de philologie et d'histoire* 5 (1926): 801–70, did not check the authenticity of the documents they used for dating the phenomenon, in a field where forgeries are abundant. To the references given in n. 30, add O. Guillot, *Le comte d'Anjou et son entourage au XIe siècle*, vol. 1 (Paris, 1972), p. 371; E. Magnou-Nortier, "La

place du concile du Puy (v. 994) dans l'évolution de l'idée de paix," *Mélanges Dauvillier* (1979): 506, who found the first mention of *malae consuetudines* in the Acts of the Council; Bonassie (134), p. 590, who observes that *usus* and *exactiones* occasionally appeared about 1010 and became current about 1040–50, when authority disintegrated; Dollinger (79), p. 189; and for the empire in general, Franz (80), p. 29.

33. "Historia Walciodorensis monasterii," *Monumenta Germaniae Historica, Scriptores*, vol. 14, p. 529. G. Despy, *Les chartes de l'abbaye de Waulsort* (Brussels, 1957), p. 340, notes that the original charter of 1070, summarized by the chronicler, does not mention *questus*. Would they have been imposed between 1070 and 1150?

34. R. Sanfaçon, *Défrichements*, p. 17. English documents mentioned by Miller and Hatcher (103) speak of "arbitrary customs." And the Statutes of Verona published by Castagnetti, *Le comunità rurali dalla soggezzione alla giurisdizione cittadino* (Verona, 1983), annex 22, speak of "innumerosae extorsiones dominorum" (the lord's countless extortions).

35. On that concept, see Genicot, "La Loi," *Typologie des sources du moyen âge occidental* 22 (1977): 19.

36. P. Petot, "L'origine de la mainmorte servile," *Revue historique de droit français et étranger* 19 (1940/41): 300–01.

37. A. Dumas, "Quelques observations sur la grande et la petite propriété à l'époque carolingienne," *Revue historique de droit français et étranger* 4th (1926): 638, collected and commented on the main passages of Carolingian documents concerning the *exactiones*.

38. Castagnetti (114), p. 236.

39. Genicot (47), vol. 3, VI and 66.

40. Ibid., vol. 2, p. 125.

41. Ibid., vol. 3, p. 86.

42. Miller and Hatcher (103), p. 236.

43. Raftis (106), p. 107; M. Morgan, *The English Lands of the Abbey of Bec* (Oxford, 1946), pp. 105–09.

44. Miller and Hatcher (103), p. 147.

45. Bonassie and Guichard (22), p. 111.

46. H. Platelle, *Le temporel de l'abbaye de Saint-Amand des origines à 1340* (Paris, 1962), p. 224; Searle (109).

47. Genicot (47), vol. 3, p. 113.

48. A. Verhulst, "Das Besitzverzeichnis der Genter Sankt-Bavo von circa 800," *Frühmittelalterliche Studien* 5 (1971): 208–10 and nn. 62, 63.

49. Fumagalli (119), p. 139; Tabacco (118), p. 200.

50. *Wort und Begriff Bauer*, ed. R. Wenskus, H. Jankuhn, and K. Grinda, in *Abhandlungen der Akademie der Wissenschaften zu Göttingen, Philo. histo. Klasse*, 3 Folge, 89, 1975. All the uses of the words designating categories of men (*rusticus, servus, homme de poesté, de taille, villain*, etc.) should be collected and interpreted as K. Baldinger did for northern and eastern France in several works, most recently "Der freie Bauer im Alt- und Mittelfranzösischen," *Frühmittelalterliche Forschungen* 13 (1979): 125–49. For Bavaria, see Dollinger (79), p. 385.

51. The existence in the central Middle Ages of "charges caractéristiques du servage" has been vigorously and, in my opinion, convincingly contested by L. Verriest, *Institutions médiévales* (Mons et Frameries, 1946–57). It is still asserted by scholars like K. H. Spiess (81), vol. 1, p. 169, according to whom the twelfth century saw the constitution of a "new" class of unfree men whose "mark of serfdom" was being submissive to *capitatio, mortimanus*, and *forismaritagium*.

52. A rule formulated about 1383 and quoted in Genicot (47), vol. 3, pp. 70, 114.
53. R. Boutruche, *Seigneurie et féodalité* (Paris, 1970), pp. 2, 78, dates the connection from the thirteenth century. I am more convinced by R. Homet, "Remarques sur le servage en Bourbonnais au XVe siècle," *Journal of Medieval History* 10 (1984): 195–207, who proved that tallage was a mark of serfdom in central France in the fifteenth century.
54. Sanfaçon, *Défrichements*, p. 67; J. P. Poly, *La Provence et la société féodale, 879–1166: Contribution à l'étude des structures dites féodales dans le Midi* (Paris, 1976), p. 108.
55. B. Dodwell, "The Free Peasantry of the Hundred Rolls," *Economic History Review* 13–14 (1943/44): 165–66; R. H. Hilton, *The Economic Development of Some Leicestershire Estates in the Fourteenth and Fifteenth Centuries* (Oxford, 1947), p. 9.
56. Fourquin (69), vol. 1, p. 479.
57. J. B. Hardley, "Population Trends and Agricultural Developments from the Warwickshire Hundred Rolls of 1279," *Economic History Review* 11, 2d series (1957/58): 8–18.
58. Castagnetti (114), p. 235; Montanari (125), p. 89; I. Guérin, *La vie rurale en Sologne aux XIVe et XVe siécles* (Paris, 1960).
59. A theory advanced particularly by P. Petot, "L'évolution numérique de la classe servile en France du IXe au XIVe siècle," in *Recueils Jean Bodin, 2, Le servage*, 2d ed. (1959), p. 165; For the *servage réel*, see p. 76.
60. Franz (80), p. 131.
61. *Monumenta Germaniae Historica, Scriptores*, vol. 14, p. 526.
62. *La Chronique de Saint-Hubert dite Cantatorium*, ed. K. Hanquet (Brussels, 1906), p. 39.
63. On the origins and evolution of the *placita generalia*, see R. van Caenegem, *Geschiedenis van het Strafprocesrecht in Vlaanderen van de XIe tot de XIVe eeuw* (Brussels, 1956), pp. 93–100. For Italy, Castagnetti (114), p. 221, describes the *placitum* presided over by the count and recording the *jus curiae* through the witness of local *jurati*.
64. *La Chronique de Saint-Hubert*, p. 226.
65. D. Brouwers, *Cens et rentes* (Namur, 1911), p. 330; for France, where it was rare, see P. Duparc, "Le sauvement," *Bulletin philologique et historique (jusqu'en 1610)* (1961): 389–433; and, on the *commendise*, which was an individual *sauvement*, P. Duparc, "La commendise ou commende personnelle," *Bibliothèque de l'École des Chartes* 69 (1961): 50–112.
66. This is suggested by Jacob (12), p. 338.
67. In that way, communities became, to use the German vocabulary, *unmittelbar*, or without any intermediate lord between them and the prince.
68. Genicot (47), vol. 3, p. 48.
69. Spiess (81), vol. 1, pp. 163, 197. P. W. Henning, *Das vorindustrielle Deutschland, 800–1800* (Paderborn, 1974), p. 69, estimates that, in the central Middle Ages, agriculture absorbed 2.1 million people; the *Ostsiedlung* (emigration to the East), 0.4 million; and the towns no more than 0.8 million. Some figures on this point are given in ch. 5.
70. Perrin (33), p. 675; Bur (60), p. 392.
71. Genicot (47), vol. 3, p. 154; W. Steurs, "Les franchises du duché de Brabant au moyen âge," *Bulletin de la Commission royale des anciennes lois et ordonnances de Belgique* 25 (1971–72): 215; Steurs, "Seigneurie et franchises dans le duché de Brabant au moyen âge: L'exemple de Dongelberg," in *Wavre 1222–1972: Colloque historique. Actes* (Wavre, 1973), p. 80; J. M. Cauchies, "Les chartes du village de Sirault (1239–1243)," *Annales du Cercle d'histoire et d'archéologie de Saint-Ghislain* 4 (1986):

113; Mariotte-Loeber (72), p. 16; Bonassie and Guichard (22), p. 85; Durand (135), pp. 208, 213; Fourquin (69), vol. 1, p. 483.

72. C. J. Joset, *Les villes au pays de Luxembourg, 1196-1383* (Brussels and Louvain, 1940), pp. 113, 116.

73. Sivery (9), pp. 329-37, is inclined to contrast two kinds of villages in Hainault: old ones, derived from the Carolingian *villa*, where the lord kept the upper hand, and new ones, resulting from reclamation, which enjoyed a liberal regime. Of course, the distinction fits old and "colonial" Germany.

74. Castagnetti (114), p. 239; Fournier (67), p. 226; C. Higounet, *Paysages et villages neufs du moyen âge* (Paris, 1975), pp. 245-54, 347-53; Grava (22), p. 193.

75. According to T. Evergates, *Feudal Society in the Bailliage of Troyes under the Counts of Champagne, 1152-1284* (Baltimore, 1975), pp. 46, 57, 138-39, the evolution was partially reversed in Champagne: the count granted charters until about 1250: before 1230, for economic aims; after 1230, for political aims. One wonders whether he thought only of profiting by the increasing mobility of the rural population and of preventing the setting up of the cities. On the point of economic aims, P. D. A. Harvey, "English Archaeology after the Conquest: A Historian's View," in *Twenty Years of Medieval Archaeology* (Sheffield, 1983), p. 77, rightly suggests discriminating towns and villages from "local markets, centers, which differed from villages in having among their inhabitants a substantial proportion of traders and craftsmen whose services would be drawn on by the privileges of the surrounding area."

76. Among many scholars, C. Petit-Dutaillis, *Les communes françaises* (Paris, 1947), p. 82, and G. Duby, *La société dans la région mâconnaise aux XIe et XIIe siècles*, (Paris, 1953), p. 601, defend the classical theory of the priority of urban concessions. But many others—like R. Grand, *Les paix d'Aurillac* (Paris, 1945), Introduction; J. M. Font-Rius, "Un problème de rapports: gouvernement urbain en France et en Catalogne (XIIe et XIIIe siècles)," *Annales du Midi* 69 (1957): 293-306; J. Yver, "Le droit privé des villes de l'Ouest de la France, spécialement des villes normandes," in *Recueil Jean Bodin*, Vol. 8. *La Ville: Le droit privé* (Brussels, 1957), p. 153—claim that the emancipation of the countryside was parallel to the enfranchisement of the towns.

77. Higounet and Ourliac (22), pp. 9, 19; other references are in Genicot (51), p. 101, and Genicot (47), vol. 3, p. 156.

78. Mayer (29), p. 471.

79. A charter of 1394 for Floriffoux, a small village near Namur, states that a part of it is declining because "icelle ville n'estoit poinct toute en franchise" (this village was not entirely enfranchised). Archives de l'État à Namur, Abbaye de Floreffe, no. 4, f. 147.

80. P. de Saint-Jacob, "Études sur l'ancienne communauté rurale en Bourgogne," *Annales de Bourgogne* 13 (1941): 186-87; Bader (77), vol. 1, p. 107; M. P. van Buytenen, *Het friese dorp in de middeleeuwen rechtshistorisch verkend* (Drachten, 1961); Gaier (43).

81. L. Verriest, "A qui ont bénéficié les 'chartes-lois' du moyen âge," *Tijdschrift voor Rechtsgeschiedenis* 5 (1924): 432-44.

82. C. G. Roland, *Recueil des chartes de l'abbaye de Gembloux* (Gembloux, 1921), pp. 68, 81; Genicot (47), vol. 3, p. 140.

83. Fossier (65), pp. 99-105; Mariotte-Loeber (72), p. x.

84. On these *cerocensuales*, too often confused with *servi*, see Genicot (47), vol. 3, pp. 238-47.

85. Ibid., pp. 247-53.

86. Leicht (123), p. 126; Aureggi (11), p. 226.
87. Castagnetti (114), pp. 241−43.
88. Jones (121), p. 402.
89. L. Genicot, in J. Gilissen, *La coutume, Typologie des sources du moyen âge occidental* (Turnhout, 1982), 69−73; *Deutsche ländliche Rechtsquellen: Probleme und Wege der Weistumsforschung,* ed. P. Blickle (Stuttgart, 1977). In England, the customs were preserved in the memories of the people; where they were written down, it was, according to Miller and Hatcher (103), p. 104, because the lord hoped to reshape them as he wished.
90. Archives de l'État à Namur, Commune de Loyers, Histoire et administration.
91. G. Despy, *Les campagnes du Roman Pays de Brabant au moyen âge: la terre de Jauche aux XIVe et XVe siècles* (Louvain, 1981), notes that the records delivered by the aldermen assigned to the lord some taxes which were not, or were no longer, levied.
92. Hilton (96), pp. 159−61; Z. Razi, "The Struggle between the Abbots of Halesowen and Their Tenants in the Thirteenth and Fourteenth Centuries," in *Social Relations and Ideas: Essays in Honour of R. H. Hilton* (Cambridge, 1983), pp. 151−67.
93. Ourliac (22), p. 19.
94. Hilton, *Economic Development of Some Leicestershire Estates,* p. 75.
95. The debate on the English economy in the thirteenth century and its social effects was opened by M. M. Postan in 1937 and continued in the *Cambridge Economic History of Europe,* vol. 2, ch. 4 (Cambridge, 1952); it was pursued by A. R. Bridbury, *Economic Growth: England in the Later Middle Ages* (London, 1962), and was evaluated by B. Lyon, "Encore le problème de la chronologie des corvées," *Le Moyen Âge* 69 (1963): 615−30, and by E. Miller, "The English Economy in the 13th Century: Implications of Recent Researches," *Past and Present,* no. 28 (1964): 21−40.
96. R. H. Hilton, "Social Structure of Rural Warwickshire in the Middle Ages," *Dugdale Society Occasional Paper* 9 (1950), reprinted in (95). But Hilton (96), pp. 135, 159, also speaks of the thirteenth century as witnessing "a slow erosion of the personal status of the peasants and the increase of their services by the joint pressure of the lords' and kings' courts." This statement would also be appropriate for the later Middle Ages.
97. Pallares Mendez and Portela Silva (137), p. 59; Mattoso, "Senhorias monasticas do Norte de Portugal nos séculos XI a XIII," in (133), pp. 175−82; Bonassie and Guichard (22), p. 89.
98. P. de Beaumanoir, *Coutumes de Clermont en Beauvaisis,* ed. P. Salmon (Paris, 1900), p. 227; B. Huppertz, *Raüme und Schichten bauerlicher Kulturformen in Deutschland* (Bonn, 1933), p. 231. Genicot (47), vol. 3, p. 214 distinguishes "real" serfdom, based on breathing the lord's air (*Luft macht eigen*) or on the exploitation of a field or of a type of field, and gives many references.
99. Among the studies, see P. Kriedte, "Spatmittelalterliche Agrarkrise oder Krise des Feudalismus," *Geschichte und Gesellschaft* 7 (1981): 42−68; R. Brenner, "The Agrarian Roots of European Capitalism," *Past and Present* 97 (1982): 16−133.
100. Thoen (52), pp. 1063−89, shows that for Flanders.
101. Duby (5), pp. 482−83, 576−80; Hilton (95); Blaschke (12), p. 82 (for Germany); J. L. Salch, "Réactions seigneuriales, banalités et vie économique du château alsacien au bas moyen âge," in (133), p. 186; Rotelli (127), p. 157; R. Pastor, *Resistencias y luchas campesinas en la época del crecimiento y consolidación de la formación feudal: Castilla y León, siglos X−XIII* (Madrid, 1980); Bonassie and Guichard (22), p. 111 (for the Kingdom of Valence); Portela Silva (139), p. 325 (for Galicia); M. Berthe, "Taux et évolution du prélèvement seigneurial en Navarre aux XIVe et XVe

siècles: le cas du domaine royal," in (140), p. 74 (the taxes were fixed but, as they were collective, they weighed more heavily because of depopulation). For Île de France, G. Fourquin, *Les campagnes de la région parisienne à la fin du moyen âge* (Paris, 1964), p. 189, and for the county of Namur, Genicot (47), vol. 3, p. 115, do not set forth such a deterioration of the manorial regime; for Flanders, Thoen (52), p. 1037, does not see a demographic or economic collapse. On the "agrarian crisis of the Middle Ages," its factors and effects, see Genicot (45).

102. P. Grossi, *Locatio ad longum tempus: Locazione e rapporti reali di godimento nella problematica del diritto comune* (Naples, 1963), explains that concessions were perpetual because civilization privileged property. But this concept did not only characterize the rural regime; it had general bearing and deeper roots: for the people of the Middle Ages, everything, every structure, was conceived as perpetual.

103. Blickle and Haverkamp (81), vol. 1, p. 244; vol. 2, p. 341.

104. Thoen (102), p. 1056: these *tenures révocables* appeared in the late thirteenth century.

105. Harvey (92).

106. C. Howell, "Peasant Inheritance Customs in the Midlands 1200–1700," in *Family and Inheritance: Rural Society in Western Europe, 1200–1800*, ed. J. Goody, J. Thirsk, and E. P. Thompson (Cambridge, 1976), p. 133.

107. Montanari (125), p. 94.

108. G. Piccinni, "In merito a recenti studi sulla mezzadria nella Toscana medievale," *Bullettino Senese di Storia Patria* 99 (1982): 336–52. Herlihy and Klapisch-Zuber (120), p. 271, calculate that, in the *contado* of Florence, the *mezzadri* in four parishes still increased from 25.3 percent of the families in 1427 to 29.6 percent of the families in 1469.

109. Jones (121), p. 237.

110. Herlihy and Klapisch-Zuber (120), p. 278.

111. W. Roesener, "Grundherrschaften des Hochadels in Südwestdeutschland im Spätmittelalter," in (81), vol. 2, pp. 87–176, esp. 169; Blickle, Last, and Haverkamp (81), vol. 1, pp. 253, 429; vol. 2, p. 330; H. H. Maurer, "Masseneide gegen Abwanderung im 14 Jahrhundert," *Zeitschrift für Würtembergische Landesgeschichte* (1980): 30–99.

112. Menzel and Prange (81), vol. 1, pp. 547, 600.

113. Jones (121), p. 246; Pastor, *Resistencias y luchas*, proves that the lord dominated peasants and communities in the late Middle Ages.

114. Castagnetti (114), pp. 242–43; Leicht (123), p. 146.

115. H. von Voltelini, "Der Gedanke der allgemeinen Freiheit in den deutschen Rechtsbüchern," *Zeitschrift der Savigny-Stiftung für Rechtsgeschichte, Germanistische Abteilung* 57 (1937): 182–209.

116. E. A. Serrarrens, "Kommunisme in de Middelnederlandsche Letterkunde," *Tijdschrift voor Taal en Letteren* 16 (1928): 87.

117. Hilton (93), pp. 120–21.

118. Thoen (52), p. 1052; J. P. Cuvillier, *L'Allemagne médiévale*, vol. 2 (Paris, 1984), p. 424.

119. Ourliac (22), p. 19.

120. J. R. Madicott, "The English Peasantry and the Demands of the Crown, 1294–1341," *Past and Present*, suppl. no. 1, (1975).

121. Thoen (52), p. 1053.

122. The theories on the phenomenon in all aspects are summed up in Genicot (45).

123. Wunder (85), p. 77.

124. Genicot, "Formorture et mortemain dans le comté de Namur aprés 1431," in *Études d'histoire et d'archéologie namuroises F. Courtoy* (Gembloux, 1952), p. 504; G. Lizerand, *Le régime rural de l'ancienne France* (Paris, 1942), pp. 66–69. The same measure had been taken in 1364 in the land of Saint-Hubert, in the Ardennes, as may be seen in *Bulletin de l'Institut archéologique liégeois* 7 (1865): 513. For Provence, J. A. Durbec, "Les villages du Val de Chanan du XIe au XVe siècle," in *Bulletin philologique et historique (jusqu'en 1610), du comité des travaux historiques et scientifiques: Section de Philologie et Histoire, (1965)* (Paris, 1968), p. 99.

125. Ourliac (22), p. 20.

126. For Spain, J. Valdéon, "Tensions sociales en los siglos XIV y XV," and J. García Oro, "La nobleza gallega en el siglo XV," both (133), pp. 257–79 and 293–99, respectively; for Berry, see Michaud-Frejaville (22), p. 215; for England, Hilton (94), p. 68, notes that the crises chiefly occurred on the accession of new seignorial families.

127. G. Fourquin, *Les soulèvements populaires au moyen âge* (Paris, 1972). This essay, which is at variance with Marxist views, has been challenged, for instance by J. Baerten in *Handelingen der Koninklijke Zuidnederlandsche Maatschappij voor Taal en Letterkunde en Geschiedenis* 30 (1976): 5–16.

128. S. Epperlein, *Bauernbedrückung und Bauernwiderstand im hohen Mittelalter* (Berlin, 1960), p. 46. Less clear is the passage of the "Vita Wicberti," composed in 1071–99 and published in *Monumenta Germaniae Historica, Scriptores,* vol. 8, p. 515, which narrates that, informed of the taking away of the saint's relics, the inhabitants of Gorze, in Lorraine, "facto grege perstrepunt populari more" (flocked together and shouted as people do).

129. "Historia Walciodorensis monasterii," in *Monumenta Germaniae Historica, Scriptores,* vol. 15, p. 926; other instances are in Genicot (47), vol. 3, p. 43.

130. B. A. Slicher van Bath, "Drente's Vrijheid," *Bydragen voor de Geschiedenis der Nederlanden* 1 (1946): 170–71; Razi, "Struggle between the Abbots."

131. Hilton (96), pp. 154–56, using the court rolls; Fourquin, *Les soulèvements populaires,* referring to R. Caggese and his researches on the kingdom of Naples under Robert I (1309–43).

132. Marxist historians reject the classification into passive and active resistance. Porchnew (75), p. 63, rightly argues that there is no passive resistance and proposes to distinguish partial opposition, in the form of not performing a work or not paying a tax or violating some custom in order to get some mitigation of the regime, from emigration, which implies a rejection of the whole system, and from collective violence, which aims to destroy it. In any case, one ought not to interpret as manifestations of class warfare, as does Epperlein, *Bauernbedrückung und Bauernwiderstand,* the inclusion of securities in contracts of landed property, the insertion of an obligation to perform such and such a cultural operation in the leases, the "flight" movement to the towns or to Eastern Europe, or the abandonment of fields. All these things might be partly or entirely the result of other motives than social struggles.

133. Levett (102), p. 203, for the thirteenth century.

134. Charter of 1148 in J. Halkin and C. G. Roland, *Chartes de Stavelot-Malmédy* (Brussels, 1909), vol. 1, p. 420.

135. Perrin (33), pp. 188–89, 608–15, 620, for the twelfth century.

136. R. Boutruche, *La crise d'une société: Seigneurs et paysans du Bordelais pendant la Guerre de Cent Ans,* 2d ed. (Paris, 1965), p. 124.

137. G. C. Coulton, *The Medieval Village* (Cambridge, 1925), p. 130; A. Palmieri, "Lotte agrarie bolognesi nei secoli XIII e XIV," in *Atti e memorie della Regia Deputazione di*

storia patria per la provincia di Romagna (1923), vol. 43, pp. 7–23; S. Epperlein, "Bündnisse zwischen Bauern und Bürgern in Nordwestdeutschland im 13.Jahrhundert," *Jahrbuch für Wirtschaftsgeschichte* 1 (1962): 69; B. A. Slicher van Bath, *Boerenvrijheid* (Groningen, 1948), for Frisia.

138. Hilton (93), p. 119.
139. On the debated question of the aims and results of the *"Alliance perpétuelle,"* see G. Wirz, *Quellenwerk zur Entstehung der schweizerischen Eidgenossenschaft,* 3d sec. vol. 1 (Aarau, 1947).
140. Bonassie (134), p. 649; C. Gaier, "Analysis of Military Forces in the Principality of Liège from the Twelfth to the Fifteenth Century," *Studies in Medieval and Renaissance History* 2 (1965): 205–61.
141. Hilton (93), p. 116.
142. Blickle (81), vol. 1, pp. 244–48; Razi, "Struggle between the Abbots," p. 163; Searle (109), p. 400.
143. M. Mollat and P. Wolff, *The Popular Revolutions of the Late Middle Ages* (London, 1973). On the much debated Rising of 1381, see Hilton (94); C. Dyer in *The English Rising of 1381,* ed., R. H. Hilton and T. H. Aston (Cambridge, 1984); and J. A. Raftis, "Social Change versus Revolution: New Interpretations of the Peasants' Revolt of 1381," in *Social Unrest in the Late Middle Ages,* ed. F. X. Newman (Binghamton, 1986).
144. R. Pastor, *Conflictos sociales y estancamiento económico en la España medieval* (Barcelona, 1973), a reprint of articles published in various reviews, access to which is difficult. Nau (81), vol. 1, p. 113, notes that in Germany riots were confined to the towns until the eve of modern times. It might be more correct to say that the Empire did not suffer in the late Middle Ages from rebellions comparable with the "Jacquerie," for instance. P. Bierbauer, "Revolten im alten Reich: Ein Forschungsbericht," in *Aufruhr und Emporung: Studien zum bäuerlichen Widerstand im Alten Reich,* ed. P. Blickle (1980), pp. 1–68, mentions sixty riots during that period.
145. M. Mollat, "La réaction des pauvres à la pauvreté en France au bas moyen âge," in *Aspects of Poverty in Early Modern Europe,* ed. T. Riis (Odense, 1986), p. 84.
146. Bonassie (75), p. 47.
147. Wunder (85), p. 75.
148. *Cantatorium Sancti Huberti,* ed. K. Hanquet (Brussels, 1906), pp. 39, 103; D. Misonne, *Eilbert de Florennes. Histoire et légende* (Louvain, 1967), p. 216.
149. Klingelhofer (99), p. 193.
150. *Cantatorium Sancti Huberti,* p. 226.
151. Castagnetti (114), p. 221.
152. Wunder (85), pp. 44–45.
153. R. Jacob, "Sur la formation des justices villageoises au XIIe siècle dans la France du Nord," in (34), p. 97, advances, on the basis of evidence from Hesdin, in Artois, original views on the origins of *jurati* and *scabini:* according to him, the *jurati* preceded the *scabini,* and there was no continuity between the Carolingian *scabini* and the *scabini* of the eleventh or twelfth century. This thesis should be based on fuller evidence.
154. M. Walraet, "La charte-loi de Beaumont-en-Argonne," *Le Pays Gaumais* 3 (1942): 21–27. Other instances for Lorraine and Hainault are in C. E. Perrin, "Chartes de franchise et rapports de droits en Lorraine," *Le Moyen Âge* 42 (1946): 15. Cauchies (30), p. 196, contests the traditional interpretation of the "Loi de Beaumont"; for him, it only granted to the burghers the right of being consulted and of approving the lord's choice of their officials.
155. Bader (77), vol. 3, p. 349, mentions other kinds of nomination: joint choice by

lord and community, choice by the community submitted to the lord's agreement, and co-optation. Here as in many matters, diversity reigned. Arnould (12), p. 301, presents, for instance, two special regimes. In Saint-Simphorien, in Hainault, the two lords designated only the first alderman. In Comines, on the margin of Flanders, the lord agreed in 1390 to appoint henceforward only two aldermen, who would co-opt a third one, and the three would co-opt the fourth one, and so on. The length of the charge also varied: one year, three years, for life.

156. To judge some cases *touchant à le loy*, the aldermen of Biesmes, in the county of Namur, summoned the elders "tels et en tele quantiteit que bon leur semble de la dicte ville et franchise" (such and as numerous as it seems good to them of the said village and franchise), in J. Roland, "Les coutumes de Biesme la Colonoise," *Anciens Pays et Assemblées d' États* 83 (1966): 109.

157. van der Linden (12), p. 479.

158. Archives de l'État à Namur, Fonds Corroy, 1641, charter of 1288; L. Genicot et R. M. Allard, "Sources du droit rural du Quartier d'Entre Sambre et Meuse," *Coutumes du Pays de Liege* 5 (1981): 532.

159. Mariotte-Loeber (72), p. 30.

160. To designate the master and spokesman of the community, a charter of 1279 quoted by Nikolay-Panter (83), p. 169, uses the word *centurio:* "honesti milites, nobiles, centuriones, maiores per quos regitur universitas ville."

161. On the *jurés*, see Genicot (47), vol. 3, p. 354; on the "Heimbürger," Wunder (12), pp. 28–35.

162. Klingelhofer (99), p. 113.

163. Mayer (29), pp. 478–81, explains and discusses the theses of Dopsch, Steinbach, O. Brunner, and Bader.

164. Wunder (85), p. 75.

165. Dollinger (79), p. 10.

166. Ault (87), p. 75: "In a good many vills, one third in some regions, the landholders were not tenants of the same lord and there was therefore no one manor court which all must attend. It is wellnigh impossible to find how the inhabitants managed their affairs under an open-field system of agriculture."

167. Roland, "Les coutumes," p. 110, charter of 1414.

168. Hilton (96), p. 151.

169. Fried, "Grundherrschaft und Dorfgericht im spatmittelalterlichen Herzogtum Bayern," in (81), vol. 2, p. 307.

170. Bader (77), vol. 2, p. 285; Fossier (22), p. 42; Ault (87), p. 58. An expression frequently used in French language charters of the late Middle Ages is ambiguous: *bonnes gens* (good men) may apply to a select group who, for instance, attested the custom or checked official accounts, or it may apply to the whole people: "bonnes gens, asscavoir maieur, eschevins, mannans, surséans et habitans de nos villes," Genicot (47), vol. 3, p. 353; and Archives de l'État à Namur, Échevinage d'Anhée, no. 3, p. 197, privilège of 1392.

171. Wunder (85), pp. 45–47.

172. Buchda (12), p. 67; Ault (87), p. 65.

173. Genicot (47), vol. 3, p. 189.

174. Arnould (12), p. 299.

175. The lord frequently intervened in the designation of all or some minor officials, especially when they were concerned with the management of the landed properties; see n. 182.

176. Hilton (94), p. 90; Raftis (107), p. 111; Wunder (85), pp. 13, 45.

177. Fried (81), p. 304.

178. Wunder (85), pp. 72-73.
179. Archives de l'État à Namur, Cure de Treignes.
180. Ault (87), pp. 59-60; Hilton (22), pp. 120-23.
181. Wunder (85), p. 74, notes that the lord kept control of the *Allmende.*
182. Bader (77), vol. 2, p. 365, puts forth that the part played by the community was proportional to the rank of the officials: the community took a larger part in the appointment of lower officials. According to a charter of 1343 quoted by Nikolay-Panter (83), pp. 180-181, the *universitas* proposed three "homines probati et fide digni" to the lord, who chose one of them. In 1392, by a charter for Vedrin, near Namur (a copy of which is preserved in the Archives de l'État à Namur, Fonds Brouwers), the Count of Namur "concède de grace espécial amendes et droitures touchant aux aysements" (grants by special grace, fines, and rights relating to the commons) and the privilege of electing a warden and two managers of the commons.
183. Fournier (29), p. 244.
184. Ault (87), p. 58; Dollinger (78), p. 385.
185. E. Cam, *Liberties and Communities of Medieval England* (Cambridge, 1933), p. 134; Wunder (85), p. 75; Michaud-Frejaville (22), p. 220.
186. Poumarède (11), p. 313; G. Mor, "Universitates vallis," *Revue historique de droit français et étranger* (1957): 449.
187. Bonassie and Guichard (22), pp. 85-92; for Portugal, where the king retained his authority over his officials but, from the twelfth century, was obliged for financial reasons to concede a charter of immunity to the nobility and to religious institutions—so paving the way to "seignoralization" in the thirteenth century, see R. Durand, *Les campagnes portugaises entre Duoro et Tage aux XIIe et XIIIe siècles* (Paris, 1982).
188. M. del Carmen Carle, *Del concejo medieval castillano-leonés* (Buenos Aires, 1968).
189. Aureggi (11), p. 226; Castagnetti (114), pp. 243-44.
190. Sinatti d'Amico (11), p. 200; Jones (121), p. 245; O. Redon, "Seigneurs et communautés rurales dans la seconde moitié du XIIIe siècle," *Mélanges de l'École française de Rome: Moyen Âge et Temps modernes* 91 (1979): 651-53.
191. Ourliac and Grava (11), pp. 21, 191-96.
192. Boutin and Gramain (11), pp. 363-71, 43.
193. Wunder (85), p. 77.
194. To the instances given in n. 101, add van der Linden (12), p. 482, for Holland.
195. Blaschke (12), p. 82.
196. Hilton (96), p. 161.

4. PAROCHIA: RELIGIOUS ASPECTS

1. Fournier (41), p. 507. On the problems raised by the history of the parish, see G. Le Bras, "Pour l'étude de la paroisse rurale," *Revue d'histoire de l'Église de France* 23 (1937): 486-502, reprinted in *Études de sociologie religieuse* (Paris, 1955), vol. 1, pp. 104-14.
2. G. Duby, *La société aux XIe et XIIe siècles dans la région mâconnaise* (Paris, 1963), pp. 286-89. J. Le Goff and P. Toubert, "Une histoire sociale du moyen âge est-elle possible," in *Centième congrès national des Sociétés savantes (Paris 1975)* (Paris, 1977). Violante (41), in a more moderate way, calls the parish a *spia* in the rural setting.
3. van der Linden (12), p. 487. The three pleas are the *placita generalia* studied on p. 70.

4. Charter of 1131 in Miraeus and Foppens, *Opera diplomatica et historica* (Louvain, 1723), vol. 1, p. 383.

5. Becquet (37), p. 203.

6. Ibid., pp. 202–03, 213; Homans (98), p. 383; Miller and Hatcher (103), p. 108. According to G. Duby, *Le Moyen Âge: Histoire de France Hachette* (Paris, 1987), p. 83, the struggle against heresy in the early eleventh century was another motive for stating precisely the parochial boundaries.

7. Taylor (111), p. 120; Miller and Hatcher (103), p. 107; W. Neuss and F. W. Oediger, *Geschichte des Erzbistums Köln* (Cologne, 1964), vol. 1, p. 282: the division of dioceses into parishes became clear about 1200; J. Mattoso, *Portugal Medieval: Novas interpretaciōnes* (Lisbon, 1983); the determination of the parishes' boundaries drew to a close only in the early fourteenth century.

8. Parisse (37), p. 569: few churches were erected in the diocese of Toul during the twelfth century because of disputes between bishops and lords.

9. Kurze (37), p. 232.

10. Fournier (66), pp. 453–56; Fournier (22), p. 475.

11. In 1249, "a proborum concilio et investiti instructus" (instructed by the advice of honest men and of the curate), the chapter of Saint-Aubain in Namur obtained the partition of the parish of Biesme into two parishes, to take into account the distance from Biesme to Oret: Archives de l'État à Namur, Fonds Brouwers, Records.

12. Wunder (85), pp. 62–63; Bonassie and Guichard (22), p. 81.

13. Kurze (37), p. 233; for Spain, Orlandis (37), p. 268.

14. *Annales de la Société archéologique de Namur*, vol. 31, p. 41.

15. Toubert (130), p. 855; A. Castagnetti, *La pieve rurale nell' Italia padana* (Rome, 1976), p. 13; but Fournier (66), p. 474, states that the castles did not much modify the parochial map, which had been definitively drawn by the end of the tenth century.

16. Violante (41), pp. 1151–53.

17. Becquet (37), p. 206.

18. Violante (41), p. 1125.

19. Becquet (37), p. 202.

20. Klingelhofer (99), pp. 329, 351; Miller and Hatcher (103), p. 107: in northern England, extensive parishes were served by a sole minister and they survived; Maccarone (37), pp. 81–95; Fournier (66), p. 460.

21. A. Dierkens, "Note sur un passage de la Vita Dagoberti: Dagobert II et le domaine de Biesme," *Revue belge de philologie et d'histoire* 62 (1984): 268.

22. Grand Séminaire de Namur, no. 30, folio 90.

23. See n. 20; Aubrun (56), p. 162.

24. Genicot (51), pp. 91–92.

25. Genicot (50), p. 9.

26. Kurze (37), p. 251, writes that the parishes in Germany are generally bigger than the communal entities and that many *Landgemeinden* had "kein religiös intergrierender moment" (the commune did not exert an integrating action in religious field); thus Blaschke (12), p. 86, for Saxony. See nevertheless below, n. 31.

27. Van der Linden (12), pp. 480, 487.

28. Moorman (104), p. 12.

29. Castagnetti (114), p. 337.

30. Feine (29), p. 77, emphasizes "wie eng kirchliche und weltliche Gemeindebildung zusammen hängen nicht nur in der gemeinsamen Wurzel sondern auch im

weiteren Verlauf der Jahrhunderte. Beide gehen als Kirchspiel und Gerichtsverband Hand in Hand."

31. Moorman (104), p. 92; A. Chèdeville, *Chartres et ses campagnes* (Paris, 1973), p. 79; de la Roncière (9), p. 70.

32. Portela Silva (13), p. 219.

33. Charter from 1269 for the church of Ben-Ahin, near Huy, in Genicot (47), vol. 3, p. 256.

34. Becquet (37), p. 214, observes that Rome defended the liberty of a dying person to choose his burial place, that an indemnity might sometimes be due to the local church, and that funeral and burial did not necessarily coincide.

35. Cartulaire du Ronceroy d'Angers, quoted in (37), p. 224.

36. Maccarone (126), p. 117, notes that the omission of preaching was not explicitly sanctioned by Canon 10 of the Lateran Council, so that Ostiensis, for instance, did not include it in the major sins to be confessed by a parish priest. In the same volume, p. 499, Zafarana observes that the synodal statutes did not emphasize the obligation and that the knowledge of religion grew *come per osmosi*. As for the respect accorded to these statutes, see O. Pontal, *Les statutes synodaux*, vol. 11, *Typologie des sources du moyen âge occidental* (1975), pp. 44–50.

37. No, says Moorman (104), p. 76; yes, says D. W. Robertson, "Frequency of Preaching in Thirteenth-century England," *Speculum* 24 (1949): 376–88.

38. Robertson, "Frequency of Preaching," 380; A. Lecoy de la Marche, *La chaire française au moyen âge, spécialement au XIIIe siècle*, 2d ed. (Paris, 1886), p. 276.

39. Popular religion is a favorite theme of research today, but it is not dealt with here. On this subject, see R. Manselli, *La religion populaire au moyen âge: Problèmes de méthode et d'histoire* (Montréal, 1975); and my remarks on this book in *Revue d'histoire ecclésiastique* 71 (1976): 470–74. The French GRECO launched in 1988 a set of *Répertoires bibliographiques* on *La piété populaire en France*.

40. O. Dobiache-Rodjdestvensky, *La vie paroissiale en France au XIIIe siècle d'après les actes épiscopaux* (Paris, 1911), p. 89.

41. The communion could be material: the cemetery was often inhabited and used for feasts, markets, and so on. See L. Musset, "Le cimetière dans la vie paroissiale en Basse-Normandie (XIe–XIIIe siècle)," *Cahiers Léopold Delisle* 19 (1963): 7–27; P. Duparc, "Le cimetière séjour des vivants (XIe–XIIIe siècles)," *Bulletin philologique et historique (jusqu'en 1610) du Comité des travaux historiques et scientifiques* (1964): 492–93.

42. C. D. Fonseca, *La tradizione commerorativa nel Mezzogiorno medievale: ricerche e problemi* (Galatina, 1984); *L'Élise et la mémoire des morts dans la France Médiévale*, ed. J. L. Lamaitre (Paris, 1986); *Memoria: Der geschichtliche Zeugniswert des liturgischen Gedenkens im Mittelalter*, ed. K. Schmid and J. Wollasch (Munich, 1984).

43. Genicot (50), p. 71.

44. Archives de l'État à Namur, Archives ecclésiastiques, no. 1930; Registre des biens et rentes de l'Église de Boneffe, f. 10 v'.

45. A charter of 1235 published by S. Bormans and E. Schoolmeesters, *Cartulaire de l'Église Saint-Lambert de Liège* (Brussels, 1893), vol. 1, p. 340, narrates that "in plena parochia apud Viler [Villers-l'Évêque, near Liège], presentibus multis militibus, sinodalibus, viris et mulieribus," the knight Lambert l'Ardenois transferred to the chapter of Saint-Martin in Liège a field and a tithe, which he had claimed.

46. J. Schneider, "Le synode paroissial en Lorraine à la fin du moyen âge," in (64), pp. 179–95.

47. *Analectes pour servir à l'histoire ecclésiastique de Belgique*, vol. 11, p. 474.

48. D. Lambrecht, "De parochiale synode in het oud bisdom Doornik gesitueerd in de Europese ontwikkeling, 11e-eeuw–1559," *Verhandelingen van de Koninklijke Academie van België, Klasse der Letteren* 46 (1984).
49. N. J. Coulet, "Les visites pastorales," vol. 23 *Typologie des source du moyen âge occidental* (1977), and mise a jour, 1985; on the disappearance of the synod, see J. Avril, *Le gouvernement des évêgues et la vie religieuse dans le diocèse d'Angers (1148–1240)* (Lille and Paris, 1983), p. 642.
50. In passing, it may be added that, in Flanders and on its borders, the synod was in competition with a lay court called *Franches vérités,* lately studied by M. A. Arnould, "Les 'franches vérités' à Chièvres," *Bulletin de l'Institut archéologique liégeois* 98 (1986): 15–30.
51. A. Uyttebrouck, "L'entretien des enfants trouvés à Jauchelette (Brabant wallon) au XIIIe et au XVIIe siècle," in *La Belgique rurale du moyen âge à nos jours: Mélanges J. J. Hoebanx* (Brussels, 1985), p. 235. The correlation established by the texts between parish and village is significant.
52. L. Genicot "Une paroisse namuroise à la fin du moyen âge," *Revue d'histoire ecclesiastique* 80 (1985): 694; Touchard (9), p. 343, gives the figure of ten percent indigents, "noyau constant et irréductible," in rural Brittany at the end of the Middle Ages.
53. L. Genicot, "Sur le nombre des pauvres dans les campagnes namuroises. L'exemple du Namurois," *Revue historique* 257 (1977): 286.
54. Genicot (47), vol. 3, p. 278; M. Mollat, *Les Pauvres au moyen âge* (Paris, 1978); G. O. Oexle, "Armut und Armenfürsorge um 1200," in *Sankt Elisabeth* (Sigmaringen, 1981), pp. 71–100, supplements Mollat's work by reference to German studies.
55. C. Dereine, *Les chanoines réguliers au diocèse de Liège avant saint Norbert* (Brussels, 1952), p. 238.
56. Adam (55), p. 83. For a large city, P. de Spiegeleer, *Les hôpitaux et l'assistance publique à Liège (Xe–XVe siècle): Aspects institutionnels et sociaux* (Paris, 1987), states that municipality intervened in only one of the fifteen hospitals.
57. E. Lesne, *Histoire de la propriété ecclésiastique en France,* vol. 5, *Les écoles de la fin du VIIe siècle à la fin du XIe* (Paris, 1940), p. 420.
58. Moorman (104), pp. 104–05; Arnould (12), p. 330.
59. Moorman (104), p. 240; W. Goering, "The changing face of the village parish: pt. 2, The thirteenth century," in (10), p. 322.
60. Genicot (50), p. 116.
61. Archives de l'État à Namur, Cure de Treignes; ibid., Cure de Boneffe, no. 3, 12 v'.
62. Ibid.
63. Genicot (50), p. 95.
64. Archives de l'État à Namur, Cure de Gelbressée, no. 5. I say "probably," because the 15 percent includes a gift of an unknown amount from two parishioners.
65. P. Desportes, "Le clergé des campagnes champenoises à la fin du XIVe siècle d'après les registres de la fiscalité pontificale," *Revue d'histoire de l'Église de France* 62 (1986): 19–47.
66. Moorman (104), p. 154. The situation improved after 1300.
67. Cherubini (126), pp. 351–413.
68. For Rapp (11), p. 467, the local priest did not enjoy much support from his flock; de la Roncière (9), p. 72, and Cherubini (126) emphasize, on the contrary, his "popularity" and his "good integration into the rural community"; Olland (73), p. 499, shows the close links with the peasantry of curates and vicars, who were in most cases of peasant birth.

69. Moorman (104), p. 245.

70. On the use of literary sources, Cherubini, "Il mondo contadino nella novellistica italiana dei secoli XIV e XV," in (124), pp. 420–23, gives valuable information on method. Interesting, also, in that way is M. De Comarieu, *Image et représentation du vilain dans les chansons de gestes: Exclus et systèmes d'exclusion dans la littérature et la civilization médiévales* (Aix-en-Provence, 1978).

71. N. Coulet, *Les visites pastorales*, in *Typologie des sources du moyen âge occidental* (1985), mise à jour (1985), 5–7. According to Gaudemet (70), vol. 3, p. 163; and M. Gibbs and J. Lang, *Bishops and Reform, 1215–1272* (Oxford, 1934), p. 145, the visitations were too irregular in the thirteenth century to regenerate the clergy. For Moorman (104), p. 191, they were conducted seriously and efficiently.

72. Cherubini, "Parrochie e popolo nelle campagne dell'Italia centro-settentrionale alla fine del medioevo," in (126), pp. 353–413, examines the relation between vicar and parishioners under all aspects and states that it was "molto stretto ma tutt'altro che facile," especially in economic affairs.

73. On the secular activities of the parochial clergy, see Le Bras (30), pp. 407, 410, n. 21.

74. K. De Vries, "Les lignes de faîte du droit urbain frison au moyen âge," *Revue du Nord*, 48 (1966): 102–03.

75. D. van Overstraeten, "Les paroisses rurales en Hainaut au moyen âge d'après les archives de l'abbaye de Saint-Ghislain," *Recueil d'études d'histoire hainuyère offertes à M. A. Arnould, Analectes d'histoire du Hainaut* 1 (1983): 511.

76. Genicot (47), vol. 2, p. 301.

77. Castagnetti (114), pp. 265–66; R. Byl, *Les juridictions échevinales dans le duché de Brabant* (Brussels, 1965), p. 227, analyzes an agreement, concluded in 1298 by the Duke of Brabant and the Lord of Grimbergen, providing that the rector would make known the days of inspection of highways and streams.

78. R. Foreville, *Latran I, II, III et Latran IV (Histoire des conciles oecuméniques)*, vol. 6 (Paris, 1965), p. 357; Gaier (43), pp. 758–59.

79. Homans (98), p. 352, advances the theory that traditional celebrations marking turning points in the farming year approximately coincided with the cycle of ecclesiastical feasts.

80. Aureggi (11), p. 227.

81. L. J. van Appeldoorn, *De kerkelijke goederen in Friesland* (Utrecht, 1915), vol. 1, p. 5.

82. Bader (77), vol. 2, p. 204.

83. Ganghofer (11), p. 54.

84. Violante (41), pp. 1043, 1066, 1093.

85. G. Mollat, "La restitution des églises privées au patrimoine ecclésiastique en France du IXe au XIe siècle," *Revue d'histoire de l'Église de France*, 4th series (1949): 339–423; Orlandis (37), p. 268.

86. Gaudemet et al. (70), p. 205.

87. G. Mollat, "Le droit de patronage en Normandie du XIe au XIVe siècle," *Revue d'histoire ecclésiastique* 33 (1973): 465.

88. D. W. Sabean, *Landbesitz und Gesellschaft am Vorabend des Bauerkriesges* (Stuttgart, 1972), pp. 83–84.

89. *Annales de la Société archéologique de Namur* 32 (1913): 26.

90. Violante (41), p. 1109.

91. Ibid.

92. Le Bras (38), p. 155; S. Schroecker, *Das Kirchenpflegrecht* (Padeborn, 1934), pp. 70–79; M. Gramain, "Les institutions charitables dans les villages du Bitterois aux

XIIe et XIIIe siècles," in (64), p. 114, notes that from the twelfth century the parishioners or some of them took part in the management of the properties of the church.

93. Moorman (104), p. 143; C. Drew, *Early Parochial Organisation* (London, 1954).

94. Bader (77), vol. 2, p. 205; Wunder (12), p. 33; Ault (87), p. 54.

95. Archives de l'État à Namur, Cure de Treignes.

96. Arnould (12), p. 299.

97. The classic work is G. G. Meerseeman, *Ordo Fraternitatis: Confraternite e pietà dei laici nel medioevo,* 3 vols. (Rome, 1977).

98. Fossier (8), p. 175.

99. For brotherhoods as frameworks to dominate the common people, see Fossier (7), p. 364; as a means of rising in society, see Zardin (131), p. 247; as a social and political organization, see Hilton (22), p. 121.

100. Charles de la Roncière, "Les confréries en Toscane—Florence et sa campagne— aux XIVe et XVe siècles d'après les travaux récents," *Ricerche per la storia religiosa di Roma* 5 (1974): 50–64; Zardin (131); Genicot, "Une paroisse namuroise."

101. R. Boutruche, *La crise d'une société: Société et paysans du Bordelais pendant la Guerre de Cent ans* (Paris, 1947), p. 124.

102. G. le Bras, "Les confréries chrétiennes," *Revue historique de droit francais et étranger,* 4th series (1940/42): 310; Rapp (40), p. 141.

103. de la Roncière (9), p. 73; Zafarina (126), p. 535; for Belgium, Genicot, "Une paroisse namuroise."

104. According to Adam (55), p. 35, the entry tax was generally high. In this paragraph, I present the conclusions of my monograph on Floreffe, which is confirmed by other studies.

105. See also Zardin (131), pp. 70, 245.

106. Rapp (40), p. 128, forwards the theory that the confraternities brought together the poor and isolated people, who combined their meager means to pay for funeral and prayers.

107. P. Duparc, "Confréries du Saint-Esprit et communautés d'habitants au moyen âge," *Revue historique de droit francais et étranger,* 4th series, 36 (1958): 349–68, 555–85.

108. Thesis of Grava (22), p. 194.

109. Genicot, "Une paroisse namuroise," pp. 710–01; Sivery (9), p. 332.

110. Archives de l'État à Namur, Archives ecclésiastiques, no. 604, f. 54 v'.

111. N. Coulet, "Les visites pastorales," p. 31.

112. Archives de l'État à Namur, Fonds Brouwers, Record pour Oret.

113. Term used in a charter of 1187 for a community in Alsace analyzed by Kurze (37), p. 48.

114. *Analectes pour servir à l'histoire ecclésiastique de Belgique,* 2d sec. fasc. 6, p. 26.

115. F. Gescher, "Synodales: Studien zur kirchlichen Gerichtsverfassung und zum deutschen Ständewesen des Mittelalters," *Zeitschrift der Savigny-Stiftung, Kanonistische Abteilung* 29 (1940): 374, 392.

116. According to two *Weistümer* of 1410 and 1450 for two villages of central Germany analyzed by W. Stoermer, "Grundherrschaften des hoheren und niederen Adels im Main-Tauber-Raum," in (81), vol. 2, p. 41, in the first village any *Dorfgenosse*— noble or not—was bound to attend the yearly *Gerichtstagen* and submit to the *Gemeideordnungen;* and in the second one, any person dwelling in the village was unfree, even if he was of noble origin, but no noble could be mayor or preside over the court.

117. Verhulst (12), p. 230.
118. Blaschke (12), pp. 82–83.
119. Durand (135), p. 207.
120. J. Imbert, *Les hôpitaux en droit canonique* (Paris, 1947), p. 63.
121. J. Tousseart, *Le sentiment religieux en Flandre à la fin du moyen âge* (Paris, 1963), p. 326.
122. The registers of the Souverain Bailliage preserved in the Archives de l'État à Namur, no. 524, report, for instance, on f. 42 v′, that the new lord of Jemeppe-sur-Sambre was in 1423 "mis à la cloque" (put to the bell).

5. IN TERRA: EXTERNAL ASPECTS

1. Hilton (93), p. 118.
2. Jacob (34), pp. 97–117.
3. Bourin (11), p. 355.
4. Bader (77), vol. 2, p. 240.
5. Ibid., p. 250; Mayer (29), p. 468; García de Cortázar (4), col. 1295.
6. van der Linden (11), pp. 479, 483, notes the constitution in Holland about 1200 of *hoogheemraadschappen:* intercommunal associations for building dams and for judging all cases, civil or criminal, regarding the water system.
7. Wunder (85), p. 40.
8. Berthe (83), p. 80.
9. J. Fernández Viladrich, "La comunidad de villa y tierra de Sepúlveda durante la edad media," *Anuario de Estudios Medievales* 8 (1972/73): 199–224.
10. Genicot (47), vol. 3, p. 199.
11. E. Fiumi, "Sui rapporti tra città e contado nell'età comunale," *Archivio storico italiano* 115 (1956): 18–68, speaks of the "fiscal oppression" of the cities.
12. D. M. Nicholas, *Stad en platteland in de middeleeuwen* (Bussum, 1971), pp. 99, 105.
13. A. Barrios García, *Estructuras agrarias y de poder en Castilla: el ejemplo de Ávila (1085–1320)* (Salamanca, 1983/84).
14. *The Cambridge Economic History of Europe*, vol. 2, p. 327; Duby (5), p. 229; H. Patze, *Die Entstehung der Landesherrschaft in Thüringen* (Cologne and Graz, 1962), vol. 1, p. 494.
15. Jones (122), p. 370; N. S. B. Grass, *The Evolution of the English Corn Market from the Twelfth to the Eighteenth Century* (Cambridge, Mass., 1915), p. 167, puts forward the theory that in the thirteenth century, these merchants were mainly inhabitants of the village and were even local farmers who bought corn; L. Genicot, "Une paroisse namuroise," *Revue d'histoire ecclésiastique*, 80 (1985): 719, confirms this for the late Middle Ages.
16. M. Mestayer, "La clientèle d'un cirier douaisien du XVe siècle," in *Valenciennes et les anciens Pays-Bas: Mélanges Paul Lefrancq* (Valenciennes, 1976), pp. 203–07.
17. L. Genicot and R. M. Allard, *Sources du droit rural du quartier d'Entre-Sambre-et-Meuse* (Brussels and Louvain, 1968), p. 153.
18. B. Gille, in *Histoire générale des techniques*, ed. M. Daumas (Paris, 1962), vol. 1, p. 502; O. Paulinyi, "Die anfänglichen Formen des Unternehmens in Edelberg-bau zur Zeit des Feudalismus," *Acta Historica* 12 (1966).
19. E. Sabbe, *De belgische vlasnijverheid.* Vol. 1, *De zuidnederlandsche vlasnijverheid tot het Verdrag van Utrecht* (Brussels, 1943), p. 48.
20. H. van Werveke, "Landelijke en stedelijke nijverheid. Bijdrage tot de oudste

geschiedenis van de vlaamse steden," in *Verslag van de algemene vergadering der leden van het Historisch Genootschap gehouden te Utrecht op 30 Oct. 1950* (Utrecht, 1951), pp. 37–51.

21. H. Kellenbenz, "Industries rurales en Occident de la fin du moyen âge au XVIIIe siècle," *Annales, Économics, Sociétés, Civilisations* 18 (1963): 833–82.

22. E. Carus-Wilson, in *The Cambridge Economic History of Europe*, vol. 2, p. 374.

23. Italian scholars differ on the question of the number and activity of artisans in the villages and the influence of the urban revival in that country. G. Calasso, in *Rivista storica italiana*, vol. 70 (1958), p. 321, asserts that craftsmen moved to the towns; Jones (122), p. 293, holds that the progress of trade increased their number in the countryside.

24. When and where did family names become hereditary or indicate birthplace or profession? The problem is raised by P. Bougard and M. Gysseling, *L'impôt royal en Artois (1295–1302)* (Louvain, 1970). For them, names had become hereditary as early as the end of the thirteenth century.

25. Bentzien (18), p. 90.

26. Pesez, "L'archéologie du village médiéval en France," in (23), p. 90; Clarke (89), p. 46.

27. Brouwers, *Cens et rentes du comte de Namur* (Namur, 1911), vol. 2, p. 49. The list roughly coincides with the inventory analyzed in *The Cambridge Economic History of Europe*, vol. 2, p. 326, of the goods of a trader of Bonifacio in 1238.

28. Among many works, T. H. Hollingsworth, "Historical Studies of Migration," *Annales de démographie historique* (1970): 87–97; P. Dollinger, "Les recherches de démographie historique sur les villes allemandes du moyen âge," in *La démographie médiévale: Sources et méthodes: Actes du Premier Congrès de l'Association des médiévistes de l'Enseignement supérieur public* (1970), pp. 115–16; C. Higounet, "Mouvements de population dans le Midi de la France du XIe au XVe siècle d'après les noms de personne et de lieu," *Annales, Économies, Sociétés, Civilisations* 8 (1953): 1–24; R. Comba, "Emigrare nel medioevo: Aspetti economico-sociali della mobilità geografica nei secoli XI–XVI," in (129), pp. 45–74.

29. L. Genicot, "Ville et campagne dans les Pays-Bas médiévaux," in *Acta historica et archaeologica medievalia* 7–8 (1986–87): 170, analyzes the documentation.

30. Y. Minet, "Les inscriptions des registres aux bourgeois de Douai au XVe siècle (1391–1506)," Ph.D. diss., University of Louvain, 1973. This work should be compared with P. Desportes, "Réceptions et inscriptions à la bourgeoisie de Lille aux XIVe et XVe siècles," *Revue du Nord* 42 (1980): 541–71.

31. *Town Origins: The Evidence from Medieval England*, ed. J. F. Benton (Boston, 1968).

32. J. Le Goff, in *Histoire de la France urbaine*, ed. G. Duby (Paris, 1980), p. 197, who reproduces the figures calculated by Desportes for Reims; out of 600 place-names of families paying tallage from 1304 to 1328, 506 referred to places less distant than twenty kms, most of them being villages.

33. For K. H. Spiess, "Zur Landflucht im Mittelalter," in (81), vol. 1, p. 164, and for other German scholars, escaping from serfdom was one of the reasons for fleeing the countryside.

34. J. Plessner, *L'émigration de la campagne à la ville libre de Florence au XIIIe siècle* (Copenhagen, 1934); G. Luzzatto, "L'inurbamento delle popolazioni rurali in Italia nei sec. XII e XIII," in *Studi di storia e diritto in onore di E. Bestan* (Milan, 1937–39), vol. 2, pp. 185–203; A. Grohmann, *Città e territorio tra medioevo ed età moderna (Perugia, sec. XIII–XVI)* (Perugia, 1981).

35. *The History of the King's Works*, ed. H. M. Colvin (London, 1963), p. 183.

36. S. Thrupp, "The Problem of Replacement-Rates in Late Medieval English Population," *Economic History Review* (1965): 105.
37. On this contract, Genicot (47), vol. 1, pp. 275–76; W. Ogris, *Der mittelalterliche Leibrentenvertrag* (Vienna and Munich, 1961).
38. Duby (5), p. 253; L. Verriest, "Étude d'un contrat privé de droit médiéval: le bail à cheptel vif à Tournai (1297–1314)," *Revue de Nord* (1946): 267–97.
39. Wunder (85), p. 68.
40. H. M. Cam, "The Community of the Vill," in *Medieval Studies Presented to Rose Graham*, ed. V. Ruffer and A. J. Taylor (Oxford, 1950), pp. 1–14.
41. Wunder (85), p. 75.
42. O. Brunner, *Land und Herrschaft*, 4th ed. (Munich, 1959), p. 186.
43. Zerner-Chandavoine (22), p. 197.
44. H. Gilles, *Les États du Languedoc au XVe siècle, Bibliothèque méridionale* 2d series, 40 (1965): 96.
45. P. Blickle, *Deutsche Untertanen: Ein Widerspruch*, (Stuttgart, 1981).
46. A. Dierkens, "La création des doyennés et des archidiaconés dans l'ancien diocèse de Liège (début du Xe siècle?)," *Le Moyen Âge* 4th series, 4 (1986): 345–65; J. Semmler, "Mission und Pfarrorganisation in den rheinischen, mosel- und maaslandischen Bistümern (5. 10.Jahrhundert)," in (41), pp. 813–88.
47. Goering (10), p. 328.
48. C. Levasseur, "Les églises rurales de la vallée de la Meuse au moyen âge," *L'information historique* (1966): 207; L. F. Genicot, *Les églises mosanes du XIe siècle* (Louvain, 1972), vol. 1, p. 219.

CONCLUSIONS

1. Postan (104), pp. 220, 243–46; E. Sabbe, "Grondbezit en landbouw, economische en sociale toestanden in de Kastelenij Kortrijk op het einde van de XIVe eeuw," *Handelingen van de Koninklijke Geschied—en Oudheidkundige Kring van Kortrijk*, new series 15 (1936): 436; Harvey (91), p. 131 and app. 6; Olland (73), p. 443.
2. Haverkamp (81), vol. 2, p. 344.
3. Sivery (9), p. 330.
4. Verhulst (12), pp. 236–46, which should be compared to and supplemented by Gilissen, "Étude historique comparative des communautés rurales," in (12), pp. 716–820, and by my own plan for studying the origins of the rural community (see Appendix). I confess that in my good colleague and friend Verhulst's excellent contribution, I do not find altogether happy his use of the adjective *suprastructurel* to describe any structure not based on possession or exploitation of the land.
5. Gilissen (12), p. 721, puts forth the theory that collective ownership or use of the soil is indispensable to make a rural community, but this is because, to some extent artificially, he distinguishes rural community and village community. On the same subject, he asserts, on p. 760, that "common feeling is not necessary to create a rural community"; but on p. 775 he writes that "the members of the rural community ought to be conscious of belonging to it."
6. According to Klingelhofer (99), p. 429, the manors were created from the ninth century, and lordships, from the tenth.
7. Fossier (7), p. 288, distinguishes three stages in economic progress from 990. But his schema does not apply to all countries.
8. Higounet (75), p. 45, for southern France; Bonassie (75), p. 47, for Catalonia.

9. Fossier (75), p. 29, sees the birth of the rural community as follows: creation of a parish, obligation to reside on the spot, common oath for maintaining peace, and collective economic duties and performances. K. Bosl, *Gebhardt Handbuch der deutschen Geschichte*, 8th ed. (Stuttgart, 1954), p. 668, proposes another schema for the emergence of towns: maintaining peace by *conjuratio* (the common oath); administering justice by *jurati* (its own judges); organizing defense and, to do so, imposing taxes; finally, dealing with external affairs. The results of such attempts to trace a universal line of evolution are interesting but questionable.

10. G. Duby, *Le Moyen Âge d'Hugues Capet à Jeanne d'Arc, Histoire de France Hachette* (Paris, 1987), p. 98.

11. Fossier (7), p. 288, sketches an immense and impressive panorama, distinguishing south and north, west and east, center and periphery, according to four criteria: demographic expansion; *incastellamento*, or building of keeps and castles; broadening of kindred; and the relations between town and country.

APPENDIX

1. This point is detailed in *L'archéologie du village médiéval* (Louvain and Ghent, 1967), p. 17.

2. Ibid., p. 16.

BIBLIOGRAPHY

GENERAL

1. *Archeological Approach to Medieval Europe.* Ed. K. Biddick. Kalamazoo, 1984.
2. *L'archéologie du village médiéval.* Louvain and Ghent, 1967.
3. *The Cambridge Economic History of Europe.* Vol. 1. *The Agrarian Life of the Middle Ages.* 2d ed. Ed. M. M. Postan. Cambridge, 1966.
4. *"Dorf."* In *Lexikon des Mittelalters.* Vol. 3, col. 1266–1311. Stuttgart and Zurich, 1986.
5. G. Duby. *L'économie rurale et la vie des campagnes dans l'Occident médiéval.* 2 vols. Paris, 1962.
6. ———. *Guerriers et paysans, VIIe–XIIe siècles: Premier essor de l'économie européenne.* Paris, 1973.
7. R. Fossier. *Enfance de l'Europe: Aspects économiques et sociaux.* Vol. 1. *L'homme et son espace.* Paris, 1982.
8. ———. *Paysans d'Occident: XIe–XIVe siècles.* Paris, 1984.
9. *Horizons marins, itinéraires spirituels (Ve–XVIIIe siècles).* Vol. 1. *Mentalités et sociétés.* Paris, 1987.
10. *Pathways to Medieval Peasants.* Ed. J. A. Raftis. Toronto, 1981.
11. *Recueils de la Société Jean Bodin pour l'histoire comparative des institutions: Les communautés rurales.* Vols. 43, 1984.
12. Ibid, vol. 44 (1987).
13. W. Roesener. *Bauern im Mittelalter.* Munich, 1985.
14. B. A. Slicher van Bath. *The Agrarian History of Western Europe (A.D. 500–1850).* 2d ed. London, 1966.
15. *Villages, Fields and Frontiers: Studies in European Rural Settlement in the Medieval and Early Modern Periods.* Ed. B. K. Roberts and R. E. Glasscock. Oxford, 1981.

TOPICS

Economy

16. W. Abel. *Die Wüstungen des ausgehenden Mittelalters.* 3d ed. Stuttgart, 1976.
17. G. P. Bognetti. *Studi sulle origini del comune rurale.* Milan, 1978.
18. U. Bentzien. *Bauernarbeit im Feudalismus: Landwirtschaftliche Arbeitsgeräte und-verfahren in Deutschland.* Berlin, 1980.
19. G. Bois. *Crise du féodalisme: Économie rurale et démographie en Normandie orientale du début du XIVe siècle au milieu du XVIe siècle.* Paris, 1976.

20. J. Chapelot and R. Fossier. *Le village et la maison au moyen âge*. Paris, 1980.

21. *Châteaux et peuplements en Europe occidentale du Xe au XIIIe siècle*. Premières journées internationales d'histoire du Centre culturel de l'Abbaye de Flaran, 1979. Auch, 1980.

22. *Les communautés villageoises en Europe occidentale du Moyen Âge aux Temps modernes*. Quatrièmes journées internationales d'histoire du Centre culturel de l'Abbaye de Flaran, 1982. Auch, 1984.

23. *Family and Inheritance*. Ed. J. Goody, J. Thirsk, and E. P. Thompson. Cambridge, 1976.

24. *Le Grand Domaine aux Époques Mérovingienne et Carolingienne: Die Grundherrschaft im frühen Mittelalter*. Ghent, 1985.

24b. B. A. Hanawalt. *The Ties that Bound. Peasant Families in Medieval England*. New York–Oxford, 1986.

25. *Histoire de la famille*. Vol. 1. *Mondes lointains, mondes anciens*. Ed. A. Burguière, C. Klapisch-Zuber, M. Segalen, and F. Zonabend. Paris, 1986.

26. *Historisch-genetische Siedlungsforschung: Genese und Typen ländlicher Siedlungen und Flurformen*. Ed. H. J. Nitz. Vol. 300 of *Wege der Forschung*. 1974.

27. *Medieval Settlement: Continuity and Change*. Ed. P. H. Sawyer. London, 1976.

28. "Le paysage rural: Réalités et représentations." *Revue du Nord* 52 (1980).

28b. "Villa-Curtis-Grangia." *Landwirtschaft zwischen Loire und Rhein von der Römerzeit zum Hochmittelalter*. Ed. W. Janssen and D. Lohrmann. Munich, 1983.

Law

29. *Die Anfänge der Landgemeinde und ihr Wesen*. Vorträge und Forschungen. Vols. 7 and 8. Stuttgart, 1964.

30. *La charte de Beaumont et les franchises municipales entre Loire et Rhin*. Nancy, 1988.

31. *Les libertés urbaines et rurales du XIe au XIVe siècle*. Colloque international. Spa 1966. Brussels, 1968.

32. *La maison forte au moyen âge*. Ed. M. Bur. Paris, 1986.

33. C. E. Perrin. *Recherches sur la seigneurie rurale en Lorraine d'après les plus anciens censiers, IXe–XIIe siècles*. Paris, 1935.

34. *Les structures du pouvoir dans les communautés rurales en Belgique et dans les pays limitrophes*. Spa 1986. Brussels, 1988.

Religion

35. N. Coulet. *Les visites pastorales. Typologie des sources du moyen âge occidental*, fasc. 23. Turnhout, 1977, mise à jour 1985.

36. A. Dierkens. "Quelques aspects de la christianisation du pays mosan à l'époque mérovingienne." In *La civilisation mérovingienne dans le bassin mosan: Actes du Colloque international d'Amay-Liège 1985*. Liège, 1986.

37. *Le istituzioni ecclesiastiche della "Societas christiana" dei secoli XI–XXI: Atti della sesta Settimana internazionale di studio: Milano 1974.* Milan, 1977.
38. G. Le Bras. *L'Église et le village.* Paris, 1976.
39. ———. *Institutions ecclésiastiques de la Chrétienté médiévale.* Vol. 12 of *Histoire de l'Église depuis les origines jusqu'à nos jours fondée par.* A. Fliche and V. Martin. Paris, 1959 and 1964.
40. F. Rapp. *L'Église et la vie religieuse en Occident à la fin du moyen âge.* Vol. 25 of *Nouvelle Clio.* 3d ed. Paris, 1983.
41. *Settimane di studio del Centro italiano di studi sull'alto medioevo.* Vol. 28. *Cristianizzazione ed organizzazione ecclesiatica delle campagne nell'alto medioevo: espansione e resistenze: Spoleto 1980.* Spoleto, 1982.

COUNTRIES

Austria

42. O. Stolz. *Rechtsgeschichte des Bauernstandes und der Landwirtschaft in Tirol und Vorarlberg.* Bolzano, 1949.

Belgium

43. C. Gaier. "La fonction stratégico-défensive du plat pays au Moyen Âge dans la région de la Meuse moyenne." *Le Moyen Âge* 69 (1963).
44. L. Genicot. "Art und Ausmasz der Mobilität von Grund und Boden im Spätmittelalter." In *Wirtschaftliche und soziale Strukturen im säcularen Wandel: Festschrift für W. Abel.* Hanover, 1974.
45. ———. *La crise agricole du bas moyen âge dans le Namurois.* With M. S. Bouchat and B. Delvaux. Louvain, 1969.
46. ———. "Défrichements et désertions: Sur les débuts de la crise agricole du bas moyen âge dans le Namurois." In *Liber amicorum Jan Buntink.* Louvain, 1981.
47. ———. *L'économie rurale namuroise au bas moyen âge.* Vol. 1. *La seigneurie foncière.* Vol. 2. *Les hommes, La noblesse.* Vol. 3. *Les hommes, Le commun.* Louvain and Namur, 1943, 1960, and 1982.
48. ———. "La dimension moyenne des exploitations paysannes dans le Namurois à la fin du XIIIe siècle." *Études rurales* (1962).
49. ———. *La noblesse dans l'Occident médiéval.* London, 1982.
50. ———. *Une source mal connue de revenus paroissiaux: les rentes obituaires: L'exemple de Frizet.* Louvain la Neuve, 1980.
51. ———. *Le XIIIe siècle européen.* Vol. 18 of *Nouvelle Clio.* 2d ed. Paris, 1984.
52. E. Thoen. *Landbouwekonomie en bevolking in Vlaanderen gedurende de late Middeleeuwen en het begin van de Moderne Tijden: Testregio: de kasselrijen van Oudenaarde en Aalst.* 2 vols. Gent, 1988.
53. M. J. Tits-Dieuaide. "Les campagnes flamandes du XIIIe au XVIIIe siècle ou les succès d'une agriculture traditionnelle." *Annales, Économies, Sociétés, Civilisations;* hereafter *AESC* (1984).

54. H. van der Wee and E. van Cauwenberghe, *Productivity of Land and Agricultural Innovations in the Low Countries, 1200–1800.* Louvain, 1978.

France

55. P. Adam. *La vie paroissiale en France au XIVe siècle.* Paris, 1964.
56. M. Aubrun. *L'ancien diocèse de Limoges, des origines au milieu du XIe siècle.* Fasc. 21. *Institut d'Études du Massif Central.* Clermont-Ferrand, 1981.
57. ———. *La paroisse en France des origines au XVe siècle.* Paris, 1986.
58. F. Bange. "L'ager et la villa: Structures du paysage et du peuplement dans la région mâconnaise à la fin du haut moyen âge (IXe–XIe siècles)." *AESC* 39 (1984).
59. M. Bloch. *Les caractères originaux de l'histoire rurale française.* New ed. Paris, 1952.
60. M. Bur. *La formation du comté de Champagne, v. 950–v. 1150.* No. 54 of *Mémoires des Annales de l'Est.* Nancy, 1977.
61. A. Déléage. *La vie rurale en Bourgogne jusqu'au début du onzième siècle.* 3 vols. Mâcon, 1941.
62. G. Demians d'Archimbaud. *Rougiers, village médiéval de Provence: Approche archéologique d'une société rurale méditerranéenne.* 6 vols. Université de Lille, 1980.
63. G. Demians d'Archimbaud and M. Finot. "L'organisation de la campagne en Provence occidentale: indices archéologiques et aspects démographiques (XIe–XVe siècles)." *Provence historique* 27 (1977).
64. *L'encadrement religieux des fidèles au moyen âge et jusqu'au Concile de Trente. La paroisse–le clergé–la pastorale–la dévotion.* T. I. *Actes du 109e Congrès national des sociétés savantes, Dijon, 1984: Section d'histoire médiévale et de philologie.* Paris, 1985.
65. R. Fossier. *La terre et les hommes en Picardie jusqu'à la fin du XIIIe siècle.* 2 vols. Louvain, 1968.
66. G. Fournier. *Le peuplement rural en Basse Auvergne durant le haut moyen âge.* 2d series, fasc. 52. *Publications de la Faculté des Lettres de Clermont-Ferrand.* Paris.
67. G. Fournier and P. F. Fournier. "Villes et villages neufs au XIIIe siècle en Auvergne: A propos des fondations d'Alphonse de Poitiers." *Journal des Savants* (1985).
68. G. Fourquin. *Les campagnes de la région parisienne à la fin du moyen âge.* Paris, 1964.
69. *Histoire de la France rurale.* Ed. G. Duby and A. Wallon. Vols. 1 and 2. Paris, 1975.
70. *Histoire des institutions françaises au moyen âge.* Ed. F. Lot and R. Fawtier. Vol. 3. *Institutions ecclésiastiques.* By J. Gaudement, J. F. Lemarignier, and G. Mollat. Paris, 1962.
71. M. T. Lorcin. *Les campagnes de la région lyonnaise aux XIVe et XVe siècles.* Lyon, 1974.
72. R. Mariotte-Loeber. *Ville et seigneurie: Les chartes de franchises des comtes de*

Savoie: Fin XIIe siècle–1343. Vol. 4 of *Mémoires et documents publiés par l'Académie florimontane*. Annecy, 1973.

73. H. Olland. *La baronnie de Choiseul à la fin du moyen âge, 1485–1525*. Nancy, 1980.

74. J. Schneider. *La ville de Metz aux XIIIe et XIVe siècles*. Nancy, 1950.

75. *Le village en France et en URSS des origines à nos jours*. Vol. 2 of *Travaux de l'Université de Toulouse-Le Mirail*. 1975.

Germany

76. W. Abel. *Geschichte der deutschen Landwirtschaft vom frühen Mittelalter bis zum 19. Jahrhundert*. 3d ed. Stuttgart, 1978.

77. K. S. Bader. *Studien zur Rechtsgeschichte des mittelalterlichen Dorfes*. Vol. 1. *Das mittelalterliche Dorf als Friedens-und Rechtsbereich*. Vol. 2. *Dorfgenossenschaft und Dorfgemeinde*. Vol. 3. *Rechtsformen und Schichten der Liegenschaftsnutzung im mittelalterlichen Dorf*. Cologne and Graz, 1957, 1962, and 1973.

78. P. Dollinger. *Der bayerische Bauernstand vom 9. bis 13. Jahrhundert*. Munich, 1982.

79. ———. *L'évolution des classes rurales en Bavière depuis la fin de l'époque carolingienne jusqu'au milieu du XIIIe siècle*. Paris, 1949.

80. G. Franz. *Geschichte des deutschen Bauernstandes vom frühen Mittelalter bis zum 19. Jahrhundert*. Stuttgart, 1970.

81. *Die Grundherrschaft im späten Mittelalter*. Ed. H. Patze. Vol. 27 of *Vorträge und Forschungen*. 2 vols. Sigmaringen, 1983.

82. K. S. Kramer. "Gemeinwesen in Schleswig-Holstein." *Kieler Blätter zur Volkskunde* 9 (1977).

83. M. Nikolay-Panter. *Entstehung und Entwicklung der Landgemeinde im Trierer Raum*. Bonn, 1976.

84. W. Stoermer. *Früher Adel: Studien zur politischen Führungschicht im fränkisch-deutschen Reich vom 8. bis 11. Jahrhundert*. No. 6 of *Monographien zur Geschichte des Mittelalters*. 2 vols. Stuttgart, 1973.

85. H. Wunder. *Die bauerliche Gemeinde in Deutschland*. No. 1483 of *Kleine Vandenhoeck-Reihe*. Göttingen, 1986.

Great Britain

86. *Agrarian History of England and Wales*. vol. 1. Ed. H. P. R. Finberg. Cambridge, 1972.

87. W. O. Ault. *Open Field Farming in Medieval England: A Study of Village By-Laws*. London and New York, 1972. Abridged version of "Open Field Husbandry and the Village Community: A Study of Agrarian By-Laws in Medieval England." In *Proceedings of the American Philosophical Society*, 1965.

88. L. Cantor. *The English Medieval Landscape*. London, 1982.

89. H. Clarke. *The Archaeology of Medieval England*. London, 1984.

90. E. B. Dewindt. *Land and People in Holywell-cum-Needingworth*. Toronto, 1972.
91. P. D. A. Harvey. *A Medieval Oxfordshire Village: Cuxham 1200–1400*. Oxford, 1965.
92. ———. *Peasant Land Market in Medieval England*. Oxford and New York, 1984.
93. R. H. Hilton. *Class Conflicts and the Crisis of Feudalism: Essays in Medieval Social History*. London, 1985.
94. ———. *Bond Men Made Free: Medieval Peasant Movements and the English Rising of 1381*. London, 1973.
95. ———. *The English Peasantry in the Later Middle Ages*. Oxford, 1975.
96. ———. *A Medieval Society: The West Midlands at the End of the Thirteenth Century*. 2d ed. London, 1967.
97. ———. "Peasant Movements Before 1381." *Economic History Review* 2d series, 2, 1949.
98. G. C. Homans. *English Villagers of the Thirteenth Century*. Cambridge, Mass., 1942.
99. E. C. Klingelhofer. "Manor, Villa and Hundred: Rural Development in the Region of Micheldever Hampshire, 700–1100. Ph.D. diss., The Johns Hopkins University, 1985.
100. E. A. Kosminsky. *Studies in the Agrarian History of England in the Thirteenth Century*. Oxford, 1956.
101. R. Lennard. *Rural England, 1086–1135: A Study of Social and Agrarian Conditions*. 2d ed. Oxford, 1965.
102. A. E. Levett. *Studies in Manorial History*. Oxford, 1938.
103. E. Miller and J. Hatcher. *Medieval England: Rural Society and Economic Change, 1086–1348*. London, 1978.
104. J. H. R. Moorman. *Church Life in England in the Thirteenth Century*. Cambridge, 1946.
104b. M. M. Postan. "Village Livestock in the Thirteenth Century." *Economic History Review* 15 (1962/63).
105. ———. *Medieval Economy and Society: An Economic History of Britain in the Middle Ages*. London, 1972.
106. J. A. Raftis. *Assart Data and Land Values: Two Studies in the East Midlands, 1200–1350*. Toronto, 1974.
107. ———. *Tenure and Mobility: Studies in the Social History of the Medieval English Village*. Toronto, 1964.
108. J. C. Russell. *British Medieval Population*. Albuquerque, 1948.
109. E. Searle. *Lordship and Community: Battle Abbey and Its Banlieu, 1066–1538*. Toronto, 1974.
110. J. M. Steane. *The Archaeology of Medieval England and Wales*. Athens, Ga., 1985.
111. C. Taylor. *Village and Farmstead: A History of Rural Settlement in England*. London, 1983.
112. J. Z. Titow. *English Rural Society, 1200–1350*. London, 1969.

Italy

113. *Brucato: Histoire et archéologie d'un habitat médiéval en Sicile.* Ed. J. M. Pesez. Rome, 1984.

114. A. Castagnetti. *Le comunità rurali dalla soggezione signorile alla giurisdizione del comune cittadino.* Verona, 1983. Partially reprinted in *Le campagne medievali prima e dopo il mille.* Bologna, 1985.

115. ———. *L'organizzazione del territorio rurale nel medioevo.* 2d ed. Bologna, 1982.

116. L. Chiappa Mauri. "La costruzione del paesaggio agrario padano: La grangia di Valera." *Studi storici* 2 (1985).

117. R. Comba. *Metamorfosi di un paesaggio rurale: Uomini e luoghi del Piemonte sud-occidentale fra X e XVI secolo.* Turin 1983. This is a collection of essays published between 1970 and 1978 and includes a bibliographical supplement.

118. *Forma di potere e struttura sociale in Italia nel medioevo.* Ed. G. Rossetti. Bologna, 1977.

119. V. Fumagalli. *Terra e società nell'Italia padana.* Turin, 1976.

120. D. Herlihy and C. Klapisch-Zuber. *Les Toscans et leurs familles.* Paris, 1978.

121. P. Jones. *Economia e società nell'Italia medievale.* Turin, 1980.

122. ———. "Per la storia agraria italiana nel medioevo: Lineamenti e problemi." *Rivista storica italiana* 76 (1964).

123. P. S. Leicht. *Operai, Artigiani, Agricoltori in Italia dal Secolo VI al XVI.* Milan, 1946.

124. *Medioevo rurale: Sulle trace de la civiltà contadina.* Ed. V. Fumagalli and G. Rossetti. Bologna, 1980.

125. M. Montanari. *Campagne medievali: Struttura produttiva, raporti di lavoro, sistemi alimentari.* Turin, 1984.

126. *Pievi e parrochie in Italia nel basso medioevo (sec. XIII–XV): Atti del VI Convegno di storia della chiesa in Italia.* Florence, 1981; Rome, 1984.

127. C. Rotelli. *Una campagna medievale: Storia agraria del Piemonte fra il 1250 e il 1450.* Turin, 1973.

128. A. Settia. *Castelli e villagi nell'Italia padana: Popolamento, potere e sicurezza fra IX e XIII secolo.* Naples, 1984.

129. *Strutture familiari, epidemie, migrazioni nell'Italia medievale.* Ed. R. Comba, G. Piccinni, and G. Pinto. Naples, 1984.

130. P. Toubert. *Les structures du Latium médiéval: Le Latium méridional et la Sabine du IXe siècle à la fin du XIIe siècle.* 2 vols. Rome, 1973.

131. D. Zardin. *Confraternite e vita di pietà nella campagna lombarda tra '500 e '600: La pieve di Paraliago-Legnano.* Milan, 1981.

Netherlands

132. B. A. Slicher van Bath. *Mens en land in de Middeleeuwen: Bydrage tot een geschiedenis der nederzettingen in Oosterlijk Nederland.* 2 vols. Assen, 1944.

Portugal and Spain

133. *Actas de las I Jornadas de metodologia aplicada de las ciencias historicas.* Vol. 2. *Historia medieval.* Santiago de Compostella, 1975.
134. P. Bonassie. *La Catalogne du milieu du Xe à la fin du XIe siècle.* 2 vols. Toulouse, 1975.
135. R. Durand. "Village et seigneurie au Portugal, Xe–XIIIe siècle." *Cahiers de civilisation médiévale* 30 (1987).
136. J. A. García de Cortázar. *La historia rural medieval: Un esquema de análisis estructural a traves del ejemplo hispanocristiano.* Santander, 1978.
137. M. C. Pallares Mendez and E. Portela Silva. *El bajo valle del Miño en los siglos XII y XIII: Economia agraria y estructura social.* Santiago de Compostella, 1971.
138. R. Pastor de Togneri. *Conflictos sociales y estancamiento económico en la España medieval.* Barcelona, 1973.
139. E. Portela Silva. *La region del obispado de Tuy en los siglos XII a XV: Una sociedad en la expansion y en la crisis.* Santiago de Compostella, 1976.
140. *Les Espagnes médiévales: Aspects économiques et sociaux. Mélanges offerts à J. Gautier Dalché.* No. 46 of *Annales de la Faculté des Lettres et Sciences humaines de Nice.* 1983.

INDEX

Composed by G & S Typesetters, Inc.
in Baskerville text and display

Printed by Thomson Shore, Inc.
on 50-lb Glatfelter Offset paper
and bound in GSB Natural Finish

Designed by Laury A. Egan